D1565911

Libri dell'autore:

Research in Physiology - A Liber Memorialis, curato da F. F. Kao, K. Koizumi e M. Vassalle.

Cardiac Physiology for the Clinician, curato da M. Vassalle.

Excitation and Neural Control of the Heart, curato da M. N. Levy e M. Vassalle.

Chandler McCuskey Brooks: The Scientist and The Man, curato by M. Vassalle.

Diario di un Fisiologo del Cuore. (Include saggi filosofici)

Emozioni Perdute/Lost Emotions. (Poesie)

L'Enigma della Mente: Aforismi/The Riddle of the Mind: Aphorisms.

La Realtà dell'Io: Aforismi/The Reality of the Self: Aphorisms

Books by the author:

Research in Physiology - A Liber Memorialis, edited by F. F. Kao, K. Koizumi and M. Vassalle.

Cardiac Physiology for the Clinician, edited by M. Vassalle.

Excitation and Neural Control of the Heart, edited by M. N. Levy and M. Vassalle.

Chandler McCuskey Brooks: The Scientist and The Man, edited by M. Vassalle.

Diario di un Fisiologo del Cuore. (Includes philosophical essays)

Emozioni perdute/Lost Emotions. (Poems)

L'Enigma della Mente: Aforismi/The Riddle of the Mind: Aphorisms.

La Realtà dell'Io: Aforismi/The Reality of the Self: Aphorisms

Mario Vassalle

La Realtà dell'Io
Aforismi

The Reality of the Self
Aphorisms

New York 2000

AVVERTENZA

Il testo originale italiano degli aforismi è stampato sulle pagine pari e la traduzione inglese sulle pagine dispari, in modo da rendere più facile il confronto dei testi italiano e inglese per coloro che desiderassero farlo. Per la compilazione dell'indice analitico, gli aforismi sono stati numerati successivamente. Per un eventuale confronto, lo stesso numero identifica lo stesso aforisma in italiano e nella traduzione inglese. La numerazione degli aforismi comincia col numero 1001, dal momento che questi aforismi sono una continuazione di quei mille che ho già pubblicato nel libro intitolato "L'Enigma della Mente: Aforismi".

La fotografia in copertina è stata presa da Roberto M. Vassalle e mostra una cava di marmo nei pressi di Gorfigliano nelle Alpi Apuane (Lucca, Italia). Nella fotografia, la masse di marmo tagliate dalla montagna vogliono simbolizzare l'analisi dei vari aspetti della mente che normalmente sono nascosti nella sua complessità sotto le apparenze talvolta ingannevoli della superficie: le venature, la trama, la struttura, le sfumature, i difetti e la purezza delle parti interne non si vedono finché non si opera una dissezione sistematica del tutto.

NOTICE

The original Italian text of the aphorisms is printed on the even pages and the English translation on the odd pages, as to make the comparison of the Italian and English texts easier for those who wish to do so. The aphorisms have been sequentially numbered for the compilation of the index. For a possible comparison, the same number identifies the same aphorism in Italian and in the English translation. The numeration of the aphorisms begins with the number 1001, since these aphorisms are a continuation of the one thousand ones that I have already published in the book entitled: "The Riddle of the Mind: Aphorisms".

The photo on the cover was taken by Roberto M. Vassalle and it shows a marble quarry in the vicinity of Gorfigliano in the Apuane Alps (Lucca, Italy). In the photo, the blocks of marble cut out of the mountain are meant to symbolize the analysis of the various aspects of the mind that normally are hidden in its complexity under the sometimes misleading appearance of the surface: the veins, texture, structure, nuances, faults and purity of the inner parts are not seen until a dissection of the whole is systematically carried out.

Alla memoria

di

mia madre, Antonietta, mio padre, Giuseppe,

e

mio fratello Massimo

To the memory

of

my mother, Antonietta, my father, Giuseppe,

and

my brother Massimo

INDICE / TABLE OF CONTENTS

Ringraziamento

Desidero ringraziare mia moglie, Anna Maria, mia figlia Francesca e mio figlio Roberto per avermi pazientemente aiutato a correggere il manoscritto.

Acknowledgments

I wish to thank my wife, Anna Maria, my daughter Francesca and my son Roberto for their patient help in correcting the manuscript.

PREFAZIONE

Nel "Diario di un Fisiologo del Cuore" (pubblicato in italiano nel 1992) ho riportato pensieri che ho sviluppato nel tempo. Come indico nella prefazione di quel libro, è un diario della mente che si rivolge anche a quei problemi generali che hanno sempre interessato la mente umana. Per esempio, la natura del tempo, spazio, movimento, realtà, Io, religione, mente, ecc. La trattazione non né rigida né sistematica e già in quel libro vi sono numerosi aforismi mescolati ai vari argomenti trattati.

Per ragioni che non so neanch'io, la forma di espressione offerta dagli aforismi ha finito per attrarmi in maniera prevalente, forse perché gli aforismi sono concisi, vari e al punto. Il risultato è stato che nel 1996 ho pubblicato una raccolta di mille aforismi in un libro intitolato "L'Enigma della Mente: Aforismi". Vi esprimo idee circa la mente e la natura umana che sono nate dall'osservazione di me stesso e degli altri.

Ma non si può scegliere di non pensare più: non si pensa più solo quando la mente cessa di essere creativa e originale. Pensando, la mente persegue quelle domande che la interessano. Alcune di queste domande sono poste dalla necessità di comprendere quei fattori che, inconsciamente ma potentemente, influenzano la quotidiana interazione tra stimoli e risposte. Questo desiderio di comprendere mi ha fatto scrivere altri aforismi che pubblico in questo libro, aggiungendoli a quei mille che ho già pubblicati nell'Enigma della Mente.

Li ho pensati perché spinto dal mio interesse nella fisiologia della mente ed il suo ruolo essenziale nell'ordine generale delle cose. Li ho scritti perché sentivo la necessità di formularli esplicitamente. E li pubblico nella speranza che possano essere utili anche ad altri nel loro sforzo di definire la *realtà dell'Io* [il proprio], un processo meno semplice di quanto sembri. Vi si oppongono spesso le cure della vita quotidiana, quelle cure che peraltro sono lo stimolo a cercare panorami più vasti di quelli imposti dagli orizzonti limitati della nostra attività. Un'attività che (per quanto possa piacere) è pur sempre ristretta ad un campo specializzato.

In che senso gli aforismi aumentano la nostra comprensione? Quando ci si guarda nello specchio, ci si riconosce subito, ma non ci si conosce di più: ci si vede più o meno come ci vedono gli altri. Quando si leggono gli aforismi, ci si guarda nello specchio, se non dell'anima, certo della mente. Quando se ne riconoscono le verità, ci si conosce di più, perché si diventa coscienti di quelle verità. Vi si vedono illuminati aspetti della realtà del nostro Io che fino allora erano rimasti fuori, non da noi, ma dal cerchio di luce della nostra coscienza nella penombra indefinita delle cose non pensate. Quelle cose che, come falde nascoste, alimentano la sorgente della consapevolezza e influenzano tante delle nostre azioni.

Naturalmente, il desiderio di capire o di capirsi non è obbligatorio. Ma il desiderio di ignorare o di ignorarsi non è naturale. Pertanto questi aforismi possono essere veduti come sondaggi di differenti aspetti di quella mente che ciascuno di noi condivide con tutti gli altri. Naturalmente, non è necessario che tu sia d'accordo con tutti gli aforismi: è sufficiente che questi stimolino l'interesse a ragionare e a conoscere. Inoltre, anche il non essere d'accordo aiuta ad autodefinirsi: si diventa coscienti della propria diversità e si cercano le ragioni che la giustifichino.

Mi rendo conto che non tutti gli aforismi che ho scritto sono aforismi in senso stretto. Ma mi rendo anche conto della necessità che vi siano pause nella varietà, e che la verità non si identifica né si esaurisce nella logica. Inoltre, talvolta ho dovuto elaborare un pensiero oltre i limiti di un aforisma per chiarirne i risvolti filosofici.

Se, nel leggerli, ne trai quel piacere che deriva dal comunicare con la propria mente, anch'io ne trarrò quella soddisfazione che deriva dal comunicare con altre menti. Mi auguro solamente che tu debba essere intrattenuto tanto dalle domande quanto dalle risposte.

Mario Vassalle

New York, 26 Maggio 2000

PREFACE

In the "Diario di un Fisiologo del Cuore" ("Diary of a Physiologist of the Heart") I have expressed thoughts that I developed in the course of time. As indicated in the preface of that book, it is a diary of the mind that addresses those general problems that always have interested the human mind. For example, the nature of time, space, movement, reality, the Self, religion, mind, etc. The treatment of these topics in neither rigid nor systematic and already in that book there are numerous aphorisms intermingled with the various topics considered.

For reasons that I myself ignore, the form of expression offered by the aphorisms eventually attracted me in a prevalent manner, perhaps because the aphorisms are concise, varied and to the point. The result has been that in 1996 I published a collection of a thousand aphorisms in a book entitled "The Riddle of the Mind: Aphorisms". There, I express ideas about the mind and human nature that were born by the observation of myself and of others.

However, one can not choose not to think any longer: we stop thinking when the mind ceases to be creative and original. In thinking, the mind pursues those questions that interest it. Some of these questions are raised by the necessity of understanding those factors that, unconsciously but powerfully, influence the daily interplay between stimuli and answers. This desire to understand drove me to write new aphorisms that I publish in this book, adding them to those one thousand already published in the Riddle of the Mind.

I conceived them because I was driven by my interest in the physiology of the mind and its essential role in the general order of things. I wrote them because I felt the need to explicitly formulate them. And I publish them in the hope that they might also be useful to others in their effort toward defining *the reality of the Self* [their own], a process less simple than it might appear. Are often opposed to it the vicissitudes of the daily life, those vicissitudes that are the very stimulus to seek panoramas wider than those imposed by the limited horizons of our activity. An activity that (no matter how much we like it) is necessarily circumscribed to a specialized field.

In which way do aphorisms augment our understanding? When we look in the mirror, we immediately recognize ourselves, but we do not know ourselves more: we see ourselves more or less as others see us. When we read the aphorisms, we look at ourselves in the mirror, if not of the soul, certainly of the mind. When we recognize their truths, we know ourselves more, because we become conscious of those truths. We see illuminated in them aspects of the reality of our Self that until then had remained outside, not of us, but of the circle of light of our consciousness in the indefinite twilight of un-thought things. Those things that, as hidden sources, feed the spring of consciousness and influence so many of our actions.

Of course, the desire of understanding or of understanding oneself is not obligatory. But the desire of ignoring or of ignoring oneself is not natural. Therefore, these aphorisms can be seen as probes of different aspects of that mind that each one of us shares with everybody else. Naturally, it is not necessary that you should agree with all of them: it is sufficient that they stimulate the interest to reason and to know. Furthermore, even disagreeing helps in defining oneself: one becomes aware of his diversity and seeks the reasons that justify it.

I realize that not all the aphorisms that I wrote are aphorisms in a strict sense. However, I also realize the necessity that there should be pauses in variety, and that the truth does not identify with nor exhausts itself in logic. Furthermore, sometimes I had to elaborate a thought beyond the limit of an aphorism in order to clarify its philosophical implications.

If, in reading them, you get out of them that pleasure that derives from communicating with one's own mind, I too will get that satisfaction that derive from communicating with other minds. I only wish that you should be entertained by the questions as well as by the answers.

Mario Vassalle

New York, 26 May 2000

Riproduco qui questa **Prefazione**, scritta per **"L'Enigma della Mente: Aforismi"**, poiché in breve delinea le mie idee circa gli aforismi.

Gli aforismi sono verità in capsula, che sono più penetranti per essere espresse concisamente. Spesso individuano un aspetto di comportamento che, per essere enunciato nella sua essenzialità, colpisce immediatamente: vi riconosciamo verità che non avevamo formulato. Per questo, gli aforismi contribuiscono a chiarire noi a noi stessi, dato che siamo tutti partecipi della natura umana e pertanto soggetti alle sue leggi.

Una limitazione degli aforismi è che colgono aspetti isolati della verità, senza fornire spiegazioni o elaborazioni. Inoltre, gli aforismi hanno due nemici importanti.

Uno è la tentazione di dire cose brillanti, ma non vere. A questo spinge la demagogia che non risparmia neanche alcune delle menti più acute, le quali confondono l'aforisma col paradosso. In tal caso, la nostra personalità sostituisce l'obiettività con il piacere di una scelta personale, volta più a impressionare che a convincere.

L'altro è la deformazione della realtà che deriva dal vedere tutto secondo le nostre convinzioni personali. Allora si può dire anche la verità, ma non tutta la verità. Una verità parziale o isolata assume connotazioni diverse per non essere vista in un contesto più generale o nell'equilibrio di altre verità taciute. Per esempio, della natura umana si possono vedere solo i difetti. Ma i difetti possono essere una necessità vitale per la nostra umanità. Questo facilmente spiega perché siano universali e insopprimibili. Lo stesso può essere detto delle virtù. Ma c'è chi si concentra prevalentemente o sugli uni o sulle altre.

Nonostante queste limitazioni, gli aforismi ci spiegano quello di cui abbiamo esperienza ma non coscienza esplicita, quello che non abbiamo mai analizzato e tanto meno formalmente espresso. Sono come lampi di luce che illuminano diversi aspetti dell'**enigma della mente**, e pertanto permettono di conoscere meglio noi stessi. Dal momento che siamo quello di cui la nostra mente ha coscienza, il conoscerci meglio aumenta la nostra realtà. Alla loro maniera, anche gli aforismi contribuiscono a farci crescere: come sovrapponendo mattone su mattone alla fine si costruisce una casa, tutti insieme contribuiscono a definire l'edificio della mente nella sua complessità e contraddizioni.

Ma gli aforismi sono un po' come i cioccolatini: per gustarli, bisogna assaggiarne pochi per volta. Altrimenti, se ne fa un'indigestione. Negli intervalli, si può sempre riflettere.

New York, 26 Maggio 1996   Mario Vassalle

I reproduce here this **Preface**, written for "**The Riddle of the Mind: Aphorisms**", as it briefly outlines my ideas about aphorisms.

Aphorisms are truths in a capsule, which are more penetrating because they are expressed concisely. Often, they identify an aspect of behavior that, being enunciated in its essentiality, immediately strikes the mind: we recognize truths that we had not formulated. For this reason, aphorisms contribute to clarify us to ourselves, since we all share in human nature and, therefore, are subject to its laws.

The limitations of aphorisms are that they highlight isolated aspects of truth, without providing explanations or elaboration. In addition, the aphorisms have two important enemies.

One is the temptation of saying brilliant but untrue things. This may result from demagoguery, which does not spare even some of the sharpest minds, who confuse aphorism with paradox. In that case, one's personality substitutes objectivity with the pleasure of a personal choice, aiming more to impress than to convince.

The other is the deformation of the truth that derives from seeing everything according to our personal convictions. What we then say may still be the truth, but not the whole truth. A partial or isolated truth assumes a different connotation for not being viewed in a more general context and in the balance of other unstated truths. For example, one may only see the faults of human nature. But our faults may be a vital necessity for our humanity. The same can be said of virtues. But some concentrate on the former and some on the latter.

These limitations notwithstanding, aphorisms explain to us that of which we have experience but not an explicit awareness, that which we never have analyzed and even less formally expressed. They are like lightning that illuminates different aspects of the **riddle of the mind**, and therefore permit us to better know ourselves. Since we are what our mind is aware of, a better knowledge of ourselves increases our reality. In their own way, aphorisms also contribute to make us grow: as laying brick over brick eventually builds a house, all together they contribute to define the edifice of the mind in its complexity and contradictions.

But aphorisms are a little bit like chocolates: to enjoy them, one must taste a few of them at a time. Otherwise, indigestion results. In the intervals, one can always reflect.

Mario Vassalle

New York, 26 May 1996

La Realtà dell'Io
Aforismi

Come ricercatore, ho cercato la verità sopra a tutto.
Come filosofo, ho posto la verità sull'altare della logica.
Come poeta, ho messo l'altare della logica sulle fondamenta delle emozioni.

The Reality of the Self
Aphorisms

As a scientist, I sought the truth above all.
As a philosopher, I placed the truth on the altar of logic.
As a poet, I put the altar of logic on the foundations of emotions.

1001. Gli aforismi sono le risposte alle domande che avremmo potuto (e talvolta dovuto) porci.

1002. È più triste non avere nessuna illusione che avere alcune delusioni.

1003. Spesso si cerca l'originalità nell'imitazione (per esempio, nel seguire la moda del momento): ci si crede originali solo perché l'imitazione è personale.

1004. La vanità contribuisce notevolmente a rendere il rispetto di se stessi, se non legittimo, per lo meno plausibile.

1005. Cambiando continuamente con l'età, il nostro corpo impone alla mente sempre nuovi atteggiamenti logici ed emotivi, dettati dalle sue modificazioni fisiologiche e precedenti esperienze. Si cambia perché siamo destinati a non durare.

1006. Un'analisi deve essere oggettiva, ma quello che è analizzato generalmente non lo è. L'analisi studia quello che gli interessi determinano. E gli interessi, spirituali o materiali non possono (e non devono) essere oggettivi se vogliamo avere una nostra realtà.

1007. Una serie di frasi acute non risultano necessariamente in un saggio acuto. Si può essere brillanti, ma superficiali.

1008. Ignoriamo quello di cui non siamo consapevolmente coscienti (anche se ne abbiamo esperienza).

1009. Prestiamo a Dio gli attributi della nostra umanità per sentirci più vicini alla sua divinità.

1010. Il balletto porta alla fusione dell'essere con il ritmo e l'estro della grazia, e il solo vigore fisico porta solo ai gesti meccanici della ginnastica. Per questa ragione, le ballerine sono in genere assai più brave dei ballerini: la grazia naturale della femminilità. Non a caso, alcuni ballerini sono effeminati, ma nessuna ballerina è mascolinizzata.

1011. Se uno è ostile, non perdona neanche di essere perdonato.

1012. Non ha peccati solo chi è amorale.

1001. Aphorisms are the answers to the questions that we could have (and sometimes should have) asked ourselves.

1002. It is sadder not to have any illusion than to have some disillusions.

1003. Often we seek originality in imitation (for example, in following the current fashion): we believe to be original only because our imitation is personal.

1004. Our vanity considerably contributes to make self-respect, if not legitimate, at least plausible.

1005. Changing continuously with age, our body imposes on the mind ever-new logical and emotional attitudes, dictated by its physiological modifications and preceding experiences. We change because we are destined not to last.

1006. An analysis must be objective, but what is analyzed generally is not. The analysis studies what interests determine. And the interests, spiritual or material, can not (and must not) be objective if we want to have a reality of our own.

1007. A series of acute sentences do not necessarily result in an acute essay. One can be brilliant, but superficial.

1008. We ignore that of which we are not consciously aware (even if we have experienced it).

1009. We lend God the attributes of our humanity to feel closer to his divinity.

1010. Ballet leads to fusion of the being with the rhythm and whims of grace, while physical vigor alone leads only to the mechanical gestures of gymnastics. For this reason, generally ballerinas are much better than male dancers: the natural grace of their femininity. Not by chance, some male dancers are effeminate, but no ballerinas are masculine.

1011. If one is hostile, he does not pardon even being pardoned.

1012. Only the amoral has no sins.

1013. La stoltezza giustifica tutto. Che colpa ci può essere nel non essere capaci di capire?

1014. Le nostre obiezioni a quello che ci conviene sono così deboli che facilmente si trasformano in scuse plausibili.

1015. In tutto quello che si fa, la necessità del ritmo impose la presenza di pause.

1016. L'estrema lucidità si deve guardare dall'aridità.

1017. Se non sei soddisfatto del tuo passato, cambia il tuo presente.

1018. Per molti, la matematica non è stimolante perché è troppo rigidamente coerente. Due più due fa quattro che si sia felici, eccitati, tristi, stanchi, innamorati, spaventati, assonnati, ecc. I numeri rimangono impassibili anche quando noi non lo siamo più.

1019. Si vive più pienamente nella gioventù, perché solo allora il rigoglio delle virtù e vizi trasforma facilmente le emozioni in passioni.

1020. Si può essere molto ragionevoli in cose molto piccole; e poco ragionevoli in quelle molto grandi.

1021. Certe lodi a Dio rasentano l'offesa. Nel suo nome, si disprezza la vanità di questo mondo, implicitamente affermando che Dio ha fatto un mondo vano. In realtà, è dalla perfezione di tante opere umane che s'innalzano le più alte lodi a Dio.

1022. Come per una cometa, la "coda" del nostro passato svanisce gradualmente negli anonimi spazi della dimenticanza.

1023. Deviando l'attenzione su se stesse, le eleganze nello scrivere possono essere un ostacolo alla comprensione logica. L'eleganza colpisce sempre piacevolmente, ma l'estetica è indifferente alla verità. Tuttavia, un errore non cessa di essere tale solo per essere espresso elegantemente.

1024. La natura si rinnova continuamente solo attraverso il ciclo della vita e della morte. Ogni primavera è nuova solo se si creano nuovi fiori e nuove fragranze.

1013. Foolishness justifies everything. What fault can there be in being incapable of understanding?

1014. Our objections to what is convenient for us are so weak that without difficulty they change into plausible excuses.

1015. In everything that we do, the necessity of rhythm demands the presence of pauses.

1016. Extreme lucidity must guard from aridity.

1017. If you are dissatisfied with your past, change your present.

1018. For many, mathematics is uninspiring because it is too rigidly consistent. Two plus two is four whether we are happy, excited, sad, tired, in love, afraid, sleepy, etc. Numbers remain impassible even when we do not.

1019. We live more fully in our youth, because only then does the bloom of virtues and vices easily transform our emotions into passions.

1020. One can be very reasonable in very small matters; and not very reasonable in big matters.

1021. Certain praises of God are borderline offenses. In his name, the vanity of this world is despised, implicitly affirming that God made a vain world. In actuality, it is from the perfection of many human accomplishments that the highest praises to God arise.

1022. Like for a comet, the "tail" of our past gradually vanishes in the anonymous spaces of forgetfulness.

1023. By diverting the attention to itself, elegance in writing may be an obstacle to logical comprehension. Elegance always strikes pleasantly, but aesthetics is indifferent to truth. Nevertheless, a mistake does not cease to be such only because it has been elegantly expressed.

1024. Nature continuously renews itself only through the cycle of life and death. Every springtime is new only if new flowers and new scents are created.

1025. La fede trova nell'umiltà la soluzione di molti dei suoi dubbi, perché nell'umiltà trova quelle verità più profonde ed intime che la logica neanche sospetta e in ogni caso non saprebbe capire.

1026. Si reagisce all'inesperienza con i tratti innati del proprio carattere. Si chiedono al nostro istinto quei consigli che la nostra mancanza di esperienza non ci può dare.

1027. Lo specchio ci permette di vedere la parte fisica del proprio Io dal di fuori, come la vedono gli altri. Ma le conclusioni che se ne traggono possono essere alquanto diverse.

1028. Il concetto di qualità si applica anche ai difetti. Per esempio, l'ipocrisia può essere ovvia, mediocre, abile o artistica (se non addirittura diabolica).

1029. L'umorismo delle persone rozze fa ridere solo loro. Ma quelli pensano la stessa cosa dell'umorismo delle persone educate.

1030. Le apparenze regali dei grandi nascondono le sottostanti miserie umane; anzi, per contrasto, le prime esagerano le seconde.

1031. Per essere indifferenti al male, bisogna essere indifferenti anche al bene. Ma essere indifferenti al bene non può che essere male.

1032 Se nello spazio oltre un certo punto non vi fossero più corpi celesti, vi dovrebbe essere il vuoto. E il vuoto dove finisce? Con che cosa confina? Probabilmente, con la pazzia.

1033. Talvolta l'abilità è al servizio del carattere, e talvolta è il contrario. Ma, a differenza del carattere, l'abilità può essere disposta a servire qualsiasi padrone, buono o cattivo.

1034. Dietro le meraviglie della natura, vi è un'intelligenza insondabile.

1035. L'Io ufficiale è il risultato di un accurata selezione delle variabili che costituiscono l'Io intimo.

1036. Il pensare intensamente dà profondità allo sguardo, come se gli occhi, rivolti all'interno, si acuissero nello sforzo di penetrare le nebbie che mascherano la verità.

1025.   Faith finds in humility the solution to many of its doubts, because in humility it finds those deeper and intimate truths that logic does not even suspect and in any case would not grasp.

1026.   People react to inexperience with the innate traits of their character. We ask our instincts the advice that our lack of experience can not give us.

1027.   The mirror allows us to see the physical part of our Self from the outside, as others see it. But the conclusions that are drawn can be rather different.

1028.   The concept of quality is also applicable to defects. For example, hypocrisy can be obvious, mediocre, skillful or artistic (if not altogether diabolical).

1029.   The humor of coarse people is funny only for them. But they believe the same thing about the humor of educated people.

1030.   The royal appearance of the great hides the underlying human miseries; nay, by contrast, the former exaggerates the latter.

1031.   To be indifferent to evil, one has to be indifferent to good. But to be indifferent to good can not be but evil.

1032.   In space, if beyond a certain point there were no more celestial bodies, there should be the vacuum. Well then, where would the vacuum end? With what would it border? Probably, with madness.

1033.   Sometimes ability is at the service of character, and sometimes it is the contrary. But, unlike character, ability may be ready to serve any master, good or bad.

1034.   Behind nature's marvels, there is an unfathomable intelligence.

1035.   The official Self is the result of the accurate selection of the variables that make up the intimate Self.

1036.   Thinking intensively adds depth to the glance, as if the eyes, inwardly directed, became sharper in the effort to penetrate the haziness that masks the truth.

1037. Un ambizioso non prova devozione verso nessuno, eccetto verso se stesso. Ma l'aspetta dagli altri.

1038. Non bisogna fare l'errore di identificare il perseguire il proprio utile con l'egoismo. Non si può perseguire che il nostro utile (in senso lato), perché assolutamente non avrebbe senso perseguire quello che ci danneggia o ci rende infelici. Quello che consideriamo "utile" è quello che ci dà piacere e ci dà piacere perché si confà con il nostro carattere e bisogni. Ma, in alcuni individui (egoisti), la ricerca dell'utile consiste solo nel vantaggio personale, anche se a danno di altri. Invece, nella maggior parte degli individui (persone normali), la ricerca dell'utile consiste nel loro vantaggio senza danno ad altri (come ottenere un buon salario, promozioni, la stima di sé, riconoscimenti, ecc.). Volta a volta, in differenti individui, la ricerca dell'utile consiste (e deve consistere) più nel dare che nel ricevere: include anche il piacere che deriva da generosità, sacrificio, negazione di se stessi, altruismo, comprensione, perdono, affetto, abnegazione, eroismo, ecc. Per es., persegue il proprio utile sia chi non si cura dell'inquinamento della natura causato dalla sua fabbrica (egoisti) sia chi combatte per la protezione dell'ambiente (altruisti). Il primo persegue un utile immediato e personale a scapito di tutti gli altri, il secondo un utile a lunga scadenza e generale. Dunque, si persegue tutti quello che ci dà piacere, e si è egoisti solo quando il nostro piacere comporta il vantaggio personale a scapito degli altri. Ragionevolmente, tutti dovremmo cercare il nostro utile, ma in maniera responsabile. La differenza può sembrare piccola, ma è fondamentale.

1039. Ci si consola pensando che tutti hanno impulsi negativi. Ma si dimentica che alcuni hanno il merito di superarli e altri la colpa di soccombervi.

1040. Non negheremo a Dio quell'intimità a cui noi riteniamo di avere diritto: l'intimità della sua grandezza.

1041. Una mente depressa prima di tutto perde la vivacità della creatività. Diventa oppressa da una tristezza pervadente che è tanto più opprimente quanto meno è oggettivamente giustificata.

1042. Tanto il parlare quanto il tacere dovrebbero essere una scelta deliberata. Il merito sta nel fare volta a volta la scelta giusta.

1037.   An ambitious person does not feel devotion toward anybody, except toward himself. But he demands it from others.

1038.   One must not make the mistake of identifying the pursuit of one's own advantage with selfishness. One has to pursue his own interests (in their broadest meaning), because it absolutely would make no sense to pursue what damages us and makes us unhappy. What we consider "useful" is what gives us pleasure and it does so because it agrees with our personality and needs. Therefore, in some individuals (the selfish), the search for profit consists only in personal advantage even if to others' detriment. In most individuals (normal persons), the search for the useful consists in their advantage without damage to others (such as a good salary, promotions, self-esteem, honors, etc.). In different occasions in different individuals, the search for profit consists (and must consist) more in giving than in receiving: it also includes the pleasure that derives from generosity, sacrifice, self-denial, altruism, pardon, comprehension, affection, abnegation, heroism, etc. E.g., pursue their own interests both those who do not care about the pollution of nature caused by their factory (the selfish) and those who vigorously fight for environmental protection (the unselfish). The former pursue an immediate and personal advantage, to the detriment of everybody else; the latter a long term advantage for everyone. So, we all pursue what gives us pleasure, and are selfish only when our pleasure results in our personal advantage to the detriment of others. Sensibly, we all should seek our advantage, but responsibly. The difference may seem small, but it is fundamental.

1039.   We console ourselves in thinking that everybody has negative impulses. But we forget that some have the merit of overcoming them and others the fault of yielding to them.

1040.   We should not deny God that intimacy to which we believe to be entitled: the intimacy of his greatness.

1041.   A depressed mind first of all loses the vivacity of its creativity. It becomes oppressed by a pervasive sadness that is as oppressive as it is objectively unjustified.

1042.   Both speaking and remaining silent should be a deliberate choice. Merit consists in making the right choice each time.

1043. Con la morte di un parente stretto muore anche tutto quel suo mondo che viveva in noi: resta solo il lento svanire dei ricordi.

1044. Probabilmente con simile frequenza, o si parla di quello che non si sa o si tace quello che si sa.

1045. Se vogliamo diminuire la nostra invidia, aumentiamo il nostro merito. Ma non l'aumenteremo diminuendo il merito altrui.

1046. Pensionati per cento, duecento, trecento, quattrocento... anni? In mancanza di morte naturale, la disperazione ci farebbe ricorrere al suicidio.

1047. L'oscurità di certe teorie può essere il risultato tanto di una grande confusione di idee quanto di una grande profondità di pensiero. Non capisce o chi scrive o chi legge.

1048. La creatività è spontanea, ma la sua espressione deve essere disciplinata. Lo impone la qualità dell'espressione.

1049. Che ci piaccia o no, le fondamenta dei nostri diritti sono i nostri doveri.

1050. Nella brevità, si elimina il non-essenziale. E non è poco.

1051. Nel regno animale, il mondo fisico diviene progressivamente più vasto man mano che aumentano la qualità e quantità dei recettori sensoriali e delle strutture cerebrali riceventi. Il mondo di un volpe è certo più vasto di quello di una lucertola, e quello di una lucertola più vasto di quello di un verme.

1052. Quando ci si dichiara figli di Dio, si assume (o si presume) che Dio sia d'accordo.

1053. È ipercritico soprattutto chi è insoddisfatto di se stesso.

1054. Non è la nebbia che è triste, ma il suo diradarsi. Similmente, è triste non l'avere sogni malinconici, ma il non averne nessuno.

1055. È importante creare il nuovo, anche se non tutto il nuovo che viene creato è importante.

1043.   With the death of a close relative, all of his world that lived in us also dies: only the slow fading of memories remains.

1044.   Probably with a similar frequency, we either speak about what we do not know or keep silent about what we know.

1045.   If we want to decrease our envy, let us increase our merit. But we will not increase our merit by decreasing that of others.

1046.   Retired for one hundred, two hundred, three hundred, four hundred... years? For lack of natural death, despair would drive us to suicide.

1047.   The obscurity of certain theories can be the result of either a great confusion of ideas or a great depth of thought. Either the writer or the reader fails to understand.

1048.   Creativity is spontaneous, but its expression must be disciplined. The quality of expression demands it.

1049.   Whether we like it or not, the foundations of our rights are our duties.

1050.   In brevity, the non-essential is eliminated. And that it is not little.

1051.   In the animal kingdom, the physical world becomes progressively larger as the quality and quantity of the sensory receptors and receiving brain structures increase. The world of a fox is certainly larger than that of a lizard, and that of a lizard is larger than that of a worm.

1052.   When we declare ourselves children of God, we assume (or presume) that God agrees with us.

1053.   Hypercritical is mostly that person who is dissatisfied with itself.

1054.   It is not the mist that it is sad, but its clearing up. Similarly, it is sad not to have melancholy dreams, but not having any dreams at all.

1055.   It is important to create the new, even if not all the new that is created is important.

1056. Gli opposti sono oscillazioni in più e in meno della normalità. Se la normalità si "sposta", gli opposti la seguono: d'estate si considera fresca la stessa temperatura che d'inverno si considera calda.

1057. Nello specchio dell'anima, i difetti sono l'immagine speculare delle virtù. Per questo, non possono esistere separatamente. Non potremmo essere buoni se non fossimo capaci di essere cattivi.

1058. È necessario per noi intuire Dio piuttosto che conoscerlo, dal momento che siamo incapaci persino di guardare direttamente il sole senza esserne accecati.

1059. Spesso ci riesce difficile ammettere che abbiamo sbagliato, come se, difendendo un nostro sbaglio, non lo facessimo più grave.

1060. La mente è spinta a cercare nell'ambiente esterno e interno stimoli gradevoli dal fatto che ne deriva piacere. Per questo, si cerca un buon ristorante, si seleziona un buon vino, si legge della poesia, si ragiona con la filosofia, si desidera essere con la persona amata, ecc. Gli stimoli che danno piacere sono diversi per ogni mente o per la stessa mente in tempi differenti: questo è un fattore essenziale nel determinare il comportamento individuale.

1061. Non la vanità, ma l'interesse può essere alla base della pomposità: si cercano i vantaggi del rispetto che derivano da una formale pretesa di importanza.

1062. Ci piacciono soprattutto le canzoni che ci fanno sognare, quelle che ci fanno rivivere alcune delle nostre emozioni più care.

1063. Prolungando la vita, vincendo le malattie e rendendo le cose più facili, la scienza coltiva indirettamente l'egoismo collettivo e individuale. Una delle limitazioni della scienza è che non si rivolge alle cose dello spirito, perché le considera estranee alla sua sfera. Per questo, un'epoca scientifica è intellettualmente interessante, ma può essere emotivamente arida.

1064. Il significato della vita sarebbe assai diminuito se il nostro modo di sentire non conoscesse volta a volta l'esaltazione delle vette e la depressione degli abissi. Inoltre, le vette sono più alte quando gli abissi sono più profondi. E reciprocamente.

1056. Opposites are plus and minus oscillations of normality. If normality "shifts", opposites follow it: during summer we consider cool the same temperature that during the winter we consider warm.

1057. In the mirror of the soul, defects are the mirror image of virtues. For that reason, they can not exist separately. One could not be good if he were not capable of being bad.

1058. It is necessary for us to have an intuition rather than knowledge of God, since we are incapable even of directly looking at the sun without being blinded by it.

1059. Often we find it difficult to admit that we made a mistake, as if, in defending a mistake of ours, we did not make it more serious.

1060. The mind is driven to seek in the external and internal environment agreeable stimuli by the fact that it derives pleasure from them. For this reason, we look for a good restaurant, we select a good wine, we read poetry, we reason with philosophy, we desire to be with our beloved, etc. The stimuli that give pleasure are different for each mind or for the same mind at different times: this is an essential factor in determining individual behavior.

1061. Not vanity, but interest may be at the basis of pomposity: the advantages of respect are sought which derive from a formal pretense of importance.

1062. We most like the songs that put us in a dreaming mood, those that make us re-live some of our most cherished emotions.

1063. By prolonging life, conquering diseases and making things easier, science indirectly encourages collective and individual selfishness. One of the limitations of science is that it does not address the matters of the spirit, because it considers them foreign to its realm. For this reason, a scientific era is intellectually interesting, but may be emotionally arid.

1064. The meaning of life would be much diminished if our way of feeling were not to experience from time to time the exhilaration of the peaks and the depression of the abysses. Furthermore, the peaks are higher when the abysses are deeper. And conversely.

1065. Se è vero che gli animali non hanno l'intelligenza dell'uomo, è anche vero che non ne hanno la stoltezza.

1066. Poiché gli altri ci vedono soprattutto dal di fuori e noi ci si vede soprattutto dal di dentro, non meraviglia che l'Io percepito da noi e quello percepito dagli altri sembrino due persone diverse.

1067. La natura dell'utile. Se persegui il tuo utile, ti considerano egoista; e se non lo fai, ti considerano stupido. Non ti criticano solo quando quello che fai è utile a loro.

1068. L'egoismo altrui ci offende tanto più quanto più siamo egoisti noi.

1069. Per tanti, un ostacolo alla fede è la logica. Eppure, la fede è giustificata proprio dall'insufficienza della logica, quella logica che sa trovare i dubbi, ma non le soluzioni.

1070. Spesso, siamo così coraggiosi che si trova più conveniente offendere quelli che ci vogliono bene che quelli che non ce ne vogliono. Perché sappiamo che i primi ci perdoneranno e siamo tentati dall'impunità? O forse abbiamo bisogno ogni tanto di scaricare le inevitabili tensioni generate dalla lunga vicinanza? Senza rendersi conto del danno che si fa.

1071. Si vive più intensamente nell'incertezza che nella certezza. Solo nella prima vi sono emozioni, speranze e opportunità.

1072. Un innamorato polarizza verso di sé il desiderio di innamorarsi della persona amata. L'innamorato interessa proprio per il suo interesse: la persona amata è assai sensibile all'idea di essere così straordinaria per chi l'ama.

1073. Se l'universo e le sue creature fossero dovuti al caso, il caso meriterebbe di essere divinizzato (se non altro, per essere così straordinariamente ordinato). In deferenza a tale dio, comportarsi a caso dovrebbe essere di gran lunga superiore al ragionare.

1074. Siamo così instabili nelle nostre emozioni che oggi ci si considera eroi e domani mostri. Ma le dimensioni delle nostre emozioni stabiliscono i limiti delle oscillazioni: piccole emozioni, piccole oscillazioni.

1065. If it is true that animals do not have the intelligence of man, it is also true that they do not have his foolishness.

1066. Since others see us mostly from the outside and we see ourselves mostly from the inside, it is not surprising that the Self perceived by us and that perceived by others seem to be two different persons.

1067. The nature of interest. If you pursue your interest, they say that you are egoist; if you do not, they say that you are stupid. Only when what you do is in their interest, they do not criticize you .

1068. The egoism of others offends us more the more egotistic we are.

1069. For many, logic is an obstacle to faith. Yet, faith is justified by the very insufficiency of logic, that logic which can find the doubts, but not the solutions.

1070. Often, we are so courageous that we find it more convenient to offend those who love us than those who do not. Is it because we know that the former will pardon us and we are tempted by impunity? Or perhaps we need occasionally to discharge the inevitable tensions generated by the long vicinity? Without realizing the damage that we do.

1071. We live more intensively in uncertainty than in certainty. Only in the former there are emotions, hopes and opportunities.

1072. A lover polarizes toward himself the desire of the beloved to fall in love. The lover elicits interest because of his very interest: the beloved is very sensitive to the idea of being so extraordinary for the lover.

1073. If the universe and its creatures were due to chance, chance would deserve to be deified (if nothing else, for being so extraordinarily ordered). In deference to such a god, behaving randomly should be far superior to reasoning.

1074. We are so unstable in our emotions that today we consider ourselves heroes and tomorrow monsters. But the dimensions of emotions establish the limits of the oscillations: small emotions, small oscillations.

1075. Tanto nell'arroganza che nell'umiltà si cerca il proprio Io, sia pure con mezzi opposti. La stessa motivazione prende strade opposte a seconda del temperamento, ma non con lo stesso merito.

1076. Nell'ignavia, l'inerzia della mente fa sì che le poche domande che si pone siano senza risposta. Se vi è una risposta, è solo il ricorrente eco della domanda.

1077. Nella nostra debolezza vi è qualcosa di patetico, la malinconia delle cose umane.

1078. L'essere sedotti dalle proprie parole risulta in una prosa che si compiace di se stessa, ma non riesce a compiacere il lettore perché la bellezza elude le pretese di una pseudo eleganza.

1079. Alcuni sono sinceramente pronti ad aiutarti ad avere successo solo finché sono convinti che non avrai successo.

1080. Si perdona veramente non quando si ignorano le offese, ma quando vi si risponde con sincera gentilezza e generosità. Questo si può fare solo quando si ama (e fintanto che si ama).

1081. Uno degli antidoti più efficaci contro la noia è la lotta. E forse è il più importante.

1082. Se non abbiamo un'intensa vita interiore, si cerca l'indipendenza e invece si trova la solitudine. Se l'abbiamo, si cerca la solitudine e si trova l'indipendenza.

1083. La demagogia è spesso turgida, in genere disonesta e mai elegante.

1084. Una delle prove più importanti dell'esistenza di Dio è la mente umana: solo Dio avrebbe potuto farla. Semplicemente, non c'è la benché minima possibilità che sia dovuta al caso. Il caso può essere fortunato, ma non ha mai una genialità così incommensurabile.

1085. Quello che ci fa adatti ad una cosa ci fa disadatti ad altre. La forza in un campo è debolezza in tutti gli altri campi. Chi compone musica eroica è in generale poco adatto a fare musica per balletti: è troppo forte per essere sufficientemente delicato. Altri sono troppo delicati per essere sufficientemente forti.

1075. In arrogance as well as in humility one seeks his Self, although with opposite means. The same motivation takes opposite paths according to one's temperament, but not with the same merit.

1076. In indolence, inertia of the mind causes the few questions that it asks itself to remain without answer. If there is an answer, it is only the recurring echo of the question.

1077. In our weakness there is something pathetic, the melancholy of human things.

1078. Being seduced by our own words leads to a prose that is pleased of itself, but fails to please the reader because beauty eludes the pretense of a pseudo elegance.

1079. Some are sincerely willing to help you to succeed only as long as they are convinced that you will not succeed.

1080. We truly pardon not when we ignore offenses, but when we answer them with a sincere kindness and generosity. We can do that only when we love (and as long as we love).

1081. One of the most effective antidotes against boredom is struggle. And, perhaps, it is the most important one.

1082. If we do not have an intense inner life, we seek independence and instead find solitude. If we do, we seek solitude and find independence.

1083. Demagogy is often turgid, generally dishonest and never elegant.

1084. One of the most important proofs of the existence of God is the human mind: only God could have made it. Simply, there is not the least chance that it might be due to chance. Chance may be lucky, but never displays such an incommensurable genius.

1085. What makes us suited for something, makes us unsuited for everything else. Strength in one field is weakness in all other fields. The composer of heroic music in general is little suited to write music for ballets: he is too strong to be sufficiently delicate. Others are too delicate to be sufficiently strong.

1086. Se si capisce, si risponde non alle azioni altrui, ma ai motivi che li muovono.

1087. L'amore è una sindrome. Come ogni sindrome, è imprevedibile e talvolta difficile a curare. Ma è una sindrome che pochi si rifiuterebbero di avere.

1088. Nell'insegnare, l'istruzione si rivolge alla memoria, e l'educazione allo sviluppo della mente.

1089. A seconda del carattere, o si invidia o si rispetta quello che noi non siamo capaci di fare.

1090. Si è spinti ad essere moralisti dall'interesse nella virtù.

1091. Senza la giustizia divina, non vi sarebbe giustizia. Ma senza la giustizia umana vi sarebbe la giungla.

1092. Le attenzioni di un innamorato seducono tanto più facilmente quanto più la persona amata è predisposta a volersi innamorare.

1093. Si è più tolleranti quando si è molto buoni, o comprensivi, o poco meritevoli, o del tutto indifferenti.

1094. La logica delle emozioni è di non averne alcuna.

1095. Troviamo affascinanti quelli di cui siamo innamorati. E fintanto che lo siamo.

1096. Essere moderati può essere ragionevole (per es., nel mangiare, bere o fumare) come può non esserlo (per es., nel non esigere abbastanza da noi stessi).

1097. Se ti fosse stato chiesto di creare gli esseri umani, come li avresti fatti? Risposta imbarazzata ad una domanda imbarazzante? Ma allora, come giustificheremo tutte le nostre critiche? Forse, con la limitatezza della nostra comprensione?

1098. Come pendoli, si oscilla tra il male e il bene. Se si smette di oscillare, ci si ferma in una posizione intermedia, non tanto equidistante dal bene e dal male quanto indifferente a tutti e due.

1086. If we understand, we respond not to the actions of others, but to the motives that drive them.

1087. Love is a syndrome. Like every syndrome, it is unpredictable and sometimes difficult to treat. But it is a syndrome that few would refuse to experience.

1088. In teaching, instruction addresses the memory, and education the development of the mind.

1089. Depending on our character, we either envy or respect in others that which we are not capable of doing.

1090. One is driven to be a moralist by the interest in virtue.

1091. Without divine justice, there would be no justice. But without human justice, there would be chaos.

1092. The attentions of a lover seduce more easily the more the beloved is predisposed to falling in love.

1093. One is more tolerant if he is very good hearted, or understanding, or little meritorious, or entirely indifferent.

1094. The logic of emotions is to have none.

1095. We find fascinating those with whom we are in love. And as long as we are in love.

1096. To be restrained may be reasonable (for example, in eating, drinking or smoking) or it may not be (for example, in not demanding enough from ourselves).

1097. If you had been asked to create human beings, how would you have made them? An embarrassed answer to an embarrassing question? But then, how will we justify all our criticisms? Perhaps, with the limitation of our comprehension?

1098. As pendulums, we oscillate between evil and good. If we stop oscillating, we stop in an intermediary position, not so much equidistant from good and evil as indifferent to both.

1099. L'essere compiaciuti della propria semplicità è già una forma di arroganza.

1100. Si generalizza perché la mente desidera intensamente di capire le leggi generali, ma inevitabilmente lo si fa secondo le proprie tendenze personali. Anche se vere, le generalizzazioni non possono che riflettere una personale realtà che crede in valori che non tutti possono condividere. Questo non significa che la verità è personale e variabile. Significa invece che vi saranno sempre differenti convinzioni su ciò che è vero o falso. Quello che varia non è la verità, ma le convinzioni, ricordando che una convinzione non dimostra la verità di nulla. E che una verità non cessa di essere tale solo perché non vi crediamo. Al contrario, il riconoscere una verità può portare a modificare le nostre convinzioni.

1101. Qualche volta, le nostre critiche degli altri fanno ridere: quelli potrebbero dire cose molto peggiori di noi.

1102. Una cosa è conoscere e un'altra è capire.

1103. Chi non è morale per ciò stesso non è neanche moralista; ad eccezione degli ipocriti.

1104. Se non l'amore, certo l'affetto prospera quando coltivato con considerazione, gentilezza e attenzioni: come l'ibisco, può allora produrre uno dopo l'altro fiori bellissimi.

1105. In generale, l'aforisma enuncia delle regole e il paradosso delle eccezioni. Ma anche questa regola ha le sue eccezioni.

1106. La demagogia ignora la ragione e la ragionevolezza. Ma, nel rivolgersi a passioni e interessi, non ignora la psicologia della natura umana.

1107. Anche se non diretta a noi, si è assai sensibili alle allusioni che riteniamo applicabili a noi.

1108. Tra quelli che considerano se stessi intelligenti, in effetti alcuni lo sono.

1109. I desideri sono i ragionamenti del cuore.

1099. To be complacent about one's own simplicity is already a form of arrogance.

1100. We generalize because the mind yearns to understand the general laws, but inevitably we do it according to our own personal tendencies. Even if true, generalizations can not but reflect a personal reality that believes in values that may not be agreed upon by everybody. This does not mean that truth is personal and variable. Instead, it means that there will always be different personal beliefs as to what is true or false. What varies is not the truth but our beliefs, keeping in mind that a belief does not demonstrate the truth of anything. And that a truth does not cease to be so only because we do not believe in it. On the contrary, recognizing a truth may lead us to modify our beliefs.

1101. Sometimes, our criticism of others is laughable: they could say much worse things about us.

1102. One thing is to know and another to understand.

1103. Those who are not moral necessarily are not moralists either; with the exception of hypocrites.

1104. If not love, certainly affection prospers when cultivated with consideration, gentleness and regards: like the hibiscus, it can then produce beautiful flowers one after the other.

1105. In general, an aphorism enunciates rules and a paradox exceptions. But also this rule has its exceptions.

1106. Demagogy ignores reason and reasonableness. But, in addressing passions and interests, it does not ignore the psychology of human nature.

1107. Even if not directed at us, we are rather sensitive to the allusions that we believe applicable to us.

1108. Among those who consider themselves intelligent, in fact some are so.

1109. Desires are the reasoning of the heart.

1110.   Al contrario della religione, la scienza non predica. La spiegazione è che la scienza studia l'uomo qual'è, e la religione cerca di ispirarlo a essere migliore. Ma, soprattutto, la prima studia la fissità del corpo, e la seconda vuole strutturare la malleabilità dello spirito. Vuole coltivarne la forza, cosicché gli impulsi animali e un miope egoismo non oscurino la necessità della presenza di Dio.

1111.   Invece di esprimere lo spirito di una cosa, certi paradossi vogliono semplicemente essere spiritosi.

1112.   L'ateismo dimostra la libertà concessaci da Dio. Sarebbe stato facile (quanto futile) farci tutti credenti.

1113.   La debolezza è spesso penosamente indifesa, all'interno e all'esterno.

1114.   Generalmente, i giovani trovano gli altri giovani belli, anche quando sono brutti.

1115.   Un egoismo miope è un egoismo incompetente.

1116.   L'altrui stupidità non dovrebbe stimolare la nostra. In fondo, solo un'adeguata comprensione e un migliore modo di agire non ci fanno altrettanto stupidi.

1117.   La sensibilità è un diapason che la bellezza fa vibrare.

1118.   La qualità di chi guida non è più importante di quella di chi segue. Lo si vede chiaramente dalla confusione che si genera quando tutti vogliono dirigere o quando nessuno vuole seguire.

1119.   La verità non ha aggettivi. La verità non è morale o immorale, idealista o cinica, ottimista o pessimista, ecc.: semmai lo è quello che correttamente descrive. E una descrizione deve sempre essere corretta, altrimenti non è una verità.

1120.   Dando ai nostri figli, si insegna loro a dare ai loro figli. Per lo meno se capiscono in cosa consista l'amore.

1121.   Possiamo essere stupidi in tante maniere. Neanche alla stupidità è negato il piacere della varietà.

1110. Contrary to religion, science does not preach. The explanation is that science studies man as it is, and religion strives to inspire him to be better. But, most of all, the former studies the fixity of the body, and the latter wants to structure the malleability of the spirit. Religion wants to cultivate its strength, so that animal drives and myopic selfishness do not obscure the necessity of God's presence.

1111. Instead of expressing the spirit of things, certain paradoxes simply want to be witty.

1112. Atheism proves the liberty conceded to us by God. It would have been easy (as well as futile) to make us all believers.

1113. Our weakness is often painfully defenseless, inside and outside ourselves.

1114. Generally, young people find other young people handsome, even when they are ugly.

1115. A myopic egoism is an incompetent egoism.

1116. The stupidity of others should not excite ours. After all, only an adequate comprehension and a better way of behaving do not make us as stupid.

1117. Sensitivity is a tuning fork that beauty sets into vibration.

1118. The quality of leaders is not more important than that of the followers. This is clearly seen from the confusion produced when everyone wants to lead or when nobody wants to follow.

1119. Truth has no adjectives. Truth is not moral or immoral, idealistic or cynical, optimistic or pessimistic, etc.: only what it truthfully describes may be so. And a description has to always be correct, otherwise it is not a truth.

1120. In giving to our children, we teach them to give to their children. At least, if they understand in what love consists.

1121. We can be stupid in so many ways. Not even stupidity has been denied the pleasure of variety.

1122. Che la moralità sia uno strumento dell'Ordine è dimostrato dal disordine causato dalla sua mancanza.

1123. Con tutti i suoi slanci, la passione dell'amore essenzialmente consiste in quello che si prova noi. E se non si prova più nulla, l'amore non c'è più, anche se la persona che si amava è cambiata ben poco e ci ama come prima o anche più di prima.

1124. Ci si avvicina tanto più a Dio quanto più ci si allontana dal proprio egoismo.

1125. La decenza esibisce piccole virtù e nasconde piccoli vizi; e l'indecenza si compiace sfacciatamente dei vizi, deridendo la virtù.

1126. Se tutti noi la pensassimo alla stessa maniera, ci si troverebbe l'un l'altro uniformemente noiosi. La necessità della varietà fa sì che ogni mente abbia le sue "verità" o convinzioni (che soggettivamente è la stessa cosa). Inoltre, essendo personali, le nostre "verità" e convinzioni ci permettono di cambiare opinione.

1127. Abbiamo un termostato personale anche per le nostre emozioni e pensieri: al di sopra o a di sotto del nostro livello prestabilito, non ci sentiamo più a nostro agio.

1128. Non la nostra discrezione, ma i nostri fallimenti ci fanno cauti nel disprezzare gli altri.

1129. La bellezza fisica è come una perla rara cui è negata l'immunità contro le devastazioni del tempo.

1130. Mantenendo ogni tanto un silenzio dignitoso, può darsi che ci attribuiscano di più di quanto in realtà avremmo potuto dire.

1131. Le minigonne sono coraggiose: non temono per nulla di mostrare delle gambe brutte.

1132. Non si cresce più quando si raggiungono i limiti delle nostre potenzialità. Allora si è quello che saremo mai capaci di essere.

1133. I lasciti del passato si ereditano solo attraverso la cultura. Per questa ragione, vi sono tanti diseredati.

1122.   That morality is an instrument of the Order is demonstrated by the disorder caused by its lack.

1123.   In spite of its devotion, the passion of love essentially consists of what we feel. And if we do not feel anything any longer, there is no more love, even if the beloved has changed very little and loves us as before or even more than before.

1124.   We get closer to God the further away we move from our selfishness.

1125.   Decency exhibits small virtues and hides small vices; and indecency shamelessly exhibits vices, while mocking virtue.

1126.   If all of us had the same opinions, we would find each other uniformly boring. The necessity of variety makes each mind to have its "truths" or its convictions (which subjectively are the same thing). Furthermore, being personal, our "truths" and convictions allow us to change our opinions.

1127.   We have a personal thermostat also for our emotions and thoughts: above or below our pre-established level, we do not any longer feel at ease.

1128.   Not our fairness, but our failures make us cautious in despising others.

1129.   Physical beauty is like a rare pearl to which immunity against the ravages of time is denied.

1130.   By keeping ever so often a dignified silence, they may attribute to us more than what we could actually have said.

1131.   Mini-skirts are courageous: they are not in the least afraid to uncover ugly legs.

1132.   We do not grow any more when we reach the limits of our potentialities. We are then what we will ever be capable of being.

1133.   The legacies of the past are inherited only through culture. For this reason, there are so many disinherited people.

1134. Si fa ridere quando si è o spiritosi o ridicoli. Nel primo caso, facciamo ridere la gente; nel secondo, la gente ride di noi.

1135. Con lo specchio ci si vede dal di fuori e con la mente dal di dentro. E le due immagini non sempre coincidono. Anche perché ogni volta lo specchio ci presenta un Io un poco differente (ma mai più giovane).

1136. Ogni tanto, desideriamo avere desideri delicati.

1137. Per essere sempre onesti con se stessi occorre un coraggio fermo, costante e quieto. In genere, più coraggio di quanto ne abbiamo. O di quanto ne vogliamo avere?

1138. La varietà è piacevole perché stimola diversi aspetti della mente: per questa ragione, piacciono sia la luminosità di un giorno pieno di sole sia il grigiore delle nuvole che corrono basse.

1139. Non bisogna aver paura di nulla, neanche di essere paurosi quando bisogna.

1140. Perdoniamo (o dovremmo perdonare) più facilmente quando anche noi abbiamo qualcosa da farci perdonare. Ma allora quasi sempre..?

1141. La vanità delle cose di questo mondo si ferma alla soglia degli affetti, bellezza, perfezione, fede, poesia, felicità, gentilezza, tragedie, generosità, dedizione, sacrificio, sofferenza, ecc.

1142. Come nei buoi, la faccia è placida quando la mente non ragiona.

1143. In questo mondo, né ai buoni né ai cattivi è garantito nulla, perché, se la moralità potesse essere patteggiata, si farebbe per interesse quello che dobbiamo fare per dovere.

1144. Si è facilmente sedotti dalle nuove maniere "moderne" di comportarsi. Solo dopo ci si rende conto che ogni stortura di condotta comporta gli inconvenienti del susseguente squilibrio.

1145. Non dubitiamo di un numero enorme di cose che non abbiamo mai visto (p. es., un elettrone). Ma l'incongruenza della logica può dubitare di ciò che è illogico negare (p. es., il Creatore dell'elettrone).

1134. We elicit laughter when we are either witty or ridiculous. In the first case, we make people laugh; in the second, people laugh at us.

1135. With the mirror we see ourselves from without and with the mind from within. And the two images do not always coincide. Also because every time the mirror introduces to us a slightly different (but never younger) Self.

1136. Once in a while, we desire to have delicate desires.

1137. To be always honest with oneself, a firm, unflagging and quiet courage is needed. In general, more courage than we have. Or than we want to have?

1138. Variety is pleasing because it stimulates different aspects of the mind: for this reason, we like both the luminosity of a day full of sunshine and the grayness of the clouds that run low.

1139. It is necessary not to be afraid of anything, not even of being afraid when it is necessary.

1140. We forgive (or should forgive) more easily when we also have something to be forgiven. But then almost always....?

1141. The vanity of the things of this world comes to a standstill at the threshold of affections, beauty, perfection, faith, poetry, happiness, kindness, tragedy, generosity, dedication, sacrifice, sorrows, etc.

1142. As in cattle, the face is placid when the mind does not reason.

1143. In this world, nothing is guaranteed to either good or bad people, since, if morality were to be subject to negotiation, we would do out of interest what we have to do out of duty.

1144. We are easily seduced by the new "modern" ways of behaving. Only afterwards we realize that every distortion of behavior brings about the disadvantages of the subsequent imbalance.

1145. We do not doubt of an enormous number of things that we have never seen (e.g., an electron). But the incongruity of logic may doubt what is illogical to deny (e.g., the Creator of the electron).

1146.   L'attenzione è la porta che permette alle percezioni di entrare nell'edificio della memoria.

1147.   Quando si parla con veemenza di quello che pesa sul nostro cuore, lo sfogo emotivo ci solleva e i consigli altrui ci irritano.

1148.   Prima di tutto, le cose dovrebbero essere divise in due categorie: quelle vere e quelle false.

1149.   L'idea di poter essere affascinanti ci titilla.

1150.   Se la natura umana potesse cambiare, la storia diverrebbe incomprensibile.

1151.   La varietà che vi è nella moltitudine ci rende individualmente dispensabili.

1152.   Sentimenti di poesia sono ispirati da quella bellezza che la logica superficialmente ignora.

1153.   Solo la gente superficiale non comprende la necessità e l'utilità della routine. Ma il disprezzo della routine non ci fa originali, ma solo facilmente annoiati.

1154.   Per quanto in differente misura, abbiamo i vizi e le virtù di sempre. Ma, a seconda dell'epoca, alcuni dei vizi o delle virtù prevalgono.

1155.   Nello scoprire le leggi naturali, l'uomo comunica con Dio.

1156.   Il nemico più pericoloso dell'amore non è tanto il disaccordo quanto il subentrare dell'indifferenza.

1157.   A seconda dei nostri sentimenti verso gli altri, si cercano delle scuse per giustificare sia la nostra simpatia che la nostra antipatia. E se i sentimenti cambiano, cambiano anche le scuse.

1158.   In quello a cui siamo esposti, si è colpiti soprattutto da quello a cui siamo predisposti.

1159.   Il comportamento riflette la maniera complessa con cui la natura umana affronta le sue complesse necessità, diverse per ciascuno.

1146. Attention is the door that allows perceptions to enter into the edifice of memory.

1147. When we speak with vehemence of what weighs on our heart, the emotional outlet relieves us and the advice of others irritates us.

1148. First of all, things should be divided in two categories: those that are true and those that are false.

1149. The idea that we might be fascinating titillates us.

1150. If human nature were subject to change, history would become incomprehensible.

1151. The variety that there is in the multitude makes us individually dispensable.

1152. Feelings of poetry are inspired by that beauty that logic superficially ignores.

1153. Only superficial people do not understand the necessity and usefulness of routine. But contempt of routine does not makes us original, only easily bored.

1154. Although in a different measure, we have the vices and virtues of always. But, in different eras, some vices or some virtues prevail.

1155. In discovering natural laws, man communicates with God.

1156. The most dangerous enemy of love is not so much discord as the beginning of indifference.

1157. Depending on our feelings toward others, we seek excuses to justify either our liking or our disliking. And if our feelings change, so do our excuses.

1158. To what we are exposed, we are struck most of all by that to which we are predisposed.

1159. Behavior reflects the complex manner with which human nature confronts its complex necessities, which are different for everyone.

1160. Il fatto che grandi pittori, scultori, architetti, musicisti, poeti, ecc. abbiano lasciato grandi opere ma non grandi pensieri suggerisce che forse la logica non è necessariamente l'attributo più importante della mente umana.

1161. Certi nostri difetti ci motivano più delle virtù.

1162. Nella realtà quotidiana, l'amore si esprime in piccole cose, in parole semplici, atti gentili, ondate emotive, e in affetti intensi e profondi, raramente espressi.

1163. Quando è intrattenuta, la mente diventa passiva: è il suo momento di rilassarsi ed apprezzare i frutti dell'altrui talento.

1164. Non si è timidi se non si è sensibili. In molti, le vicissitudini della vita cambiano gradualmente la sensibilità della timidezza in una sensibile abilità.

1165. Persino la moralità ha le sue mode; come del resto l'immoralità.

1166. Gli impulsi istintivi sono i binari della condotta: ciascuno ha un binario che lo porta dove è spinto ad andare, anche se qualche volta troppo tardi si scopre che si trattava di un binario morto.

1167. Si comprendono solo alcuni aspetti del mistero che ci circonda, perché noi non abbiamo la chiave passe-partout, cioè una comprensione della strategia generale.

1168. Le persone educate urlano sottovoce.

1169. Ci si stanca di ogni situazione, perché gradualmente i vantaggi si esauriscono e gli svantaggi divengono apparenti: si desidera allora l'opposto. Per es., quando nella solitudine non abbiamo più nulla da dirci, si desidera la compagnia. E quando gli svaghi della compagnia divengono noiosi, si desidera l'intimità della solitudine.

1170. Come categoria i numeri sono anonimi, eppure vengono usati proprio per stabilire l'identità di un gran numero di oggetti e persone.

1171. Anche l'anticipazione ha i suoi fremiti.

1160. The fact that great painters, sculptors, architects, composers, poets, etc., have left great works but not great thoughts perhaps suggests that logic is not necessarily the most important attribute of the human mind.

1161. Some of our faults motivate us more than virtues.

1162. In the daily reality, love is expressed in small things, in simple words, gentle acts, waves of emotions, and in intense and deep feelings, rarely expressed.

1163. When it is entertained, the mind becomes passive: it is its moment to relax and enjoy the fruits of others' talent.

1164. Timidity is associated with sensitivity. In many, the vicissitudes of life gradually change the sensitivity of timidity in a sensitive ability.

1165. Even morality has its fashions; as, for that matter, immorality.

1166. Instinctive drives are the tracks of behavior: everyone has a track that brings him where he is pushed to go, even if sometimes we discover too late that it was a dead end track.

1167. We understand only some aspects of the mystery that surrounds us, because we do not have the master key, that is a comprehension of the overall strategy.

1168. Well-bred persons scream in an undertone.

1169. We tire of every situation, because gradually the advantages become exhausted and the disadvantages apparent: we then desire the opposite situation. E.g., when in solitude we have nothing more to say to ourselves, we desire company. And when the amusements of company become boring, we desire the intimacy of solitude.

1170. As a category, numbers are anonymous. Yet, they are used precisely just to establish the identity of a large number of objects and persons.

1171. Anticipation too has its thrills.

1172. La sensibilità esige che l'ingrediente più importante dei nostri sogni debba essere la poesia.

1173. La vecchiaia comincia quando desideri, ambizioni, timori e speranze cominciano a svanire e l'indifferenza rende le emozioni stanche.

1174. Quando volontariamente si sopprime una nostra virtù, si indurisce il cuore per avere quella rigidità che ci permetta di non sentirci consciamente colpevoli o di fare marcia indietro.

1175. Poiché la logica non è infallibile, convince solo quando *si crede* ai suoi argomenti. Per questo, le sue "verità" sono accettate da alcuni e respinte da altri.

1176. La gran varietà di persone risulta dal mescolarsi di una gran varietà di caratteristiche congenite ed acquisite. Nelle singole persone, non sono tanto le caratteristiche che variano di più quanto il loro grado di sviluppo.

1177. È nel nostro interesse esigere da noi stessi più di quanto si esiga dagli altri.

1178. La giovinezza ha una sua maniera esuberante di sentire senza averne la coscienza.

1179. Si chiudono gli occhi quando si vuol essere con la propria intimità.

1180. Nella speranza manteniamo aperta la porta alla possibilità, anche contro il parere della probabilità.

1181. Se non fosse per i dubbi creati dal fatto che Dio non si manifesta direttamente e che la nostra mente è limitata, saremmo tutti forzati ad essere credenti. Questo sarebbe la fine della fede e il principio della schiavitù.

1182. L'abitudine è uno strumento di uguaglianza: entro certi limiti, ci si abitua alla miseria come alla ricchezza.

1183. Gli ipocriti sono creduti anche quando mentono e i bugiardi non sono creduti anche quando dicono la verità. Il che fa dell'ipocrita un bugiardo più abile.

1172. Sensitivity demands that the most important ingredient of our dreams should be poetry.

1173. Old age begins when desires, ambitions, fears and hopes begin to fade and indifference makes the emotions tired.

1174. When we voluntarily suppress a virtue, we harden our heart to have that rigidity that allows us not to feel consciously guilty or to pull back.

1175. Since logic is not infallible, it convinces only when *we believe* its arguments. This is why its "truths" are accepted by some and rejected by others.

1176. The great variety of persons results from the mixing of a great variety of congenital and acquired characteristics. In each person, it is not the characteristics that vary so much as their degree of development.

1177. It is in our interest to demand of ourselves more than what we demand of others.

1178. Youth has its own exuberant way of feeling without being conscious of it.

1179. We shut our eyes when we want to be with our intimacy.

1180. In hoping, we keep the door open to possibility, even against the advice of probability.

1181. If it were not for the doubts created by the fact that God does not manifest himself directly and that our mind is limited, all of us would be forced to be believers. This would be the end of faith and the beginning of slavery.

1182. Habit is a means of equalization: within certain limits, people get used to being poor as well as to being rich.

1183. Hypocrites are believed even when they lie and liars are not believed even when they say the truth. That makes the hypocrite a more skillful liar.

1184. È quanto mai straordinario che il disegno divino includa un senso di libertà. La necessità di un ordine rigido e stabile è stata conciliata con quella della responsabilità individuale. Ci è stato permesso di scegliere tra il bene ed il male, per quanto la nostra volontà si trovi spesso in balia della tempesta delle emozioni.

1185. Il senso dell'umorismo varia da individuo a individuo. Quello che non varia è la necessità di avere il senso dell'umorismo.

1186. La logica non è la sola realtà, né il solo mezzo di considerare la realtà: quando uno è illogico, non cessa di esistere. Anzi, può vivere più intensamente.

1187. L'ambizione obbliga il merito ad eccellere.

1188. È tipico dell'ignoranza di aver dell'arroganza: nemmeno si sospetta quanto poco si valga.

1189. Le prediche non sarebbero necessarie se si fosse meno deboli e fragili meno spesso.

1190. Si vede il mondo con gli occhi della propria età. Se la realtà è mentale (come in effetti è), la realtà non può avere che i connotati dello stadio di sviluppo della mente.

1191. Ci si sente liberi quando si decide "liberamente". Ma dentro di noi chi è che decide liberamente se si risponde allo stesso stimolo una volta con ira, un'altra con ragionevolezza, e qualche volta non si risponde per nulla? Sembrerebbe che spesso la "libera" decisione sia il risultato netto di vari impulsi contrastanti di cui abbiamo poco controllo.

1192. Non è illogico che i filosofi siano appassionati soprattutto da quello che non capiscono.

1193. Se non i sentimenti, certo la sentimentalità è più sviluppata nei giovani.

1194. Certe persone sono imprevedibili: non appartengono né ad uno schema generale né ad uno particolare. Magari si offendono per una lode e ridono divertite per un'offesa.

1184. It is most extraordinary that the divine design includes a sense of liberty. The necessity of a rigid and stable order has been reconciled with that of individual responsibility. We have been allowed to choose between good and evil, although our will is often at the mercy of the tempest of our emotions

1185. The sense of humor varies from individual to individual. What does not vary is the necessity of having the sense of humor.

1186. Logic is not the only reality, nor the only means to address reality: when illogical, one does not cease to exist. On the contrary, he may live more intensively.

1187. Ambition compels merit to excel.

1188. It is typical of ignorance to have arrogance: we do not even suspect how little is our worth.

1189. Preaching would be unnecessary if we were less weak and fragile less often.

1190. The world is seen through the eyes of one's age. If reality is mental (as it actually is), it can not but have the features of the stage of development of the mind.

1191. One feels free when one decides "freely". But, within ourselves, who is it that decides freely if we respond to the same stimulus at one time with anger, at another with reasonableness, and sometimes do not respond at all? It would seem that often the "free" decision is the net result of the different contrasting drives of which we have little control.

1192. It is not illogical that philosophers should be fascinated mostly by what they do not understand.

1193. If not sentiments, certainly sentimentality is more developed in young people.

1194. Some persons are unpredictable: they belong neither to a general nor to a particular scheme. They may take offense at praise and laugh amused at an offense.

1195. Una disciplina senza eccezioni soffoca la creatività.

1196. La genetica è il nostro testamento biologico: stabilisce quello che di più importante lasciamo ai nostri eredi.

1197. Bisogna essere sempre pronti ad essere se stessi, sia quando è facile sia quando è difficile.

1198. Qualche volta, si scrive solo per la propria solitudine.

1199. Prima o poi, ci si guarda nello specchio e vi si vede la vecchiaia.

1200. Ci cerca di impressionare tanto più i nostri vicini quanto meno riusciamo ad impressionare noi stessi.

1201. Per perdonare, bisogna prima superare il proprio egoismo. La generosità può dare solo quello che non è obbligata a dare.

1202. Una bontà generalizzata e costante sarebbe stucchevole come una dieta fatta solo di dolciumi. E altrettanto non fisiologica.

1203. Uno dei misteri della nostra epoca sarà il perché alcune donne non vogliano essere femminili. Il fascino di una carriera invece di una carriera di fascino?

1204. Naturalmente, si ride delle sciocchezze. Solo gli sciocchi ridono delle cose serie.

1205. Il senso dell'umorismo ci permette sia di ridere che di evitare di essere ridicoli.

1206. Il solo posto in cui ci si può nascondere al nostro Io cosciente è l'oscura cantina del subconscio. Ma, anche lì, si può essere scoperti dall'intermittente luce del faro dell'introspezione.

1207. La ripetizione degli stessi temi annuncia l'esaurimento della creatività.

1208. L'immaginazione e la fantasia sono la parte più libera della mente. Forse la sola. Creano la realtà che è esclusivamente nostra, cioè quella che ci piace di più.

1195. Discipline without exceptions stifles creativity.

1196. Genetics is our biological will: it establishes what of most importance we leave to our heirs.

1197. One must always be ready to be himself, when it is easy and when it is difficult.

1198. Sometimes, we write only for the benefit of our solitude.

1199. Sooner or later, we look in the mirror and we see old age.

1200. We try to impress our neighbors more the less we succeed in impressing ourselves.

1201. To pardon, one must first overcome his own selfishness. Generosity can only give what it is not obliged to give.

1202. A generalized and constant goodness would be sickly as a diet consisting only of sweets. And likewise non-physiological.

1203. One of the mysteries of our epoch will be the reason why some women do not want to be feminine. The fascination of a career instead of a career of fascination?

1204. Naturally, people laugh at nonsense. Only the silly laugh at serious matters.

1205. A sense of humor allows us to laugh as well as to avoid being ridiculous.

1206. The only place where we can hide from our conscious Self is the dark cellar of subconscious. But, even there, we can be detected by the intermittent beam of the lighthouse of introspection.

1207. The repetition of the same themes announces the exhaustion of creativity.

1208. Imagination and fancy are the freest part of the mind. Perhaps the only one. They create the reality that is exclusively ours, that is, the reality that we most like.

1209. Solo le emozioni più intense mantengono lo spirito giovane e la mente audace.

1210. Le offese eccitano il desiderio (o l'illusione) di essere potenti, naturalmente per potersi vendicare.

1211. Ha furia soprattutto chi è sempre in ritardo.

1212. La distinzione tra logica e fede non è così netta: quello che si crede non può essere illogico e quello che è logico deve essere credibile.

1213. La scuola degli scolari riflette quella dei maestri.

1214. Il piacere può deludere, ma la felicità si può solo rimpiangere.

1215. Il fatto che le donne contribuirono a fare sia gli eroi che la decadenza di Roma dimostra quanto grande sia la loro influenza nella formazione dell'uomo e delle sue azioni.

1216. In qualsiasi cosa si dica, si cerca quello che ci aumenta. Ma gli sciocchi in qualche maniera fanno sì da trovare in quello che dicono solo quello che li diminuisce.

1217. Si deve cercare l'essenziale per capire le leggi generali, ma l'essenza della vita è fatta in gran parte di non-essenziale: alla loro maniera, tutte le cose contribuiscono ad una vita normale.

1218. Se dobbiamo amare il prossimo come noi stessi (nonostante i suoi difetti), sembrerebbe che fosse obbligatorio amare noi stessi (nonostante i nostri difetti).

1219. Uguali opportunità rivelano solo meriti disuguali. Tra chi ha meno meriti, alcuni possono dire di voler uguali opportunità, ma in realtà vogliono non-meritati privilegi. Ma il tatto domanda che non si insista troppo su questo punto.

1220. In parte della realtà della mente, non raramente la sostanza consiste nell'apparenza. Se si distrugge l'apparenza attraverso un analisi non-sufficientemente critica, ci rimane ben poco. Pertanto, nelle cose di questa vita, non bisogna fare come i bambini che, per vedere cosa c'è dentro un giocattolo, lo distruggono.

1209. Only the most intense emotions keep the spirit young and the mind daring.

1210. Offenses excite the desire (or the delusion) of being powerful, naturally to take revenge.

1211. Those who are always late are most of the times in a hurry.

1212. Distinction between logic and faith is not so sharp: what we believe can not be illogical and what is logical has to be credible.

1213. The school of pupils reflects that of the teachers.

1214. Pleasure can disappoint, but happiness can only be regretted.

1215. The fact that women contributed to create both the heroes and the decadence of Rome shows how great is their influence in molding man and his actions.

1216. In whatever we say, we seek that which augments us. But the silly somehow in what he says only manages to find what diminishes him.

1217. We must look for the essential to understand general laws, but the essence of life is largely made of the non-essential: in their own way, all things contribute to a normal life.

1218. If we must love our neighbor as ourselves (in spite of his faults), it would seem that it should be obligatory that we love ourselves (in spite of our faults).

1219. Equal opportunities only reveal unequal merits. Some of those who have less merit may claim to want equal opportunities, but in actuality they want undeserved privileges. But tact demands that we do not insist too much on this point.

1220. In part of the reality of the mind, not rarely substance consists of appearance. If appearance is destroyed through a non-sufficiently critical analysis, very little remains. Therefore, in the things of this life, we must not act like children who, to in order to see what is inside a toy, destroy it.

1221. Non si deve credere che solo l'essenziale vada detto: sarebbe la fine della comune conversazione e di molti dotti trattati.

1222. Le devastazioni dell'età rendono difficile immaginare come la maggior parte delle persone possano essere state attraenti nella loro gioventù. Solo la gioventù dei loro figli può suggerire una tale possibilità.

1223. La debolezza considera forti anche quelli che sono solo testardi o rozzi.

1224. Capire molto ma non abbastanza è più pericoloso che capire poco: è probabile che gli sbagli siano più grandi.

1225. Con lo sguardo fisso solo sulle aspirazioni dell'anima, l'ascetismo riconosce come valide solo le emozioni dello spirito.

1226. Nei delitti passionali, quello che meraviglia di più sono le fotografie delle vittime: non si capisce come qualcuno possa aver perso la testa a causa loro.

1227. Nel tumulto della vita, vi è l'ordinata strategia del disegno divino: un tumulto pianificato. E pertanto obbligatorio. Vi appartengono sia l'ordine che il disordine, per quanto con funzioni e conseguenze differenti.

1228. Nell'algebra della mente, la somma dei piaceri non risulta necessariamente nella felicità.

1229. È vero che il pessimismo può indebolire la volontà di combattere, ma qualche volta è il contrario: una debole volontà di combattere si serve del pessimismo per giustificarsi.

1230. I modulatori del cuore sono i nostri ormoni. Sono loro che influenzano il nostro umore, fantasie, sogni e desideri. Per questo, la parabola del cuore segue quella dell'età.

1231. I bambini si adattano facilmente perché, non avendo ancora una struttura portante propria, si appoggiano alle strutture disponibili. Se la struttura a cui si appoggiano cambia (per es., adozione), cambiano anche loro.

1221. We must not think that only the essential should be said: it would be the end of common conversation and of many learned treatises.

1222. The devastation of age make it difficult to imagine how most people could have been attractive in their youth. Only the youth of their children may suggest such a possibility.

1223. The weak considers strong even those who are only stubborn or coarse.

1224. Understanding a lot but not enough is more dangerous than understanding little: the mistakes are bound to be greater.

1225. With the gaze fixed only on the aspirations of the soul, asceticism recognizes as valid only the emotions of the spirit.

1226. In crimes of passion, what is most surprising are the photographs of the victims: one can not understand how someone might have lost his head because of them.

1227. In the tumult of life, there is the orderly strategy of the divine design: a planned tumult. And therefore obligatory. Both order and disorder belong to it, although with different functions and consequences.

1228. In the algebra of the mind, the sum of pleasures does not necessarily result in happiness.

1229. It is true that pessimism may weaken the will to fight, but sometimes it is just the contrary: a weak will to fight uses pessimism to justify itself.

1230. The modulators of the heart are our hormones. They influence our mood, imagination, dreams and desires. For this reason, the parabola of the heart follows that of age.

1231. Children adapt easily, because, not having yet a main structure of their own, they lean against the available structures. If the structure upon which they lean changes (e.g., adoption), they change accordingly.

1232. Ci si giudica non in senso assoluto, ma relativamente agli altri, come quando, per esempio, ci si considera onesti, energici, attivi, ecc. Di qui, l'importanza degli standard generali di qualità.

1233. Ci si stanca di ogni condizione tanto più rapidamente quanto meno sappiamo trarne dei vantaggi, o quanto meno si apprezzano quelli che ne traggono.

1234. Il pietismo è la pietà degli imbecilli.

1235. Certe verità non ci offenderebbero se non ve ne fosse una ben precisa ragione.

1236. Si percepisce la pace di un bosco di montagna sotto la neve solo quando si smette di pensare. E si percepisce il suo silenzio solo se lo si ascolta.

1237. Osservare significa guardare, vedere e riflettere. In fondo, anche le pecore guardano.

1238. La terra estingue la sua sete al fruscio della pioggia; e si inebria d'acqua nelle inondazioni.

1239. Anche la bontà ha i suoi ornamenti, come la semplicità, gentilezza, umanità, comprensione (e talvolta un po' di malinconia).

1240. Nell'educazione dei giovani, con i concetti si educa la mente e con l'esempio il carattere.

1241. Il nostro umore è come il tempo. Volta a volta, è buono, cattivo, sereno, annuvolato, incerto, freddo, caldo, gelido, ecc.: come il tempo, varia indipendentemente dalla nostra volontà.

1242. La nascita inizia un processo per cui si cresce, si matura e si decade al ticchettio inesorabile dell'orologio della genetica.

1243. Nella lotta è necessario reclutare tutte le nostre risorse. È per questo che ci si sviluppa completamente solo combattendo.

1244. La natura umana non cambia. Cambia solo il suo comportamento a seconda delle circostanze e dei tempi.

1232.   We judge ourselves not in absolute terms, but relative to others, as, for example, when we consider ourselves honest, energetic, active, etc. Hence, the importance of general standards of quality.

1233.   We tire more quickly of any situation the less we know how to extract advantages from it, or the less we appreciate the advantages that we get out of it.

1234.   An uncritical compassion is the pity of imbeciles.

1235.   Certain truths would not offend us if there were not a definite reason.

1236.   We perceive the peace of a forest on a snow-covered mountain only when we stop thinking. And we perceive its silence only if we listen to it.

1237.   To observe means to look, see and reflect. After all, also sheep look.

1238.   The earth extinguishes its thirst at the rustle of the rain; and it gets inebriated with water in the floods.

1239.   Goodness too has its ornaments, like simplicity, gentleness, humanity, understanding (and sometimes a little bit of melancholy).

1240.   In the education of youth, the mind is educated by concepts and the character by example.

1241.   Our mood is like the weather. On and off, it is good, bad, calm, overcast, uncertain, cold, hot, icy, etc.: like the weather, it varies independently of our will.

1242.   Birth initiates a process by which we grow, peak and decay to the inexorable ticking of the clock of genetics.

1243.   In struggle, all of our resources must be recruited. It is for this reason that we completely develop only by fighting.

1244.   Human nature does not change. Only its behavior changes according to the circumstances or the times.

1245. Il piacere è una sensazione e la felicità un modo di sentire.

1246. I barbari, interni e esterni, emergono quando le civilizzazioni cominciano a decadere.

1247. La ripetizione annoia, dal momento che quello che si sa già non suscita interesse. Non dice nulla, perché non dice nulla di nuovo.

1248. È difficile essere volgari in maniera poetica. La volgarità poetica non esiste, non più di una bellezza brutta.

1249. Il declino comincia con l'erosione della qualità. Si comincia a fare quello che detta la convenienza piuttosto che quello che esigono le convinzioni. La causa prima è il declino del desiderio di eccellere e la mediocrità delle aspirazioni, che a loro volta risultano dalla mediocrità del materiale umano disponibile.

1250. Man mano che i figli crescono, il loro mondo diventa progressivamente diverso da quello dei genitori. Rimane l'intimità degli affetti, ma non quella delle idee.

1251. L'evoluzione potrebbe essere il processo con cui Dio gradualmente perfeziona la Sua creazione; o le permette di adattarsi in maniera flessibile a nuove condizioni.

1252. Il desiderio di spiritualità affonda le sue radici nelle miserie del nostro materialismo.

1253. Una grande civiltà è un fermento che continua a lievitare lo spirito umano anche quando è da lungo tempo scomparsa.

1254. Si sembra forti quando si nasconde la nostra debolezza. E deboli quando si nasconde la nostra forza.

1255. Ci si innamora perché vi siamo obbligati dalla fisiologia. E la vicinanza fisica è spesso il complice di questa necessità.

1256. C'è della musica che fa danzare, altra che fa sognare, o che commuove o esalta. I diversi tipi di musica si indirizzano a diversi aspetti emotivi del nostro essere e forse a differenti strati della mente (se non del cervello).

1245. Pleasure is a sensation and happiness a way of feeling.

1246. Barbarians, internal and external, emerge when civilizations begin to decay.

1247. Repetition bores, since what we already know does not interest us. It says nothing, because it says nothing new.

1248. It is difficult to be vulgar in a poetic manner. A poetic vulgarity does not exist, any more than an ugly beauty.

1249. Decline begins with the erosion of quality. We begin doing what convenience dictates rather than what convictions demand. The primary cause is the decline in the desire to excel and the mediocrity of aspirations, which in turn result from the mediocrity of the human material available.

1250. As children grow, their world becomes progressively different from that of their parents. What remains is the intimacy of affections, but not that of ideas.

1251. Evolution could be the process by which God gradually perfects his creation; or allows it to adapt in a flexible manner to changing conditions.

1252. The desire of spirituality sinks its roots in the pettiness of our materialism.

1253. A great civilization is a yeast that continues to leaven the human spirit even when it has long since disappeared.

1254. We seem strong when we hide our weakness. And weak when we hide our strength.

1255. We fall in love because we are forced into it by physiology. And the physical proximity is often the accomplice of this necessity.

1256. There is music that make us dance, that makes us dream, or that moves or exalts us. The different types of music address different emotive aspects of our being and perhaps different strata of the mind (if not of the brain).

1257. Lo scopo del corteggiamento è di iniziare la reciprocità dell'amore.

1258. Il comportamento è potentemente regolato da come la mente è geneticamente strutturata nel rispondere agli stimoli.

1259. La nostra superficialità e irrequietezza ci impediscono di soffermarci ad apprezzare le cose buone a cui siamo esposti.

1260. La virtù è maestra degli istinti, e spesso anche la loro vittima.

1261. Per la mente, gli opposti sono immagini speculari della stessa cosa: se si vivesse sempre sotto terra come le talpe, non si sarebbe coscienti del buio, non conoscendo la luce.

1262. La logica è il frutto della genetica, ma la genetica non viene influenzata dalla logica. Per questo, la filosofia può anche capire la natura umana, ma non può modificarla. Tutt'al più, può incoraggiare questa o quella tendenza umana (per es., stoicismo o edonismo), ma solo in quelli che vi sono per natura già predisposti.

1263. Si cerca sempre il piacere, ma chi lo trova nelle sensazioni piacevoli e chi nell'ascetismo dei sacrifici. O la stessa persona lo trova ora nell'appagamento del corpo e ora nelle rinunzie dello spirito.

1264. La superbia convenientemente non si domanda cosa mai possa giustificarla.

1265. La modestia consiste non nell'essere inconsapevoli dei propri meriti (ché quella sarebbe mancanza di comprensione), ma nella discrezione di farli riconoscere dagli altri. Per questo, la modestia vuol essere contraddetta, ma non la contraddirà certo l'invidia.

1266. Non rispondere alle offese facilita il processo di cicatrizzazione. Tuttavia, per funzionare, le offese non dovrebbero essere conservate nell'armadio della memoria come asciugamani accuratamente piegati e sovrapposti, pronti ad essere usati di nuovo.

1267. L'anarchia protesta contro tutto e tutti senza avere un suo programma. Può distruggere, ma non può costruire: per l'anarchia, il costruire sarebbe un suicidio.

1257. The aim of courtship is to initiate the reciprocity of love.

1258. Behavior is mightily regulated by the way the mind is genetically structured in responding to stimuli.

1259. Our superficiality and restlessness prevent us from pausing to appreciate the good things to which we are exposed.

1260. Virtue is the teacher of instincts, and often also their victim.

1261. For the mind, opposites are mirror images of the same thing: if we always lived underground like moles, we would not be conscious of darkness, not knowing the light.

1262. Logic is the product of genetics, but genetics is not influenced by logic. For this reason, philosophy may understand human nature, but it may not modify it. At most, philosophy may encourage this or that human tendency (e.g., stoicism or hedonism), but only in those who are by nature already so predisposed.

1263. We always seek pleasure, but some find it in pleasurable sensations and others in the asceticism of sacrifices. Or the same person finds it now in the gratification of the body and then in the denials of the spirit.

1264. Haughtiness conveniently does not ask itself what possibly could justify it.

1265. Modesty consists not in being unaware of one's own merits (since that would be lack of understanding), but in the discretion of having them recognized by others. For this reason, modesty wants to be contradicted, but envy certainly will not contradict it.

1266. Not responding to offenses facilitates the healing process. However, in order to work, offenses should not be kept in the closet of memory like carefully folded and superimposed towels, ready to be used anew.

1267. Anarchy protests against everything and everybody without having a program of its own. It can destroy, but can not build: for anarchy, to build would be suicide.

1268. I servi dei grandi signori ne assorbono l'arroganza.

1269. Chi si dichiara deluso della vita, teme la morte come tutti: quando si sente male, anche lui corre dal dottore.

1270. Una mente solo logica sarebbe come i circuiti dei pannelli elettronici: nitidamente ordinata, fredda e senza vita.

1271. Varietà e cambiamento sono le necessarie precondizioni per lo sviluppo e il progresso. Ma solo la mente umana è capace di imparare e creare. Non vi è progresso negli animali.

1272. È piuttosto divertente vedere come si risponde differentemente agli stessi stimoli quando si cambia opinione.

1273. Per essere sinceramente orgogliosi dei propri successi bisogna ignorare insinceramente i propri insuccessi.

1274. L'egoista è interessato solo al suo interesse, ma spesso non comprende quale sia. Non si può diminuire l'egoismo, ma si può diminuire la sua stupidità per mezzo di una migliore comprensione.

1275. La nostre convinzioni non tollerano di essere contraddette. Per questo, non solo non si è d'accordo con certe verità, ma non le consideriamo neanche vere.

1276. Un pensiero delicatamente bello soffonde l'anima di piacere intimo.

1277. Un mezzo potente per mantenere normale la funzione del corpo e della mente è il servomeccanismo: una deviazione dalla normalità attiva meccanismi che tendono a ristorare la normalità.

1278. La bontà più straordinaria è quella diretta verso chi non se la merita da parte di chi di bontà ne ha poca.

1279. Spesso, sono proprio quelli che non capiscono che hanno più bisogno di essere capiti.

1280. Nelle cose a cui siamo esposti, si cerca la verità che ci interessa e si formano le opinioni che si confanno alla nostra natura.

1268. The servants of the rich aristocrats absorb their arrogance.

1269. Those who claim to be disappointed by life fear death as every-body else: when not feeling well, they too hasten to see the doctor.

1270. A mind that were only logical would be like the circuits of the electronic panels: neatly tidy, cold and lifeless.

1271. Variety and change are the necessary preconditions for development and progress. But only the human mind is capable of learning and creating. There is no progress in animals.

1272. It is rather amusing to see how differently we answer the same stimuli when we change opinion.

1273. To be sincerely proud of our successes we must insincerely ignore our failures.

1274. The egoist is interested only in his own interests, but often he does not understand what his interests are. Egoism can not be decreased, but its stupidity may be decreased through a better understanding.

1275. Our convictions do not tolerate being contradicted. For this reason, not only do we not agree with certain truths, but we do not even consider them true.

1276. A delicately beautiful thought suffuses the soul with intimate pleasure.

1277. A powerful means to maintain a normal function of body and mind is the feedback: a deviation from normality activates mechanisms that tend to restore normality.

1278. The most extraordinary goodness is that directed toward those who do not deserve it by those who have little goodness.

1279. Often, it is precisely those who do not understand who need more to be understood.

1280. In the things to which we are exposed, we seek the truth that interests us and we form opinions that suit our nature.

1281. I lampioni delle strade sono piccoli patetici soli umani.

1282. Il merito non ha genere maschile o femminile, ma ha le sue specializzazioni a seconda del sesso.

1283. Per la giustizia umana, si è colpevoli solo quando ve ne sono le prove. Per la giustizia divina, si è colpevoli quando si è colpevoli.

1284. La vanità dello specchio risiede nella mente di chi vi si rimira.

1285. Richiede abilità dare risposte sensate a domande stupide.

1286. Legalmente, si è tanto più innocenti quanto più bravo è il nostro avvocato: la validità delle prove dipende anche dalla sua abilità.

1287. Certe parole sono difficili a tradursi in un'altra lingua, perché riflettono modi di pensare e agire che esistono in una popolazione ma non nell'altra.

1288. Si ama il bello, ma l'amore fa *diventare* bello quello che si ama.

1289. Quando ci correggono, o lo apprezziamo se vogliamo imparare, o ci si offende se non sappiamo o non vogliamo imparare.

1290. Se in natura esiste un'evoluzione, perché non un'involuzione? Certi uomini dalla scimmia e certe scimmie dall'uomo?...

1291. Quello che possiamo permetterci spesso è deciso non dalle nostre finanze, ma dalle nostre voglie.

1292. Il fatto che le persone e le cose non durino impedisce loro di diventare decrepite.

1293. Di notte, le emozioni assumono connotati differenti. Per es., la paura proietta ombre più lunghe e l'amore tenerezze più delicate.

1294. Sentirsi obbligati a dire la verità è una maniera sostanziale di costringersi ad agire correttamente. L'ipocrisia modera la rigida necessità di questa dura regola.

1295. Un amore deluso non è meno amore.

1281. Street lamps are small pathetic human suns.

1282. Merit has no male or female gender, but it has its specializations according to the sex.

1283. For human justice, one is guilty only when there is proof thereof. For the divine justice, one is guilty when one is guilty.

1284. The vanity of the mirror resides in the mind of the viewer.

1285. It takes skill to give sensible answers to stupid questions.

1286. Legally, one is more innocent the abler his lawyer is: the validity of the evidence also depends on the skill of the lawyer.

1287. It is difficult to translate certain words in another language, because they reflect ways of thinking and acting that exist in one population but not in the other.

1288. We love beauty, but love *makes* beautiful what we love.

1289. When others correct us, either we appreciate it if we want to learn, or we are offended if we are unable or unwilling to learn.

1290. If in nature there is evolution, why not involution? Some men from monkeys and some monkeys from man?...

1291. What we can afford is often decided not by our financial means, but by our whims.

1292. The fact that people and things do not last prevents them from becoming decrepit.

1293. At night, emotions assume different connotations. For example, fear projects longer shadows and love a more delicate tenderness.

1294. To feel obliged to say the truth is a substantial way to compel ourselves to act correctly. Hypocrisy softens the rigid necessity of this hard rule.

1295. A disappointed love is not less of a love.

1296. I nostri atti riflettono i nostri pensieri: è difficile nascondere i secondi a causa dei primi. Ma qualcuno manipola gli atti per mascherare i pensieri.

1297. La stanchezza di una lunga giornata di lavoro ottunde la mente. Il ristoro del sonno ne rinnova la freschezza e l'impazienza.

1298. L'ipocrita esibisce le sue virtù e nasconde i suoi vizi. Da questo punto di vista, siamo tutti ipocriti per quanto in misura differente.

1299. In natura, non vi può essere ordine senza leggi fisse e inderogabili. La pietà e la bontà sono parte indispensabile di quest'ordine, ma né lo determinano, né lo potrebbero determinare.

1300. C'è un tempo per tutto, anche per morire.

1301. L'amore ignora tutto (obiettività, ragionevolezza, grettezza, calcolo, rischi, convenienza, pericoli, ecc.) eccetto il suo acuto modo di sentire.

1302. Quando si pensa, si formulano i pensieri, e quando si riflette, si analizzano.

1303. Il fatto che anche noi avremmo potuto dire o fare una certa cosa non ci deve far illudere che, in effetti, l'avremmo detta o fatta.

1304. È la nostra vanità che è dispiaciuta quando si perde l'amore di una persona che non amiamo.

1305. Il tempo passa inesorabilmente perché la genetica segue il suo ciclo prestabilito. Ed è irreversibile perché la genetica non sa contare alla rovescia.

1306. L'essere immorali non giustifica l'essere immoralisti. Altrimenti, da corrotti si diventa anche corruttori.

1307. La moda contribuisce a fare di noi le marionette che caratterizzano il nostro tempo. Ma lo fa in maniera piacevole.

1308. La nostra condotta è influenzata da numerosi stimoli e determinata dallo stimolo che volta a volta prevale.

1296. Our actions reflect our thoughts: it is difficult to hide the latter because of the former. But some manipulate their actions in order to mask their thoughts.

1297. The tiredness of a long day of work dulls the mind. The restoration of sleep renews its freshness and impatience.

1298. The hypocrite displays his virtues and hides his faults. From this viewpoint, we are all hypocrites although to differing degrees.

1299. In nature, there can be no order without fixed and absolute laws. Pity and goodness are an indispensable part of this order, but they do not determine it, nor could they determine it.

1300. There is a time for everything, even to die.

1301. Love ignores everything (objectivity, reasonableness, meanness, reckoning, risks, convenience, dangers, etc.) except its acute way of feeling.

1302. When we think, we formulate thoughts, and when we reflect, we analyze them.

1303. The fact that we too could have said or done something should not delude us into believing that in fact we would have said or done it.

1304. It is our vanity that is displeased when we lose the love of a person that we do not love.

1305. Time inexorably passes because genetics follows its pre-established cycle. And it is irreversible because genetics does not know how to count in reverse.

1306. To be immoral does not justify being immoralist. Otherwise, the corrupt also becomes a corrupter.

1307. Fashion contributes to make of us the puppets that characterize our era. But it does so in a pleasant manner.

1308. Our behavior is influenced by numerous stimuli and it is determined by the stimulus that in each case prevails.

1309. L'entusiasmo è fatto soprattutto di piacevoli anticipazioni, spesso entusiasticamente esagerate.

1310. Ci sono due tipi di esperti: quelli che lo sono e quelli che se lo credono.

1311. Che penserà mai un corvo appollaiato su un lampione della autostrada? Non bisognerà dunque apprezzare la nostra mente?

1312. La poesia dovrebbe sedurre il cuore con la bellezza, e non cercare di sorprendere la mente con la stranezza.

1313. Alcuni si sentono falliti se non sono invidiati e considerano l'invidia altrui la prova del proprio successo. In genere, si tratta di persone invidiose.

1314. In politica, la "giustizia" è seduta sullo scanno del potere.

1315. Gli aforismi riflettono un sistema di pensiero e gradualmente lo definiscono. Per questo, è più facile riconoscere gli aforismi che si sono letti che predire il prossimo.

1316. Molta gente sta facilmente a dieta, eccetto quando mangia.

1317. L'uso di frasi complicate e incomprensibili da parte di una mente educata può dare un'impressione di profondità anche quando si tratta solo di confusione.

1318. La persistente ripetizione del brutto irrita e quella del bello annoia. Di qui la suprema e inderogabile necessità della varietà, e dei suoi inevitabili errori.

1319. Come una nave fende le onde del mare in tempesta, così la natura supera le successive ondate filosofiche, tenacemente avanzando sulla sua rotta prestabilita.

1320. Il candore della neve rende la luce del sole abbagliante, come la felicità rende un viso radioso.

1321. La società è intrattenuta dalla creatività di alcuni e dalle follie di tanti.

1309. Enthusiasm is mainly made up of pleasant anticipations, often enthusiastically exaggerated.

1310. There two types of experts: those who are experts and those who believe to be experts.

1311. What could a raven perched on a street lamp along the highway ever think? Should we not then appreciate our mind?

1312. Poetry should seduce the heart with its beauty, and not seek to dazzle the mind with its strangeness.

1313. Some regard themselves as failures if they are not envied and consider the envy of others as a proof of their success. In general, these are envious people.

1314. In politics, "justice" is seated on the bench of power.

1315. Aphorisms reflect a system of thought and gradually define it. For this reason, it is easier to recognize aphorisms that we have read than to predict the next one.

1316. Many people stay consistently on a diet, except when they eat.

1317. The use of complicated and incomprehensible sentences on the part of an educated mind may give the impression of depth even when there is only confusion.

1318. The persistent repetition of ugliness irritates us and that of beauty bores us. Hence, the supreme and absolute necessity of variety and its unavoidable errors.

1319. As a ship ploughs its way through the waves of a rough sea, thus nature overcomes the successive philosophical waves, tenaciously advancing on the pre-established route.

1320. The whiteness of the snow makes the light of the sun dazzling, like happiness makes a visage radiant.

1321. Society is entertained by the creativity of a few and by the follies of many.

1322. Presumibilmente, i pensieri oscuri e confusi sono tradotti con successo in un'altra lingua solo quando anche i pensieri tradotti sono oscuri e confusi.

1323. In una mente abile, le conseguenze negative di una parziale comprensione portano alle catastrofi della logica.

1324. Se si capisce solo una cosa per volta, si capisce ben poco.

1325. Tutte le cose sono necessarie all'economia generale, ma non alle economie individuali. Per esempio, è necessario che vi sia la generosità, ma è anche necessario che non tutti siano generosi. Se tutti lo fossero, sarebbe la fine della generosità.

1326. La solitudine consiste nell'assenza di scambi con altre menti. Pertanto, se non vi è comunicazione, si può essere soli anche in compagnia.

1327. Imparare è difficile perché bisogna ascoltare, leggere, osservare, riflettere, comprendere e ricordare. E agire in conseguenza. Si impara non quello che si ricorda, ma quello che diviene parte della struttura della nostra mente.

1328. L'intimo bisogno di sentimenti gentili trova conforto nella delicata bellezza delle forme, colori e profumi dei fiori.

1329. Se vuoi piacere a qualcuno, permettigli di ascoltare se stesso.

1330. La rudezza non è colpevole quando è necessaria (per esempio, contro i disonesti).

1331. La coscienza dei propri meriti ostacola l'umiltà e quella dei propri demeriti la superbia. O piuttosto meriti e demeriti ci fanno oscillare tra l'una e l'altra.

1332. La saggezza è un concetto funzionale: in certe situazioni, può essere saggio non essere "saggi".

1333. È più facile seguire il consiglio dei difetti che quello delle virtù, perché ai difetti è sufficiente la debolezza, mentre alle virtù necessita fermezza e addirittura coerenza.

1322. Presumably, obscure and confused thoughts are successfully translated in another language only when the translated thoughts are also obscure and confused.

1323. In a skillful mind, the negative consequences of a partial comprehension lead to the catastrophes of logic.

1324. If we understand only one thing at a time, we understand very little.

1325. Everything is necessary to the general economy, but not to individual economies. For example, it is necessary that there be generosity, but it is necessary that not everyone be generous. If everyone were, that would be the end of generosity.

1326. Solitude consists in the absence of exchange with other minds. Therefore, if there is no communication, one may be alone even in company.

1327. To learn is difficult because it is necessary to listen, read, observe, think, understand and remember. And act accordingly. We learn not what we remember, but what becomes part of the structure of our mind.

1328. The intimate need for gentle feelings finds comfort in the delicate beauty of the forms, colors and scents of flowers.

1329. If you want to please someone, allow him to listen to himself.

1330. Rudeness is not a fault when it is necessary (e.g., against the devious).

1331. The awareness of our merits and our faults hinders humility and haughtiness, respectively. Or, rather, merits and faults make us oscillate between the two.

1332. Wisdom is a functional concept: in certain situations, it may be wise not to be "wise".

1333. It is easier to follow the advice of our faults than of our virtues, because weakness is sufficient for faults whereas firmness and even coherence is needed for virtues.

1334. Nel nome di quello che si dovrebbe desiderare, si condanna quello che realmente si desidera.

1335. L'eroismo avrebbe ben poco significato se non fosse il superamento della debolezza umana.

1336. Nelle famiglie, la profondità degli affetti determina come ci si comporta quando vi è un disaccordo.

1337. Si può nascondere qualcosa assumendo un'espressione imperscrutabile, ma l'espressione imperscrutabile non si può nascondere.

1338. Si può ridere disinvoltamente delle cose che ci preoccupano, ma solo a spese di una maggiore ansietà.

1339. Sono più le domande che ci eludono che le risposte.

1340. Ai confini *invisibili* della nostra finezza ci aspetta la stupidità.

1341. Un presente invariabilmente mediocre non ha né passato né futuro.

1342. Il desiderio di novità (anche se in peggio) è creato o dalla ricerca di espressioni originali da parte delle nuove generazioni o dalla monotonia dell'abitudine da parte di tutti.

1343. Entro certi limiti, il disordine può essere un elemento indispensabile di libertà (e qualche volta di creatività).

1344. Vantaggi e svantaggi spesso cambiano categoria dal momento che sono relativi ai nostri mutevoli interessi.

1345. Anche la mediocrità ha diritto al rispetto di tutto quello che le è inferiore.

1346. Si eccelle in un campo, quando *per caso* la genetica sviluppa in misura esagerata una particolare facoltà della mente. Ne può risultare un grande pittore o un grande criminale.

1347. Il fruscio delle prime foglie secche spinte dal vento sono il preludio ai segreti d'autunno, come gli sguardi furtivi lo sono ai segreti di un amore che nasce.

1334. In the name of what we should desire, we condemn what we actually desire.

1335. Heroism would have little meaning if it were not the overcoming of human weakness.

1336. Within a family, the depth of affections determines how we behave when there is a disagreement.

1337. We can hide something by assuming an inscrutable expression, but the inscrutable expression can not be hidden.

1338. We may nonchalantly laugh at our worries, but only at the expense of a greater anxiety.

1339. There are more questions that elude us than answers.

1340. At the *invisible* boundaries of our cleverness, stupidity awaits us.

1341. A consistently mediocre present has neither a past nor a future.

1342. The desire of novelty (even if for the worse) is created either by the search for original expressions by new generations or by the monotony of habit on the part of everybody.

1343. Within certain limits, disorder can be an indispensable part of freedom (and sometimes of creativity).

1344. Advantages and disadvantages often change category since they are relative to our changing interests.

1345. Mediocrity too is entitled to the respect of everything that is inferior to it.

1346. One excels in a field when *by chance* genetics develops to an exaggerated degree a particular faculty of the mind. The result may be a great painter or a great criminal.

1347. The rustling of first wilted leaves pushed by the wind are the prelude to the secrets of autumn, as furtive glances are to the secrets of a love being born.

1348.   Una limitazione della finezza è che spesso non ha buon senso, anche se raramente manca di compiacenza.

1349.   Individualmente e collettivamente, abbiamo tutta la libertà che ci è *concessa*.

1350.   A causa della loro continua transizione, il presente è il futuro del passato e il passato del futuro.

1351.   La saggezza non esiste: esiste solo il desiderio di essere saggi. Ma una perfetta saggezza svuoterebbe la vita della sua vivacità e intensità emotiva. Si sarebbe così poco saggi da essere vecchi ad ogni età. Non a caso, i saggi sono di rado giovani e spesso vecchi.

1352.   L'intensità e il calore dei nostri argomenti riflette la profondità dei nostri interessi.

1353.   È difficile resistere all'amore anche perché in genere non vogliamo resistervi.

1354.   C'è sempre qualcuno pronto ad approfittare di quei vantaggi di cui noi tralasciamo di usufruire.

1355.   Il perseguire la spiritualità è fonte di indipendenza: quello che ci si nega ci fa indifferenti a quello che ci negano.

1356.   Solo le azioni umane che sono degne del passato possono sperare di avere un futuro.

1357.   La genetica pianifica il nostro sviluppo fisico e mentale servendosi della ordinata successione di cicli ormonali.

1358.   La varietà continua stanca. Si desidera ancora la varietà, ma per un po' come pausa da un continuo cambiamento.

1359.   Non è mai superficiale quello che ci interessa profondamente. Può esserlo solo per quelli che hanno interessi diversi.

1360.   I filosofi sono necessari come categoria, ma non più delle categorie dei fornai, idraulici, contadini o qualsiasi altro. Ogni categoria risponde ad un bisogno differente.

1348. A limitation of cleverness is that often it has no common sense, although it rarely lacks complacency.

1349. Individually and collectively, we have all the freedom that is *conceded* to us.

1350. Due to their continuous transition, the present is the future of the past and the past of the future.

1351. Wisdom does not exist: only the desire to be wise exists. But a perfect wisdom would empty life of its emotional poignancy and intensity. We would be so unwise as to be old at any age. Not by chance, sages are seldom young and often old.

1352. The intensity and warmth of our arguments reflects the depth of our interests.

1353. It is difficult to resist love also because in general we do not want to resist it.

1354. There is always someone ready to profit of those advantages of which we omit to make use.

1355. The pursuit of spirituality is a source of independence: what we deny ourselves makes us indifferent to what they deny us.

1356. Only the human actions that are worthy of the past can hope to have a future.

1357. Genetics plans our physical and mental development by using the orderly succession of hormonal cycles.

1358. A continuous variety tires. We still desire variety, but for a while as a pause from a continuous change.

1359. What deeply interests us is never superficial. It may be superficial only for those who have different interests.

1360. Philosophers are necessary as a category, but not more than the categories of bakers, plumbers, farmers or anybody else. Each category addresses a different need.

1361. Come nelle stagioni, il fiore della gioventù è seguito dal rigoglio della maturità, dal lento declino della vecchiaia e finalmente dalla fredda immobilità dell'inverno. Il nostro ciclo è più lungo di quello delle stagioni, ma è uno solo.

1362. Anche un'abile finezza può diventare una cattiva abitudine.

1363. Quello che si dice è in genere migliore di quello che si fa, perché esprimiamo le nostre aspirazioni, non le nostre realizzazioni.

1364. In un film, il regista crea la sua realtà ritraendo quello che gli interessa con particolari prospettive ed effetti speciali, modulati dalla musica di fondo. Lo spettatore vede la realtà che il regista gli vuol far vedere.

1365. L'Io vive solo nel presente, cioè nella somma di quello che percepisce, ricorda e anticipa. L'Io cambia continuamente cambia perché il presente cambia continuamente, man mano che le anticipazioni diventano percezioni e queste ricordi.

1366. Anche quando non si presta attenzione, la nostra sopravvivenza fisica richiede che, come un radar, le "antenne" dei nostri sensi continuamente esplorino l'ambiente. Ci si affida alle percezioni subconsce.

1367. È la sofferenza a dare significato ai piaceri. I piaceri ininterrotti portano all'infelicità, dal momento che l'abitudine li svuota di significato. In tal caso, si ha di nuovo la sofferenza (di un vuoto interiore), ma non più il rimedio.

1368. Siamo sempre inferiori alla superiorità che ci siamo assegnati.

1369. Di tanto in tanto, ci sentiamo come bambini perduti: deboli, indifesi, paurosi, ansiosi e soli.

1370. Per quanto profondi possano essere i pensieri, c'è sempre uno strato inesplorato più profondo.

1371. La noia non nasce dalla mancanza di cose interessanti, ma dall'incapacità di divenirne interessati. La conseguente mancanza di stimoli è lo stimolo che porta all'irrequietezza della noia.

1361. As for the seasons, the flower of youth is succeeded by the bloom of maturity, the slow decline of old age and finally the cold immobility of winter. Our cycle is longer than that of seasons, but it is only one.

1362. Even a subtle cleverness may become a bad habit.

1363. What we say is generally better than what we do, because we express our aspirations, not our accomplishments.

1364. In a motion picture, the director creates his own reality by portraying what interests him with unusual perspectives and special effects, modulated by background music. The spectator sees the reality that the director wants him to see.

1365. The Self only lives in the present, that is, in the sum of what we perceive, remember and anticipate. The Self continuously changes because the present continuously changes, as anticipations become perceptions and these become remembrances.

1366. Even when we do not pay attention, our physical survival demands that, like a radar, the "antennae" of our senses continuously explore the environment. We rely on subconscious perceptions.

1367. It is suffering that gives meaning to pleasures. Uninterrupted pleasures lead to unhappiness, since habit empties them of meaning. In that case, we have again the suffering (of an inner emptiness), but no longer the remedy.

1368. We are always inferior to the superiority that we have assigned to ourselves.

1369. From time to time, we feel like lost children: weak, defenseless, fearful, anxious and lonely.

1370. No matter how deep thoughts might be, there is always an unexplored deeper layer.

1371. Boredom is not caused by the lack of interesting things, but by the incapacity of becoming interested in them. The consequent lack of stimuli is the stimulus that leads to the restlessness of boredom.

1372. A ciascuno di noi sono dati dolori e gioie: cosa mai potremmo chiedere di più?

1373. Chi urla spesso raramente ragiona.

1374. Le virtù sono soprattutto delle aspirazioni dell'anima; e i vizi il fallimento di tali aspirazioni.

1375. Si vede con gli occhi e si osserva con la mente.

1376. Gli opposti si definiscono a vicenda. Per esempio, la bellezza riceve significato dalla bruttezza, e il contrario. Se le cose fossero tutte belle o tutte brutte, nessuna lo sarebbe.

1377. Se non fosse per lo specchio, per la mente l'identità del corpo sarebbe senza faccia. Eppure, è proprio la fotografia della faccia che viene usata per i documenti d'identità.

1378. Per essere in compagnia della propria mente, bisogna essere soli.

1379. La religione non elimina le nostre qualità negative, ma ne cambia la motivazione. Per esempio, la religione dirige l'odio contro i propri difetti, per quanto i fedeli qualche volta dirigano il loro odio contro gli eretici o gli infedeli.

1380. Ci si illude di influenzare gli altri quando non siamo neanche capaci di influenzare le nostre inclinazioni.

1381. È facile condannare l'ipocrisia, ma nessuna società potrebbe farne a meno. Inoltre, anche chi denuncia virtuosamente l'ipocrisia è ben lontano dall'esserne esente.

1382. Se *vogliamo* fare una cosa perché ci piace, si trova il tempo di farla anche se siamo molto occupati. Se *dobbiamo* fare una cosa che non ci piace molto, non si trova il tempo anche quando non abbiamo altro da fare.

1383. Il concetto di uguaglianza ha le sue stranezze. Si pretende che la donna venga trattata come l'uomo, ma non l'uomo come la donna. Uguaglianza a senso unico... o mancanza di rispetto verso la donna? In realtà, siamo uguali quando ciascuno è se stesso.

1372.   Sorrows and joys are given to each one of us: what more could we ask for?

1373.   Those who often scream rarely think.

1374.   Virtues are most of all aspirations of the soul; and vices are the failure of those aspirations.

1375.   We see with the eyes and we observe with the mind.

1376.   Opposites define each other. For example, beauty is given meaning by ugliness, and conversely. If things were all beautiful or all ugly, none would be so.

1377.   If it were not for the mirror, to the mind the identity of the body would be without face. Yet, it is precisely the photo of the face that is used for identity papers.

1378.   To be in the company of one's own mind, one needs to be alone.

1379.   Religion does not eliminate our negative attributes, but it changes their motivation. For example, religion directs hatred against one's own faults, although believers sometimes direct their hatred against heretics or non-believers.

1380.   We delude ourselves of influencing others when we are not even capable of influencing our own inclinations.

1381.   It is easy to condemn hypocrisy, but no society could dispense with it. Furthermore, even those who righteously denounce hypocrisy are very far from being exempt from it.

1382.   If we *want* to do something because we like it, we find the time for it even when we are very busy. If we *must* do something that we do not like very much, we do not find the time even if we have nothing else to do.

1383.   The concept of equality has its oddities. They insist that a woman should be treated as a man, but not a man as a woman. One way equality... or lack of respect toward the woman? In reality, we are equal when each one is his or her Self.

1384. Il "nuovo" è fatto in gran parte di cose insignificanti e in piccola parte di cose perfette: in questa maniera si accontentano tutti.

1385. Le parole sono toccanti quando si rivolgono a qualcosa a cui siamo o sensibili o sensibilizzati. Siamo più recettivi a quello che ci turba dentro.

1386. L'abitudine comporta risposte riflesse e pertanto permette all'attenzione di concentrarsi su nuovi stimoli.

1387. I grandi problemi morali tormentano solo le anime più elevate. La maggior parte di noi ignora tali problemi, come se fossero nere nuvole perdute nell'oscura volta del cielo in una notte senza luna.

1388. Le sole leggi eterne sono quelle naturali.

1389. Che la bruttezza sia l'indispensabile piedistallo della bellezza lo si vede nei musei: per mancanza di confronto, l'accumulo di cose belle dopo un po' satura e stanca.

1390. Non ci disturbano per nulla quei difetti degli altri che ci fanno comodo.

1391. Ciascuno è tentato solo da quello che desidera. Di qui, la piacevole varietà delle tentazioni.

1392. Una mente suggestionabile ingenuamente trova il fascino del mistero nell'oscurità di certe teorie confuse.

1393. Si possono dare buoni consigli, ma non la capacità di apprezzarli o di metterli correttamente in pratica. Inoltre, gli altri considerano buoni quei consigli che coincidono con quello che desiderano fare.

1394. Per non trovare risposte è sufficiente non domandarsi nulla.

1395. Nelle questioni di religione, il non credere ha i suoi dubbi come il credere. Ma, nel negare Dio, si dovrebbe soprattutto temere che l'universo e le sue leggi ci rendano ridicoli.

1396. Le nostre convinzioni più profonde ci obbligano ad agire in conseguenza. Quando non lo si fa, siamo forzati a sentirci infelici.

1384. The "new" is made up largely of meaningless things and in small part of perfect things: in this fashion, everybody is contented.

1385. Words are touching when they are directed to something to which we are either sensitive or sensitized. We are more receptive to what troubles us within.

1386. Habit involves reflex responses and therefore allows attention to concentrate on new stimuli.

1387. Great moral problems torment only the most lofty souls. Most of us ignore these problems, as if they were black clouds lost in the obscure vault of the sky in a night without moon.

1388. The only everlasting laws are the natural ones.

1389. That ugliness is the indispensable pedestal to beauty is seen in museums: for lack of comparison, the accumulation of beautiful things after a while saturates and tires.

1390. The defects of others that we find useful do not disturb us in the least.

1391. Everyone is tempted only by what he desires. Hence, the pleasant variety of temptations.

1392. An impressionable mind naïvely finds the fascination of mystery in the obscurities of certain confused theories.

1393. We can give good advice, but not the capacity of appreciating it or correctly acting on it. Furthermore, others consider good the advice that coincides with what they wish to do.

1394. Not to find answers it is sufficient not to ask ourselves anything.

1395. In matters of religion, not believing has its doubts like believing. But, in denying God, we should most of all fear that the universe and its laws should make us ridiculous.

1396. Our deepest convictions oblige us to act accordingly. When we do not do it, we are forced to feel unhappy.

1397. Stranamente, nei cani l'espressione degli occhi non partecipa alle loro più calorose manifestazioni di affetto.

1398. Bisogna accettarsi per quello che siamo, anche quando la nostra natura non vuole accettarsi per quello che è.

1399. Si è più propensi a perdonare gli sbagli dell'inesperienza della gioventù. Vi si rivede la nostra gioventù e i suoi errori.

1400. Quando siamo oggettivi, si vede quello che si guarda; se si hanno degli interessi, si vede solo quello che vogliamo vederci.

1401. I consigli più difficili sono quelli che bisogna dare a se stessi.

1402. Quello che si presta facilmente all'abuso è soggetto a potenti inibizioni.

1403. Anche chi è ostile alla religione pratica molti dei suoi valori etici: si può disubbidire alla religione, ma non alla genetica.

1404. L'abilità è il cervello della forza.

1405. Si vive delle nostre esperienze e del loro ricordo. Per questo, le cose piacevoli sono importanti anche se sono transitorie.

1406. Un'intuizione coglie l'essenza di un'idea, ma solo una definizione formale può esprimerne con chiarezza la struttura e giustificarne la correttezza. Dopo tutto, ci sono anche le intuizioni sbagliate.

1407. I santi hanno i loro poveri come i ricchi hanno i loro gioielli: non è più facile rinunciare a questi che a quelli.

1408. Si può non essere moralisti solo per indifferenza verso la morale.

1409. Quello che non possiamo ottenere dall'esterno, lo cerchiamo nell'interno della mente. Se la mente non può percepire quello che desidera, cerca di crearlo con l'immaginazione. Questo è reso possibile dal fatto che sia la realtà percepita che la realtà immaginata sono mentali. Creando mentalmente delle immagini, si sostituisce l'una con l'altra, per quanto le persone normali si rendono conto della sostituzione.

1397. Strangely, in dogs the expression of the eyes does not participate to their warmest manifestations of affection.

1398. We must accept ourselves for what we are, even when our nature does not want to accept itself for what it is.

1399. We are more inclined to pardon the mistakes of the inexperience of youth. We see in it our youth and its errors.

1400. When objective, we see what we look at; if we have interests, we see only what we want to see in it.

1401. The most difficult advice is that which we have to give to ourselves.

1402. What easily lends itself to abuse is subject to potent inhibitions.

1403. Even those who are hostile to religion practice many of its ethical values: one can disobey religion, but not genetics.

1404. Ability is the brain of strength.

1405. We live of our experiences and their memory. For this reason, pleasant things are important even if they are transient.

1406. An intuition seizes the essence of an idea, but only a formal definition can express with clarity the structure and justify the correctness of the idea. After all, there are also wrong intuitions.

1407. The saints have their poor like the rich have their jewels: it is not easier to renounce the former than the latter.

1408. One may not be a moralist only because of his indifference toward morals.

1409. What we can not obtain from outside, we seek inside the mind. If the mind can not perceive what it desires, the mind seeks to create it by means of imagination. This is made possible by the fact that both perceived and imagined reality are mental. Mentally creating images, we substitute the former with the latter, although normal people are aware of the substitution.

1410. La finezza psicologica è misurata prima di tutto dall'abilità di comprendere la propria mente.

1411. È meglio un desiderio non soddisfatto che una soddisfazione non desiderata.

1412. L'acidità è corrosiva, soprattutto per chi ce l'ha.

1413. Non si può essere sicuri di nulla, neanche della propria incertezza. E spesso non vogliamo essere sicuri, specialmente circa le cose che si temono.

1414. Inevitabilmente, quello che si fa influenza quello che si farà, perché quello che si fa diventa parte di noi, che piaccia o no.

1415. È improbabile che un carattere forte abbia inibizioni deboli, anche perché la forza delle inibizioni contribuisce a quella del carattere.

1416. Il mondo è nella nostra mente: anzi, la nostra mente è il mondo, un mondo a cui i nostri affetti, emozioni, desideri e speranze danno un significato personale.

1417. Servomeccanismi: la volontà di combattere porta ai successi; e il compiacimento dei successi erode la volontà di combattere.

1418. Il parlare ci fa sentire interessanti, perché ci sentiamo al centro dell'attenzione generale. Ed effettivamente siamo interessanti, se, in effetti, si dice qualcosa di interessante.

1419. Qualche volta, le stranezze hanno una loro strana attrattiva.

1420. Qualsiasi cosa si dica, vi sarà sempre chi non capisce, interpreta male, distorce, diminuisce o esagera quello che si è detto.

1421. Nel limpido chiarore della luna tra gli alberi di un bosco, c'è il fascino della silenziosa luminosità delle ombre.

1422. I tempi moderni rimangono estranei all'età avanzata: si osservano, ma non si vivono; e non piacciono dove sono differenti. In contrasto, i nostri ricordi sentimentali amano i tempi passati, dimenticandone i lati negativi.

1410. Psychological finesse is measured first of all by the ability of understanding one's own mind.

1411. It is better to have an unsatisfied desire than an undesired satisfaction.

1412. Acidity is corrosive, especially for those who have it.

1413. One can not be sure of anything, not even of one's own uncertainty. And often we do not want to be sure, especially about the things that we fear.

1414. Inevitably, what we do influences what we will do, because what we do becomes part of us, whether we like it or not.

1415. It is improbable that a strong character has weak inhibitions, also because the strength of inhibitions contributes to that of character.

1416. The world is in our mind: rather, our mind is the world, a world to which our affections, emotions, desires and hopes give a personal meaning.

1417. Feedback mechanisms: the will to fight leads to successes; and the complacency of successes erodes the will to fight.

1418. Talking makes us feel interesting, because we feel at the center of the general attention. And in actuality we are interesting, if we actually say something interesting.

1419. Sometimes, strangeness has a strange attractiveness.

1420. No matter what one says, there will always be those who misunderstand, misinterpret, distort, belittle or exaggerate what was said.

1421. In the limpid gleam of the moon among the trees of a forest, there is the fascination of the silent luminosity of shadows.

1422. Modern times remain foreign to advanced age: they are observed, but not lived; and they displease where they are different. In contrast, our sentimental memories cherish past times, forgetting their negative aspects.

1423. La statistica è la scienza che sa tutto di noi tutti e nulla di ciascuno di noi.

1424. Avere una sola buona qualità può essere solo un difetto.

1425. Un problema della matematica è che non ha un'equazione per la felicità.

1426. Con le bugie ripetute si può nascondere tutto, eccetto il fatto che si mente.

1427. L'acutezza fa dire talvolta cose che sarebbero giuste se quello che non si è considerato non le facesse sbagliate. Questa incapacità di una visione globale spiega perché singole verità acute possano poi risultare assurde in un contesto generale.

1428. L'invidia nasce dal fatto che l'opinione di noi stessi viene modificata dall'opinione che siamo forzati ad avere degli altri. E se quella è troppo buona, ne siamo dispiaciuti per esserne diminuiti.

1429. Gli aforismi indagano non la fisiologia del cervello, ma quella della mente.

1430. La felicità è uno stato d'animo determinato non da valori assoluti, ma dal rapporto tra quello che si desidera e quello che si ottiene. Per questo, è più facile essere felici quando si desidera poco. Ma l'intensità della felicità è proporzionale a quella del desiderio.

1431. L'indifferenza fa tutto più faticoso; e la noia lo fa addirittura estenuante.

1432. La mente percepisce i dati particolari e ne estrae il significato comune, formulandone l'essenziale. Pertanto, l'essenziale è un'astrazione della mente (ed esiste solo lì), ma i dati particolari mancano della consapevolezza che deriva dall'analisi.

1433. L'irrequietezza cronica nasce dall'incapacità di apprezzare quello che si ha o di sviluppare un interesse che assorba. O dal non sapere quello che si vuole.

1434. Si vuole essere amati soprattutto da chi si ama.

1423. Statistics is the science that knows everything about all of us and nothing about each of us.

1424. To have only one good quality can only be a fault.

1425. A problem with mathematics is that it does not have an equation for happiness.

1426. With repeated lies one can conceal everything, except the fact that one lies.

1427. Acuteness sometimes makes us say things that would be right if what we did not consider did not make them wrong. This incapacity of a global vision explains why single acute truths may later prove to be absurd in a general context.

1428. Envy is caused by the fact that the opinion of ourselves is modified by the opinion that we are forced to have of others. And if the latter is too good, we are displeased because we feel diminished.

1429. Aphorisms investigate not the physiology of the brain, but that of the mind.

1430. Happiness is a state of mind determined not by absolute values, but by the ratio between what we desire and what we obtain. For this reason, it is easier to be happy when we desire little. But the intensity of happiness is proportional to that of desire.

1431. Indifference makes everything more fatiguing; and boredom makes it altogether exhausting.

1432. The mind perceives the particular data and extracts their common meaning, formulating their essential. Therefore, the essential is an abstraction of the mind (and it exists only there), but the particular data lack the consciousness that derives from the analysis.

1433. Chronic restlessness results from the incapacity of appreciating what we have or of developing an absorbing interest. Or from not knowing what we want.

1434. We want to be loved mostly by those whom we love.

1435. Il lamentarsi di un problema è raramente la sua soluzione, poiché il lamentarsi (oltre lo sfogo emotivo) non conduce a nulla.

1436. I tentativi di novità sono tanti e quelli che piacciono di più diventano la moda. Per un po' di tempo.

1437. Quello che ci nascondono eccita la nostra curiosità. E pertanto il nostro pettegolezzo.

1438. Come una sorgente che sgorga dalle rocce, la creatività è nutrita da innumerevoli falde nascoste.

1439. La decadenza è facilitata dalla sterilità di un egoismo senza freni che si ribella alle regole fisse di un gioco obbligato.

1440. Un aforisma deve essere prima di tutto vero, ma poi anche acuto. È la sua acutezza che stimola la mente. È come un lampo che illumina improvvisamente (e forse altrettanto brevemente) aspetti differenti della mente umana.

1441. Il fatto che io non sia d'accordo con te non significa che io abbia ragione. E il fatto che tu non sia d'accordo con me non significa che io abbia torto.

1442. Una sfacciataggine spontanea e genuina può essere più attraente di una calcolata e falsa modestia.

1443. Le cose di questo mondo sono eterne solo nelle convinzioni e speranze della gioventù.

1444. Le ambizioni nascoste che attribuiamo agli altri somigliano stranamente alle nostre ambizioni nascoste. Non ci si rende conto che le altrui ambizioni non solo possano essere completamente diverse, ma anche molto più grandi.

1445. La mancanza di spirito si rimedia facilmente avendo l'accortezza di tacere.

1446. Ci si esprime confusamente di proposito quando vogliamo far comprendere quello che non è conveniente dire esplicitamente o quando non vogliamo farci comprendere.

1435. Complaining about a problem is rarely its solution, since complaining (beyond emotional relief) leads nowhere.

1436. Attempts at novelty are many and those which we like the most become the fashion. For a little while.

1437. What they hide from us excites our curiosity. And therefore our gossip.

1438. As a spring that gushes out of the rocks, creativity is nourished by endless hidden sources.

1439. Decadence is facilitated by the sterility of an unrestrained egoism that rebels against the fixed rules of an obligatory play.

1440. An aphorism must first of all be true, but then also keen. It is its keenness that stimulates the mind. It is like lightning that suddenly (and perhaps as briefly) illuminates different aspects of the human mind.

1441. The fact that I do not agree with you does not mean that I am right. And the fact that you do not agree with me does not mean that I am wrong.

1442. A spontaneous and genuine effrontery may be more attractive than a calculated and false modesty.

1443. The things of this world are eternal only in the beliefs and hopes of youth.

1444. The hidden ambitions that we attribute to others strangely resemble our hidden ambitions. We do not realize that the ambitions of others not only could be completely different, but also much greater.

1445. The lack of wit is easily remedied by having the perspicacity of keeping silent.

1446. We purposely express ourselves in a confused way when we want something to be understood that is not convenient to explicitly say or when we do not want to be understood.

1447.   La moda ha sempre delle novità perché deve; e del buon gusto quando può.

1448.   Se si potessero eliminare i peccati, ci sarebbe certo qualcuno che li inventerebbe di nuovo.

1449.   Naturalmente si persegue la felicità attraverso quello che ci dà piacere: che senso avrebbe il perseguire l'infelicità attraverso quello che ci dispiace? Ma, altrettanto naturalmente, non bisogna confondere il piacere con le sensazioni piacevoli. Anche la sofferenza può dare piacere, per quanto non come tale, ma come mezzo per ottenere la felicità. Per esempio, nello sviluppo spirituale; o nei sacrifici che si fanno per chi si ama.

1450.   Per un attore, saper interpretare abilmente tutte le parti comporta la rinuncia a sviluppare un'immagine personale. Potendo impersonare tutti, alla fine non si identifica con nessuno. È proprio la sua versatilità che rivela l'attore professionale e previene la creazione di un mito e di un'immagine personali che la gente impara ad amare.

1451.   La stupidità invita la disonestà dell'altrui approfitto.

1452.   Le nostre reazioni emotive ci impediscono di vedere le opportunità che si nascondono nelle difficoltà.

1453.   Per non essere sempre annoiati, bisognerebbe non annoiarsi troppo facilmente.

1454.   Le pene che si sopportano con più fermezza sono quelle degli altri.

1455.   Ciascuna azione individuale è determinata da fattori ben precisi, come desideri, istinti, interessi, doveri, opinioni, necessità, convinzioni, impulsi, obblighi, paure, ideali, ecc. Le analisi teoriche influenzano le azioni individuali, ma sono uno sforzo per capire, non una molla per agire.

1456.   Le modificazioni dell'umore sono un'indispensabile sorgente di varietà nel comportamento.

1457.   Se non c'è capacità, il desiderio del fantastico genera solo il bizzarro.

1447. Fashion always has novelties because it must; and good taste when it can.

1448. If sins could be eliminated, there would be certainly someone who would re-invent them.

1449. Naturally, we pursue happiness through what gives us pleasure: what sense would it have to pursue unhappiness through what displeases us? But, as naturally, pleasure should not be confused with pleasurable sensations. Even suffering may give pleasure, although not as such, but as a means to obtain happiness. For example, in spiritual development; or in the sacrifices that we make for those we love.

1450. For an actor, to be able to skillfully interpret any role results in the failure to develop a personal image. Being able to play everybody, in the end he does not identify himself with anybody. It is his very versatility that reveals the professional actor and prevents the creation of a personal myth and image, that people come to cherish.

1451. Stupidity invites the dishonesty of others to take advantage of it.

1452. Our emotional reactions prevent us from seeing the opportunities that are hidden in hardships.

1453. In order not to be always bored, one should not become bored too easily.

1454. The sorrows that we bear with more firmness are those of others.

1455. Each individual action is determined by precise factors, like desires, instincts, interests, duty, opinions, necessities, convictions, drives, obligations, fears, ideals, etc. Theoretical analyses influence individual actions, but they are an effort to understand, not a drive to act.

1456. The modifications of mood are an indispensable source of variety in behavior.

1457. If there is no ability, the desire of the fantastic generates only the bizarre.

1458. L'ateismo è una illogica mancanza di fede. La logica ci forza a trarre le conseguenze dalle meraviglie che si vedono. Si può non credere in Dio solo rifiutandosi di guardare, vedere e ragionare. L'agnosticismo "scientifico" è ancora più sorprendente dell'ateismo, perché la scienza rivela meraviglie così straordinarie da essere quasi incredibili. L'agnosticismo scientifico non nega Dio ma lo ignora, per il fatto che il metodo scientifico può provare quello che è fisico, ma non quello che è metafisico. Naturalmente, l'impotenza del metodo scientifico a questo riguardo non prova nulla eccetto la sua impotenza. Per fare un esempio, sarebbe come se si ignorasse la bellezza, l'amore, la speranza, ecc. solo perché il metodo scientifico non sa provarli e misurarli. Alcuni sono così illogici da rifiutare di trarre le inevitabili conseguenze logiche delle meraviglie che vedono, considerandole un'estrapolazione non scientifica. Implicitamente, affermano che la logica non è scientifica, quella stessa logica senza la quale non vi può essere metodo scientifico.

1459. Per amare molto, bisogna non amarsi troppo.

1460. L'analisi della realtà da parte dei filosofi riflette spesso le loro vicende personali, esperienze, educazione, carattere, mode del momento, convinzioni, ecc.: si indaga quello che personalmente interessa e con conclusioni influenzate dalle proprie emozioni e esperienze. Dal che si vede che anche la logica non è immune ai riverberi emotivi della nostra umanità.

1461. Non avendo sufficiente fiducia in se stessi, alcuni cercano di nascondere il loro complesso di inferiorità simulando un complesso di superiorità, che loro per primi sanno essere una finzione.

1462. Non sempre si sbaglia di meno quando si riflette di più. Anche perché qualche volta, invece di riflettere, si farnetica in balia delle nostre emozioni.

1463. Talvolta, le nostre passioni ci appassionano indipendentemente dal loro oggetto. Diventa più importante quello che si prova che per chi si prova.

1464. Non ci si rende pienamente conto di essere mortali finché non si raggiunge la mezza età; e che, di fatto, si muore finché non si raggiunge la tarda età.

1458. Atheism is an illogical lack of faith. Logic forces us to draw the consequences from the marvels that we see. One may not believe in God only by refusing to look, see and reason. The "scientific" agnosticism is even more surprising than atheism, because science reveals to us marvels so extraordinary as to be almost incredible. Scientific agnosticism does not deny God but ignores Him, because the scientific method can only prove what is physical, but not what is metaphysical. Of course, the impotence of the scientific method in this regard does not prove anything, except its impotence. To make an example, it would be as if we were to ignore beauty, love, hope, etc., because the scientific method does not know how to prove or measure them. Some are so illogical that they refuse to draw the inescapable logical consequences of the marvels they see, considering them non-scientific extrapolations. They implicitly affirm that logic is not scientific, the same logic without which there can not be a scientific method.

1459. To love much, one must not love himself too much.

1460. The analysis of reality by philosophers often reflects their personal events, experiences, education, character, fashions of the moment, convictions, etc.: what personally interests is investigated and with conclusions influenced by one's emotions and experiences. From this, it can be seen that even logic is not immune to the emotional feelings of our humanity.

1461. Not having a sufficient self-confidence, some people try to hide their inferiority complex by simulating a superiority complex, which they are the first ones to know that it is a pretense.

1462. Not always we err less when we reflect more. Also because sometimes, instead of reflecting, we rave at the mercy of our emotions.

1463. Sometimes, we are passionate about our passions independently of their object. What we feel becomes more important than for whom we feel it.

1464. We do not fully become aware that we are mortal until we reach the middle age; and that actually we die until we reach an advanced age.

1465. I nostri desideri più intensi trovano la ragionevolezza insipida.

1466. Comportarsi semplicemente è un merito solo quando non si è semplici di natura.

1467. Quando le meraviglie della natura non ci parlano più, diventiamo orfani di Dio.

1468. Per quanto poco si possa valere, ciascuno di noi non è tanto prezioso quanto assolutamente indispensabile a se stesso.

1469. In ogni società, le differenti classi sono create dalla selezione naturale. È impossibile eliminarle, perché non si può eliminare il processo di selezione di meriti differenti. Si può solo favorire il passaggio dei vari individui da una classe all'altra sulla base del loro merito. E formalizzare il fatto che il maggior merito è solo dovuto ad un caso fortunato e pertanto non si può rifiutare agli obblighi dettati dalla necessità di equilibri sociali.

1470. La verità ha componenti oggettive e soggettive che sono ugualmente valide, le prime per tutti e le seconde per ciascuno. Una distanza di tre chilometri (verità oggettiva) è grande o piccola a seconda di chi la considera (giovane o vecchio, atleta o persona sedentaria, ecc.) (verità soggettiva). Ed un oggetto che costa un certo prezzo (verità oggettiva) è caro o meno a seconda delle nostre finanze, avarizia o prodigalità (verità soggettiva). Così, una verità soggettiva può essere anche una verità oggettiva, ma solo per una certa mente e non per tutte.

1471. Nel compromesso, si rinuncia a vincere per non rischiare di perdere.

1472. Il problema della saggezza è che non suscita emozioni. E la sua stoltezza è di cercare di eliminare quelle che ci sono.

1473. Si cerca di impressionare gli altri quando è già così difficile impressionare noi stessi. Ma forse lo si fa proprio per quello.

1474. I ribelli sono esenti dal bigottismo dell'ipocrisia, ma non dall'ipocrisia. Si può non essere ipocriti solo quando non si hanno interessi.

1465.   Our most intense desires find reasonableness insipid.

1466.   To behave simply is a merit only when one's own nature is not simple.

1467.   When the wonders of nature no longer speak to us, we become orphans of God.

1468.   No matter how little is our worth, each one of us is not so much precious as absolutely indispensable to himself.

1469.   In every society, the different classes are created by natural selection. It is impossible to eliminate them, because the process of selection of different merits can not be eliminated. One can only facilitate the passage of the various individuals from one class to another on the basis of their merit. And formalize the fact that a greater merit is only due to a fortunate chance and therefore it can not refuse the obligations dictated by the need of a social balance.

1470.   Truth has objective and subjective components that are equally valid, the former for all people and the latter for each individual. A distance of three kilometers (objective truth) is great or small depending on who considers it (young or old, athlete or sedentary person, etc.) (subjective truth). And an object that costs a given price (objective truth) is or is not expensive depending on our finances, avarice or prodigality (subjective truth). Therefore, a subjective truth may be also an objective truth, but only for a given mind and not for all.

1471.   In compromise, one gives up winning in order not to risk losing.

1472.   The problem with wisdom is that it does not excite emotions. And its silliness is to seek to eliminate those which are there.

1473.   We try to impress others when it is already so difficult to impress ourselves. But perhaps we do the former precisely because of the latter.

1474.   Rebels are exempt from the sanctimony of hypocrisy, but not from hypocrisy. One may not be hypocritical only when one has no interests.

1475. La smania di affermarsi non risparmia nessuno, anche se le dimensioni del cerchio della risonanza che ciascuno cerca variano assai.

1476. Le profezie si caratterizzano per essere oscure o ambigue: in questa maniera, è più difficile dimostrare che sono sbagliate dal momento che ognuno le può interpretare come desidera.

1477. Non si dimenticano le cose che colpiscono, offendono o interessano, perché le pensiamo ripetutamente.

1478. Quando diventa vecchia, la mente rimpiange soprattutto che il suo corpo non sia più giovane.

1479. Se si rimane normali, è solo grazie a continui aggiustamenti di cui non siamo coscienti. Il caso e le malattie ci rivelano quanto la normalità sia un processo dinamico che continuamente dipende da un precario equilibrio.

1480. Nella nostra memoria, i colori svaniscono rapidamente. Tutt'al più, rimangono i *nomi* dei colori (verde, giallo, bianco, ecc.). Solo le fotografie ci permettono di rivedere il nostro passato a colori.

1481. Del nostro passato esiste solo quello che si ricorda, e fintanto che lo si ricorda.

1482. L'abuso delle emozioni più gentili porta al cinismo, perché si delude se stessi e si perde così il proprio rispetto.

1483. Il voler essere sempre spiritosi comporta spesso l'essere insufficientemente seri.

1484. Analizzare le cose significa cercare il significato di se stessi nel contesto generale.

1485. Siamo soprattutto il prodotto della nostra ricetta genetica; come dire, della sorte e del caso.

1486. Come l'influenza, vizi e virtù sono contagiosi. Ma, come per l'influenza, alcune persone sono più resistenti al contagio (degli uni o delle altre).

1475.   The craving for recognition does not spare anybody, even if the dimensions of the circle of the resonance that each seeks considerably varies.

1476.   Prophesies are characterized by being either obscure or ambiguous: in this manner, it is more difficult to demonstrate that they are wrong, since everyone can interpret them as he wishes.

1477.   We do not forget the things that strike, offend or interest us, because we think them repeatedly.

1478.   When getting old, the mind most of all regrets that its body is no longer young.

1479.   If we remain normal, it is only because of continuous adjustments of which we are not aware. Chance and disease reveal how much normality is a dynamic process that continuously depends on a precarious balance.

1480.   In our memory, colors quickly fade. At most, only the *names* of the colors remain (green, yellow, white, etc.). Only photographs allow us to see again our past in color.

1481.   Of our past, only what we remember exists, and as long as we remember it.

1482.   The abuse of most gentle emotions leads to cynicism, because one disappoints himself and thereby loses his self-respect.

1483.   Wanting always to be witty often entails being insufficiently serious.

1484.   Analyzing things means to seek the meaning of oneself in the general context.

1485.   We are essentially the product of our genetic recipe; that is to say, of fate and of chance.

1486.   Like influenza, vices and virtues are contagious. But, as for influenza, some people are more resistant to contagion (by the former or by the latter).

1487. Si vive più intensamente con una forte passione che con mille pensieri acuti.

1488. L'importanza degli impulsi del subconscio si vede nel vuoto che si verifica quando ne siamo privati.

1489. Il cervello riceve stimoli fisici dalle molecole che sono nell'ambiente esterno e li trasforma in immagini mentali. La mente crede che queste immagini provengano dall'ambiente esterno (invece che dalla trasformazione degli stimoli nel cervello) e che gli stimoli esterni siano identici alle immagini interne. Pertanto, la mente dà valore oggettivo alle sue immagini: crede che provengano direttamente dall'esterno, dal momento che non può determinare quando le immagini sono state formate durante il processo di percezione. Ma la differenza tra stimoli esterni ed immagini interne la si vede in situazioni particolari. Se la percezione è difettosa (per esempio, ubriachezza o allucinazioni), gli stimoli esterni sono gli stessi, ma le immagini interne diventano difettose (immagini doppie o distorte). Questo dimostra che la realtà comporta una elaborazione degli stimoli esterni da parte della mente e non la loro percezione diretta e non modificata. Basta considerare che non vi sono colori o suoni (solo lunghezze d'onda) fuori della mente.

1490. Spesso si sacrifica la bellezza alla praticità, anche per motivi economici. Eppure l'utilità della praticità passa man mano che nuovi bisogni si sviluppano; e quella della bellezza resta a rallegrare tutti come un'acquisizione senza scadenza. Pertanto, anche da un punto di vista pratico e persino economico, bisogna capire che la vera praticità deve cedere alla vera bellezza. Dopo tutto, la bellezza è una forma duratura di ricchezza perché soddisfa un bisogno eterno dello spirito umano: il desiderio del bello. L'oro dei Greci è sparito da gran tempo, ma la poesia di Omero no.

1491. Essere sciocchi è male e non rendersene conto è peggio. O forse è meglio...

1492. Il voler provare tutto deriva dall'assenza di ferme convinzioni e delle conseguenti scelte.

1493. Professionalmente, dopo aver mostrato quanto si costa, non ci rimane che dimostrare quanto si vale.

1487. We live more intensely with a strong passion than with a thousand keen thoughts.

1488. The importance of the subconscious drives is seen in the vacuum that occurs when we are deprived of them.

1489. The brain receives physical stimuli from the molecules that are in the external environment and transforms the stimuli in mental images. The mind believes that these images come from the external environment (rather than from the transformation of the stimuli in the brain) and that the external stimuli are identical with the internal images. Therefore, the mind attributes an objective value to its own images: it believes that they come directly from outside, since it can not determine when the images were formed during the perception process. But the difference between external stimuli and internal images is seen in particular situations. If the perception is defective (e.g., drunkenness or hallucinations), the external stimuli are the same, but the internal images become defective (double or distorted images). This shows that reality involves an elaboration of perceived external stimuli by the mind and not their direct and unmodified perception. It suffices to consider that there are no colors or sounds (only wavelengths) outside the mind.

1490. Often, beauty is sacrificed to practicality, also for economic reasons. Yet, the usefulness of practicality passes as new needs develop; and that of beauty stays to gladden everyone as an enduring acquisition. Therefore, also from a practical and even an economic point of view, it is necessary to understand that true practicality must yield to true beauty. After all, beauty is a lasting kind of wealth because it satisfies an everlasting need of the human spirit: the desire of the beautiful. The gold of the Greeks is long gone, but not the poetry of Homer.

1491. To be silly is no good and not to be aware of it is worse. Or perhaps it is better...

1492. Wanting to experience everything derives from the absence of firm convictions and of the consequent choices.

1493. Professionally, after showing how much we cost, we have only to demonstrate how much is our worth.

1494. Riesce difficile rendersi conto che la realtà come la percepiamo è interamente una creazione della nostra mente. Le molecole del mondo fisico che originano gli stimoli non sono mentali, ma i loro stimoli sono percepiti secondo la struttura e la funzione dei recettori e della mente. Siamo fatti in tal maniera che si attribuisce alle immagini originanti dalle molecole del mondo fisico una realtà oggettiva che, di fatto, esiste solo nella nostra mente.

1495. Dal punto di vista dell'infinito, che significato possono mai avere le dimensioni del tempo o dello spazio? Come si possono misurare le dimensioni di quello che non ha né un principio né una fine?

1496. La logica è una figlia della natura che pretende di insegnare alla madre. Ma una seria limitazione della logica è che può comprendere solo quello che è logico.

1497. Chi si ammira è poco propenso ad invidiare gli altri. Lo si vede in chi ha un merito considerevole o una florida vanità o una notevole presunzione. O tutti e tre.

1498. Inesorabilmente, l'invecchiamento del corpo si trascina dietro quello della mente e del cuore.

1499. I frutti proibiti sono più desiderati degli altri, non perché necessariamente sono più buoni, ma perché eccitano la nostra curiosità.

1500. Quando le inibizioni sono fisiologiche, le disinibizioni sono patologiche. La genetica non ci permette di dimenticare la distinzione tra libertà e arbitrarietà.

1501. Si vede tutto secondo la prospettiva della nostra mente, con angoli più o meno acuti (od ottusi).

1502. I piaceri richiedono fermezza solo quando vi si rinuncia.

1503. Se fossimo più intelligenti, vi sarebbero meno teorie filosofiche.

1504. Le nuove tendenze spesso entusiasmano, anche perché, infantilmente, l'entusiasmo non prevede i pericoli e i danni dei loro lati negativi. S'impara solo se il nostro passato insegna al futuro.

1494. It is difficult for us to realize that reality as we perceive it is entirely the creation of the mind. The molecules of the physical world that originate the stimuli are not mental, but their stimuli are perceived according to the structure and function of the receptors and of the mind. We are made in such a fashion that we attribute to the images originating from the molecules of the physical world an objective reality that actually exists only in our mind.

1495. From the point of view of infinity, what meaning might possibly have the dimensions of time and space? How can one measure the dimensions of what has neither beginning nor end?

1496. Logic is a daughter of nature that wants to teach her mother. But a serious limitation of logic is that it can understand only what is logical.

1497. Those who admire themselves are little inclined to envy others. This is seen in those who have a considerable merit or a flourishing vanity or a remarkable conceit. Or all three.

1498. Inexorably, the aging of the body drags along that of the mind and of the heart.

1499. The forbidden fruits are more desired than the others, not because they necessarily taste better, but because they excite our curiosity.

1500. When the inhibitions are physiological, their removal is pathological. Genetics does not allow us to forget the distinction between freedom and arbitrariness.

1501. We see everything according to the perspective of our mind, with angles that are more or less acute (or obtuse).

1502. Pleasures demand firmness only when we renounce them.

1503. If we were more intelligent, there would be fewer philosophical theories.

1504. New trends often arouse enthusiasm, also because, childishly, enthusiasm does not foresee the dangers and damages of their negative sides. We learn only if our past teaches our future.

1505. Si deduce usando i paradigmi della logica e si scopre usando le intuizioni della creatività.

1506. Senza l'autocoscienza, non si saprebbe chi siamo. E neanche ce lo domanderemmo.

1507. I filosofi possono non seguire le religioni rivelate, ma pochi sono atei, perché la ragione impone loro la fede nell'esistenza di Dio.

1508. Le nostre potenzialità sono solo quelle che riusciamo a realizzare. Il resto è velleità.

1509. L'egoismo cieco è un difetto genetico facilitato da una limitata comprensione e una cattiva educazione. Quando è totale, non gli mancano i piaceri, ma la felicità.

1510. In ogni movimento, c'è sempre chi vuole spingere le cose un po' più oltre, verso estremi inaccettabili. Queste esagerazioni causano una reazione opposta da parte di altri, una reazione che spesso ha le stesse caratteristiche.

1511. Un'illusione deliziosa è certo migliore di una sciatta realtà.

1512. Quanto sia profondo un pentimento lo stabilisce la sua sincerità.

1513. Le nostre aspirazioni nascono dal desiderio di librarsi sulla magnanimità delle nostre speranze.

1514. Siamo più pronti a criticare quello che non capiamo che a farne un'analisi critica.

1515. Il buon senso delle scimmie si vede dal fatto nessuna scimmia si è mai vantata di aver dato origine all'uomo.

1516. Le creazioni umane richiedono uno sforzo intenso o addirittura la sofferenza. A causa della nostra limitatezza, la via verso la perfezione è lunga e difficile. In realtà, senza fine.

1517. Quale che sia il livello mentale, a nessuno sono state negate le emozioni. Ma la qualità delle emozioni è condizionata dalla finezza della mente.

1505. We deduce by using the paradigms of logic and we discover by using the intuitions of creativity.

1506. Without self-consciousness, we would not know who we are. And we would not even ask it to ourselves.

1507. Philosophers may not follow any revealed religion, but few are atheists, because reason forces on them the faith in God's existence.

1508. Our potentialities are only those which we succeed in realizing. The rest is foolishness.

1509. Blind egoism is a genetic defect facilitated by a limited understanding and a poor education. When it is total, it lacks not pleasures, but happiness.

1510. In every trend, there are always those who want to push things a little further, toward unacceptable extremes. These exaggerations result in an opposite reaction by others, a reaction which often has the same characteristics.

1511. A delightful illusion is certainly better than a slovenly reality.

1512. How deep is repentance is established by its sincerity.

1513. Our aspirations are born out of the desire to hover on the magnanimity of our hopes.

1514. We are more ready to criticize than to critically analyze what we do not understand.

1515. The common sense of monkeys is shown by the fact that no monkey has ever claimed to have given origin to man.

1516. Human creations require an intense effort or even suffering. Because of our limitations, the road toward perfection is long and difficult. Actually, endless.

1517. Whatever the mental level, emotions have been denied to no one. But the quality of emotions is conditioned by the finesse of the mind.

1518. È impossibile essere sempre felici: ne andrebbe di mezzo la felicità.

1519. Le parole sono strumenti potenti per evocare pensieri ed immagini nella mente altrui. Naturalmente, sono solo strumenti.

1520. Il movimento consiste in una successione mentale d'immagini diverse, come quelle di un cavallo che corre. Se si fermano le immagini (per es., fermando un film), il movimento sparisce; e se si accelerano, il movimento diventa più veloce del normale.

1521. I nostri desideri riempiono la mente di anticipazioni piacevoli e l'arricchiscono di intensità emotiva. Inoltre, danno significato alle nostre azioni: non avrebbe molto significato ottenere quello che non si desidera.

1522. Le inibizioni imposte dalla genetica separano il bene e il male. Senza le inibizioni, tutto diventa lecito e nulla è più lecito.

1523. Siamo così incostanti che, prima o poi, ci si stanca di essere buoni come di essere cattivi.

1524. Se fossimo tutti perfetti, saremmo insopportabili gli uni agli altri. E forse anche a noi stessi.

1525. Una tenacia risoluta sopporta anche una profonda disperazione, ignorando le emozioni che la indebolirebbero.

1526. Nella decadenza, si perde soprattutto la fede: prima in Dio, poi negli altri e infine in se stessi. E il vuoto interno che inizia il declino: *ex nihilo nihil*. Ci si arrende, prima di combattere.

1527. Le cose sono nuove o vecchie solo per la mente: per le menti di una nuova generazione, tutte le cose sono nuove, anche quelle antiche di duemila anni. Poi l'abitudine fa diventare vecchie sia le cose antiche che quelle recenti.

1528. La moderazione cresce con la grandezza delle cose a cui si applica. È per questo che anche moderazione può essere grande.

1529. L'ignoranza delle qualità che ci mancano ci protegge dal renderci tristemente conto delle nostre deficienze.

1518. It is impossible to be always happy: there could not be happiness.

1519. Words are powerful instruments to evoke thoughts and images in the mind of others. Naturally, they are only instruments.

1520. Movement consists in a mental succession of different images, such as those of a running horse. If we stop the images (e.g., by stopping a film), the movement disappears; and if we speed up the images, the movement becomes faster than normal.

1521. Our desires fill the mind with pleasurable anticipations and enrich it of emotional intensity. Furthermore, they give meaning to our actions: there would be little meaning in obtaining what we do not desire.

1522. Inhibitions imposed by genetics separate good from evil. Without inhibitions, everything becomes licit and nothing is licit any more.

1523. We are so inconstant that, sooner or later, we tire of being good as of being bad.

1524. If everyone were perfect, we would be unbearable to each other. And perhaps even to ourselves.

1525. An unflinching tenacity endures even a profound despair, ignoring the emotions that would weaken it.

1526. In decadence, most of all we lose faith: first in God, then in others, and finally in ourselves. It is the internal emptiness that initiates the decline: *ex nihilo nihil*. We surrender; before fighting.

1527. Things are new or old only for the mind: for the minds of a new generation, all things are new, even those that are two thousand years ancient. Then, habit makes both the ancient and the new things become old.

1528. Moderation grows with the greatness of the things to which it applies. This is the reason why moderation too can be great.

1529. The ignorance of the qualities that we do not have protects us from being sadly aware of what we lack.

1530. Taluni non riescono a comportarsi semplicemente, perché per loro è troppo complicato farlo. Dopo tutto, comportarsi semplicemente richiede una naturale semplicità o notevole comprensione.

1531. Alcuni sono derelitti per aver scelto la "libertà", quel senso di libertà che deriva dal rifiutarsi di sottomettersi alle asperità e agli obblighi della lotta: la "libertà" della rinuncia che deriva dal perdere prima di combattere.

1532. Ci si risente del fatto che quelli che non ci piacciono non abbiano più difetti. Per rimediare a questo, non esitiamo ad attribuire loro anche quei nostri difetti che quelli non hanno.

1533. Il sentiero della semplicità segue una linea retta. Che è anche la più breve.

1534. Il fascino del mare risiede nella grande varietà e bellezza dei suoi differenti umori, dalla lucida calma di riflessi dorati alla violenza furiosa di possenti onde spumose perseguitate dal vento impazzito.

1535. Non si rinuncia alla speranza se non per sostituirvi un'illusione.

1536. Se fossimo immortali, sarebbe facile essere coraggiosi. E invece è il contrario: solo dimostrando un coraggio eccezionale alcuni possono aspirare all'immortalità.

1537. La compassione verso assassini colpevoli implica la mancanza di compassione verso le loro vittime innocenti. Gli assassini dovrebbe ottenere il perdono non da noi (che non abbiamo ricevuto nessun danno), ma dalle loro vittime. Sfortunatamente, le loro vittime sono morte; assassinate. La pietà non consiste nel volersi sentire buoni.

1538. Ogni giorno si consuma un po' di quel filo di cui è fatto il gomitolo della vita per intesserlo nel tappeto delle nostre opere.

1539. L'amore è sempre illogico: un amore ragionevole non sembrerebbe neanche amore.

1540. Noi ignoriamo il significato dell'eternità. Soprattutto, non ci riesce concepire che non abbia un principio. L'infinito è troppo grande per la mente umana.

1530. Some people can not behave simply, because for them it is too complicated to do so. After all, to behave simply demands a natural simplicity or a considerable comprehension.

1531. Some are derelicts because they have chosen "freedom", that sense of freedom that derives from refusing to submit to the asperity and obligations of struggle: the "freedom" of giving up that derives from losing before fighting.

1532. We resent the fact that those whom we dislike do not have more faults. To remedy that, we do not hesitate to attribute them even those of our faults that they do not have.

1533. The path of simplicity follows a straight line. Which is also the shortest.

1534. The fascination of the sea resides in the great variety and beauty of its different moods, from a lucid calm of golden reflexes to the furious violence of powerful foamy waves haunted by a mad wind.

1535. One does renounce hope if not to substitute it with an illusion.

1536. If we were immortal, it would be easy to be courageous. Instead, it is the converse: only by displaying an exceptional courage a few can aspire to immortality.

1537. Compassion toward guilty murderers implies lack of compassion toward their innocent victims. Murderers ought to obtain their pardon not from us (who received no damage), but from their victims. Unfortunately, the latter are dead; murdered. Pity does not consist in wanting to feel good.

1538. Every day we use up a little of that yarn of which the clew of life is made up to knit it in the carpet of our deeds.

1539. Love is always illogical: a reasonable love would not even seem to be love.

1540. We ignore the meaning of eternity. Above all, we are not able to conceive that it did not have a beginning. Infinite is too big for the human mind.

1541. Ci sono tante maniere per essere insignificanti e nessuna e particolarmente difficile.

1542. I dettagli sono necessari: basta non perdercisi.

1543. La maniera più stupida di essere aggressivi è di esserlo stupidamente.

1544. Una fine psicologia è la chiave che penetra e influenza l'altrui mente. Ma quest'ultima spesso ne previene l'intrusione sbarrando la porta con il chiavistello dei propri interessi.

1545. Spesso, le virtù sono desiderabili e i vizi desiderati.

1546. Quando fa comodo, si "legalizzano" i vizi come "diritti". E li si giustifica nel nome della modernità. Non si legalizzano come virtù, perché quello implicherebbe una valutazione morale, che invece vogliamo accuratamente evitare.

1547. Il bene ed il male non risparmiano né i buoni né i cattivi, dal momento che bene e male sono relativi a ciascuna mente. Per questo, non sono necessariamente lo stesso bene e male per tutti. Per esempio, un furto è male per il derubato e bene per il ladro. E la prigione è male per il ladro e bene per il derubato.

1548. La fatuità della raffinatezza considera non distinte e inappropriate le emozioni intense e sincere (perché la imbarazzano). In genere, vi reagisce pubblicamente deridendole con un riso che suona falso; e talvolta in privato con le lacrime (di compassione per il suo vuoto interno privo di significato).

1549. Quello che ci deumanizza non sono i nostri peccati, ma la mancanza del senso di colpa.

1550. La verità è inflessibile. E pertanto talvolta è dura e sgradita. Ne segue che non raramente il dire la verità (o tutta la verità) può essere "inopportuno".

1551. Alcuni confondono la poesia con le espressioni strane, con il suono di cose non comuni e talvolta incomprensibili: cercano uno stile personale quando sarebbe necessario prima di tutto aver stile.

1541.　There are so many ways to be insignificant and none is particularly difficult.

1542.　Details are necessary: as long as one does not get lost in them.

1543.　The most stupid way to be aggressive is to be stupidly so.

1544.　A fine psychology is the key that penetrates and influences others' mind. But the latter often prevents the intrusion by locking the door with the bolt of its own interests.

1545.　Often, virtues are desirable and vices are desired.

1546.　When it is convenient, we "legalize" vices as "rights". And we justify them in the name of modernity. We do not legalize them as virtues, since that would imply a moral evaluation, which instead we seek to carefully avoid.

1547.　Good and evil spare neither good nor bad people, since good and evil are relative to each mind. For this reason, they are not necessarily the same good or evil for everyone. For example, a theft is evil for the robbed and good for the thief. And prison is evil for the thief and good for the robbed.

1548.　The fatuity of refinement considers sincere and intense emotions as undistinguished and unbecoming (because they embarrass it). Generally, it reacts publicly by deriding them with a laugh that sounds false; and sometimes in private with tears (of self-compassion for its meaningless internal vacuity).

1549.　What dehumanizes us is not our sins, but the lack of a feeling of guilt.

1550.　Truth is inflexible. And therefore sometimes it is hard and disagreeable. Hence, not rarely, to say the truth (or the whole truth) may be "inappropriate".

1551.　Some confuse poetry with strange expressions, with the sound of uncommon and sometimes incomprehensible things: they seek a personal style when it would be necessary first of all to have style.

1552. Si eviterebbero le delusioni evitando le illusioni. Ma è difficile evitare le illusioni perché sono troppo legate alla speranza. E ancora di più al desiderio di creare nella nostra mente con l'immaginazione quello che desideriamo.

1553. Abbiamo sempre bisogno dell'irrequietezza di un qualche desiderio insoddisfatto. Se poi succede di non aver desideri, si desidera di averne.

1554. Si perde la fiducia nel futuro quando si perde la fiducia in se stessi, dal momento che per futuro intendiamo il nostro futuro.

1555. Quando si fa solo quello che ci piace (e non quello che dovremmo fare), non ci rimane che sperare che ci piacciano anche le conseguenze.

1556. Nel nostro interesse, la natura fa sì che si sia intermittentemente insoddisfatti di noi stessi.

1557. La natura della nostra realtà dipende anche dal fatto che, quali che siano gli stimoli fisici o mentali, si percepisce solo quello che ciascuna mente è capace di percepire. Per questo, la qualità della nostra realtà riflette quella della nostra mente.

1558. Il presumere di saperne di più delle leggi naturali dovrebbe essere motivo di ansietà: può darsi benissimo che tale presunzione nasca dal fatto che non si capisce tutto (o che non si capisce nulla).

1559. Se non fosse per la nostra debolezza, la vita sarebbe più dura. La durezza di una macchina efficiente e senza sentimenti o fallimenti.

1560. Per forza di cose, nel creare ci si esprime con uno stile personale. Lo stile di Dio è espresso nelle infinite meraviglie dell'universo.

1561. Quando si accetta la realtà come è (realismo), si rinuncia a modificarla secondo come la vogliamo (idealismo). Nel primo caso, la realtà peggiora gradualmente per mancanza di necessari stimoli. Non è neanche necessario che i nostri ideali abbiamo successo, ma è necessario che si cerchino nuove e migliori realtà. L'ordine prestabilito include anche gli idealismi irrealizzabili: questi modificano la realtà molto di più di quanto sembri.

1552.   Disillusions could be avoided by avoiding illusions. But it is difficult to avoid illusions because they are inextricably bound to hope. And even more so to the desire to create in our mind with our imagination what we desire.

1553.   We always need the restlessness of some unsatisfied desire. If we happen not to have desires, we desire to have some.

1554.   We lose confidence in the future when we lose confidence in ourselves, since by future we mean our future.

1555.   When we do only what we like (and not what we should do), we can only hope that we will also like the consequences.

1556.   In our own interest, nature sees to it that we are intermittently unsatisfied of ourselves.

1557.   The nature of our reality depends also on the fact that, whatever the physical or mental stimuli are, we perceive only what each mind is capable of perceiving. For this reason, the quality of our reality reflects that of our mind.

1558.   Presuming to know more than the natural laws should be a reason for anxiety: it is possible that such a presumption is born by the fact that we do not understand everything (or that we do not understand anything).

1559.   If it were not for our weakness, life would be harder. The hardness of an efficient machine without feelings or failings.

1560.   Necessarily, in creating one expresses himself with a personal style. The style of God is expressed in the infinite marvels of the universe.

1561.   When we accept reality as it is (realism), we renounce to modify it as we want it (idealism). In the former case, reality becomes gradually worse for lack of necessary stimuli. It is not even necessary that our ideals should be successful, but it is necessary that we seek new and better realities. The pre-established order includes also the unrealizable ideals: these modify reality far more than it would seem.

1562. L'ordinata continuità della specie umana è affidata all'amore, non al piacere. Tuttavia, c'è il piacere senza l'amore, ma non l'amore senza il piacere.

1563. Certe leggende sono deliziose: è assai di più di quanto si possa dire di molte verità.

1564. Si dimenticano tante cose, ma sarebbe peggio se non si dimenticasse nulla: ci si piegherebbe gradualmente sotto il peso di tanti ricordi inutili e polverosi, come gli abeti sotto il peso della neve.

1565. Nella confessione sincera, non si vi è solo la remissione dei peccati, ma il rinnovo delle aspirazioni e speranze dell'anima.

1566. Si possono fare continue domande, ma se non si sanno trovare le risposte, non si aumenta la conoscenza, ma piuttosto i dubbi. Se si capisse di più, si domanderebbe di meno.

1567. Gli impulsi fisiologici hanno scopi precisi, ma non manifestazioni assolutamente specifiche. Per esempio, la ricerca del piacere è fisiologica, ma la ricerca di ogni tipo di piacere non lo è. Di qui, la presenza di inibizioni che separano quello che è lecito da quello che istintivamente non è permissibile.

1568. Più che dalla comprensione, la virtù è determinata da profonde convinzioni che hanno a che fare poco con la logica e molto con la genetica.

1569. La stravaganza è spesso assai più costosa dell'eleganza. E le sue pretese cercano di mascherare la sua mancanza di sostanza.

1570. Neanche l'amore resisterebbe all'analisi spietata della logica. Questo dimostra quanto la logica posa essere limitata e, se è usata ·male, anche pericolosa.

1571. La Necessità non è un mostro duro e insensibile. La Necessità è l'espressione di un ordine indispensabile e rigido, ma include tra le sue più importanti caratteristiche anche la bellezza, varietà, delicatezza e sentimenti intensi. Basta considerare l'attrattiva dei fiori, la delicatezza dell'aurora o i sogni d'amore.

1562. The orderly continuity of the human species is trusted to love, not to pleasure. Nevertheless, there is pleasure without love, but not love without pleasure.

1563. Some legends are very charming: this is much more than what could be said about many truths.

1564. We forget many things, but it would be worse if we were not to forget anything: we would gradually bend under the weight of so many useless and dusty remembrances, as firs under the weight of snow.

1565. In a sincere confession, there is not only the remission of sins, but also the renewal of the aspirations and hopes of the soul.

1566. One can ask continuous questions, but if he is unable to find the answers, not knowledge, but rather doubts are increased. If one understood more, one would question less.

1567. Physiological drives have precise aims, but not absolutely specific manifestations. For example, the search for pleasure is physiological, but the search for any type of pleasure is not. Hence, the presence of inhibitions that separate what is licit from what instinctively is not permissible.

1568. More than by comprehension, virtue is determined by deep convictions that have to do little with logic and plenty with genetics.

1569. Extravagance is often much more expensive than elegance. And its pretense tries to mask its lack of substance.

1570. Not even love would resist the pitiless analysis of logic. This shows how limited logic can be and, if it is improperly used, even dangerous.

1571. Necessity is not a harsh and unfeeling monster. Necessity is the expression of an indispensable and rigid order, but it includes among its most important characteristics also beauty, variety, delicacy and intense feelings. It suffices to consider the charm of flowers, the delicacy of dawn or the dreams of love.

1572. L'egoismo sfrenato porta al cinismo: si cerca di giustificare il nostro fallimento dubitando degli altri. Ma il cinismo è spesso amaro, raramente felice e mai completamente sincero.

1573. Con ogni nuova generazione, il ciclo ricomincia dal principio ma da un punto di partenza diverso.

1574. L'amore non rompe il cerchio del nostro egoismo, ma vi include la persona amata. Per questo, la persona amata diventa parte di noi.

1575. Non bisogna sopravvalutare il ruolo della logica nella vita della mente. Il conoscere non sarà mai un sostituto adeguato né per il sentire né per il fare. Inoltre, ciò che è logico non è necessariamente buono o vero.

1576. Nella disciplina, la parte cosciente della mente esige l'obbedienza del resto di se stessa.

1577. La via di mezzo non può essere che un compromesso tra due estremi opposti. Pertanto, la via di mezzo si sposta se uno degli estremi si indebolisce o si rafforza; e sparisce se uno degli estremi scompare.

1578. L'autocoscienza diventa eccessiva quando è ossessiva.

1579. Si è coscienti quando si pensa, e si diventa coscienti di sé quando ci si rende conto che si pensa.

1580. Come l'acqua di una sorgente, il silenzio è puro. Incontaminato da suoni, diventa il giardino in cui i pensieri e gli affetti della mente si intrattengono con piacere senza essere disturbati.

1581. Si pensa, ma non si sa come. Ma, quali che siano i meccanismi responsabili per il pensiero, è certo che la facoltà di pensare del cervello umano è un processo tanto straordinario da doverlo considerare un miracolo.

1582. Non esisterebbe il bene se non esistesse il male. Tutti e due sono parti indispensabili del fenomeno "vita". Se qualcosa è bene, il suo contrario non può essere che male. Se vincere è bene, perdere è male. E come si potrebbe vincere, se non si potesse perdere?

1572.   An unbridled selfishness breeds cynicism: we seek to justify our failure by doubting others. But cynicism is often bitter, rarely happy and never completely sincere.

1573.   With each generation, the cycle begins again from scratch but from a different starting point.

1574.   Love does not break the circle of our egoism, but it includes in it the beloved. For this reason, the beloved becomes part of us.

1575.   One must not overestimate the role of logic in the life of the mind. Knowing will never be an adequate substitute either for feeling or doing. Furthermore, what is logical is not necessarily good or true.

1576.   In discipline, the conscious part of the mind demands the obedience of the rest of itself.

1577.   The middle road can not be but a compromise between two opposite extremes. Therefore, the middle road shifts if one of the extremes weakens or strengthens; and ceases to exist if one of the extremes disappears.

1578.   Self-consciousness becomes excessive when it is obsessive.

1579.   One is conscious when he thinks, and one becomes conscious of his Self when he realizes that he thinks.

1580.   As the water of a spring, silence is pure. Uncontaminated by noise, it becomes the garden where the thoughts and affections of the mind dwell with pleasure without being disturbed.

1581.   We think, but we do not know how. But, whatever the mechanisms underlying thinking, it is certain that the faculty of thinking of the human brain is such an extraordinary process that it has to be considered a miracle.

1582.   Good could not exist if evil did not exist. And both are indispensable parts of the phenomenon "life". If something is good, its contrary has to be bad. If to win is good, to lose is bad. And how could we win, if we could not lose?

1583. La mente cosciente può avere volta a volta una sola attività pensante, determinata dall'attenzione. Si ricevono continui stimoli dall'ambiente interno ed esterno anche quando si pensa, ma li si percepisce solo se vi si presta attenzione, smettendo di pensare quello che si pensa. Così, se si ascolta della musica, non si può pensare ad altro: è per questo che ne siamo intrattenuti. Se si pensa ad altro, non si percepisce la musica (solo un rumore). Per questa ragione, ci si rilassa meglio quando non si pensa e si pensa meglio quando nulla interferisce.

1584. Non si ama abbastanza appassionatamente se non si diventa schiavi d'amore.

1585. La "giustizia" è un concetto e pertanto un'astrazione. Ma non è necessario sapere definire la giustizia per essere giusti, dato che l'istinto ci dice volta a volta quello che è giusto. Tanto più che la "giustizia" umana (a differenza degli istinti) cambia nel tempo e nello spazio. Secondo la giustizia umana, è giusto quello che è legale. Ma le leggi sono fatte da uomini a seconda delle teorie o degli interessi che prevalgono in un dato momento.

1586. Per esistere, Tempo e Spazio hanno bisogno di un punto di riferimento: la mente umana. Vicino o lontano, destra o sinistra, passato o futuro, ecc., esistono solo in ciascuna mente e sono relativi a questa. Per esempio, il presente era il futuro per quelli che ci hanno preceduto ed sarà il passato per quelli che ci seguiranno.

1587. È più difficile capire intimamente quello di cui non si ha esperienza. Questa è una limitazione della gioventù.

1588. I piaceri del corpo sono una necessità della mente. Per esempio, chi vorrebbe sempre mangiare male o vestirsi male?

1589. Molti preferiscono la sofferenza causata da una forte passione all'indifferenza causata da mancanza di passioni.

1590. L'autocoscienza comincia non quando la mente percepisce il proprio Io, fisico e mentale, ma quando si rende conto che quello che percepisce è il proprio Io. Si trova la propria identità solo quando si diventa coscienti della propria identità. Una scimmia che si guarda allo specchio non si riconosce.

1583. The conscious mind can think only one subject at any one time, singled out by attention. Continuous stimuli are received from the internal and external environments also when we think, but we perceive them only if we focus our attention on them, stopping the pursuit of our thoughts. Thus, if we listen to music, we can not think about something else: for this reason, we are entertained by it. If we think about something else, we do not perceive the music (only a noise). For this reason, we relax better when we do not think and we think better when nothing interferes.

1584. One does not love passionately enough if he does not become a slave of love.

1585. "Justice" is a concept and therefore an abstraction. But it is not necessary to know how to define justice to be just, since instinct tells us in each instance what is just. All the more so since human "justice" (in contrast to instinct) changes in time and space. According to human justice, right is what is legal. But laws are made by men according to theories and interests that prevail in any given moment.

1586. In order to exist, Time and Space need a reference point: the human mind. Near or far, right or left, past or future, etc., exist only in each mind and are relative to it. For example, our present was the future for those who preceded us and will be the past for those who will follow us.

1587. It is more difficult to intimately understand that of which we have no experience. This is a limitation of youth.

1588. The pleasures of the body are a necessity of the mind. E.g., who would want to always eat tasteless food or wear ugly clothes?

1589. Many prefer the suffering caused by a strong passion to the indifference caused by lack of passions.

1590. Self-consciousness begins not when the mind perceives the Self, physical and mental, but when it becomes aware that what it perceives is the Self. We find our identity only when we become aware of our identity. A monkey that looks at itself in a mirror does not recognize itself.

1591. Se non si ha una mente, non si ha coscienza di sé: si esiste solo per quelli che ci percepiscono. È quanto succede nella pazzia. Similmente, una mente rudimentale rende gli animali delle "macchine biologiche", determinate da una Necessità di cui non sono per nulla coscienti.

1592. I desideri impossibili spesso si soddisfanno solo con illusioni improbabili.

1593. Quando si deve parlare di noi stessi, si è obbligati a dire la verità anche se quello che si dice ferisce il nostro orgoglio. Ma non ci è permesso di dire la verità quando ferirebbe la nostra modestia.

1594. Una simpatia reciproca prelude ad un desiderio reciproco.

1595. Le soluzioni astratte vengono proposte da menti poco pratiche. Ma le generalizzazioni hanno la funzione essenziale di ridurre la miopia delle menti troppo pratiche. Una mente pratica tende a risolvere i problemi particolari, e ad ignorare quelli generali.

1596. La mente è ordinata in strati, costituiti da percezioni, riflessi, emozioni, sensibilità, concetti, riflessioni, generalizzazioni, ecc. In molte persone, uno di questi strati prevale, determinando una caratteristica essenziale di quella persona.

1597. Alcuni non lodano gli altri per paura che quest'ultimi si rendano conto che valgono assai più di loro.

1598. Il coraggio dovremmo averlo nel superare le difficoltà, non nel crearne.

1599. Solo le emozioni più intense ci rivelano i recessi più intimi e reconditi della nostra anima.

1600. Il piacere di comprendere deriva dalla stimolante novità dei panorami che si aprono alla mente.

1601. Se si dicesse sempre la verità, tutta la verità e niente altro che la verità, la maggior parte delle conversazioni finirebbe in un litigio. È esattamente quello che succede nei tribunali (e non viene detta neanche la metà della verità).

1591. If there is no mind, there is no awareness of the Self: one exists only for those who perceive him. This is what happens in madness. Similarly, a rudimentary mind makes animals "biological machines", determined by a Necessity of which they are not aware in the least.

1592. Impossible desires are often satisfied only with improbable illusions.

1593. When we must speak of ourselves, we are obliged to say the truth even if what we say hurts our pride. But we are not permitted to say the truth when it would hurt our modesty.

1594. A reciprocal liking preludes to a reciprocal desire.

1595. Abstract solutions are proposed by unpractical minds. But the generalizations have the essential function of reducing the myopia of too practical minds. A practical mind tends to solve particular problems, and to ignore the general ones.

1596. The mind is ordered in layers, constituted by perceptions, reflexes, emotions, sensibility, concepts, reflections, generalizations, etc. In many people, one of these layers prevails, determining an essential characteristic of that person.

1597. Some do not praise others for fear that the latter might become conscious that they are much more worthy than the former.

1598. We should have courage in overcoming difficulties, not in creating them.

1599. Only intense emotions reveal to us the most intimate and hidden recesses of our soul.

1600. The pleasure of understanding derives from the stimulating novelty of the new vistas that are opened to the mind.

1601. If we were to always say the truth, all the truth and nothing but the truth, most conversations would end up in a quarrel. It is exactly what happens in the courts of law (and not even half of the truth is said).

1602. Si ama la campagna e ci si ammucchia nelle città: si preferisce la compagnia di altre menti a quella della natura. Ogni tanto, si fanno delle scampagnate, ma in compagnia di altri: raramente si ride soli.

1603. La poesia è una forma di libertà. La libertà di perseguire l'espressione della bellezza per la bellezza.

1604. Quando si ama, i sensi diventano un'espressione delicata e appassionata del reciproco amore.

1605. Le emozioni e pensieri nuovi sono come i germogli dei alberi: una promessa di fiori e di frutti.

1606. La nostra sofferenza non è mai inutile, dal momento che non si hanno mai emozioni profonde invano: l'Io diventa più maturo, per quanto allo stesso tempo qualche volta ne sia devastato.

1607. Ad una frase elegante vengono perdonate tante sciocchezze: i piaceri dell'estetica non si curano dei rigori della logica.

1608. La logica deduce, ma non intuisce. Di qui, la sua potenziale sterilità.

1609. Neanche le virtù romane poterono resistere all'assalto di dilaganti ricchezze. La natura umana può sopravvivere alla povertà, ma non ha difesa contro l'opulenza.

1610. L'ignoranza è spesso assai imbarazzante per le persone educate; per le persone ignoranti, è una maniera di essere.

1611. I filosofi si immaginano che gli altri siano infelici perché non hanno la loro stessa passione di comprendere. Non sanno che invece gli altri sarebbero infelici se forzati ad avere gli stessi interessi dei filosofi.

1612. La condotta è influenzata molto dal fatto che spesso, sbagliando, perseguiamo i mezzi (per es., il denaro o le parole) come fini.

1613. L'intimo desiderio di cedere rende ferma la debolezza.

1614. La logica è abusata dai sofismi e violentata dalle passioni.

1602. We love the country and pile up in the cities: we prefer the company of other minds to that of nature. Once in a while, we go for a picnic, but in the company of others: rarely one laughs alone.

1603. Poetry is a form of freedom. The freedom of pursuing the expression of beauty for beauty's sake.

1604. When we love, the senses become a delicate and passionate expression of the reciprocal love.

1605. New emotions and thoughts are like the buds of trees: a promise of flowers and fruits.

1606. Our suffering is never useless, since we never have deep emotions in vain: the Self becomes more mature, although sometimes it is devastated in the process.

1607. To an elegant sentence, much nonsense is pardoned: the pleasures of aesthetics do not care about the rigors of logic.

1608. Logic deduces, but does not have intuitions. Hence, its potential sterility.

1609. Not even Roman virtues could resist the onslaught of immoderate wealth. Human nature can survive poverty, but it is defenseless against opulence.

1610. Ignorance is often rather embarrassing for educated persons; for ignorant persons, it is a way of being.

1611. Philosophers imagine that others are unhappy because they do not have their own passion for understanding. They do not know that instead others would be unhappy if forced to have the same interests of philosophers.

1612. Behavior is much influenced by the fact that often, we mistakenly pursue the means (e.g., money or words) as the ends.

1613. The intimate desire of yielding makes weakness unswerving.

1614. Logic is abused by sophisms and raped by passions.

1615. Nella breve euforia prodotta dal vino, la mediocrità cede il posto ad un'ebbra magnanimità.

1616. È cosa terribile essere inutilmente giovani.

1617. La fede si basa sulla nostra intuizione di Dio.

1618. La ricerca di un'espressione originale può alla fine provare solo la mancanza di originalità.

1619. La stupidità ci umilia, ma solo se non si è troppo stupidi.

1620. La bruttezza si insinua persino nella gioventù, a maggior gloria della più rara bellezza.

1621. L'unica maniera di rallentare l'invecchiamento è di mettere a frutto la creatività che deriva dall'esperienza, così che il vecchio crea il nuovo.

1622. Sotto la spinta della graduale assuefazione, la vacuità della noia, e la ricerca di nuove sensazioni, gli abusi della licenza portano gradualmente alla perversione.

1623. Ci vuole una certa bravura per estrarre quello che è interessante da quello che è ovvio. Cioè, capire il significato recondito delle cose.

1624. Nell'essere convenzionali si evitano molti rischi, ma non quello di essere convenzionali.

1625. Non è difficile ribellarsi coraggiosamente e generosamente, eccetto che alle proprie limitazioni.

1626. Certi aforismi dovrebbero avere più significato per il futuro di chi li legge che per il passato di chi li ha scritti.

1627. Per rilassare la mente, bisogna pensare pensieri diversi da quelli connessi con la propria attività professionale (rilassamento attivo), o non pensare e invece percepire qualcosa di piacevole (rilassamento passivo).

1628. È necessario essere ragionevoli, ma anche non esserlo sempre.

1615   In the brief euphoria caused by wine, mediocrity yields to a drunken magnanimity.

1616.   It is a terrible thing to be young in vain.

1617.   Faith is based on our intuition of God.

1618.   The search for an original expression may end up proving only a lack of originality.

1619.   Stupidity humiliates us, but only if we are not too stupid.

1620.   Ugliness insinuates itself even in youth, to the greater glory of the more rare beauty.

1621.   The only way to slow down the advancing of age is to put to fruition the creativity that derives from experience, so that the old creates the new.

1622.   Under the push of a gradual assuetude, the emptiness of boredom, and the search for new sensations, the abuses of license gradually lead to perversion.

1623.   It takes some skill to extract what is interesting from what is obvious. That is to say, understand the hidden meaning of things.

1624.   In being conventional many risks are avoided, but not that of being conventional.

1625.   It is not difficult to rebel courageously and generously, except against one's own limitations.

1626.   Certain aphorisms should have more meaning for the future of those who read them than for the past of the one who wrote them.

1627.   To relax the mind, one must think thoughts different from those connected with one's professional activity (active relaxation), or not to think and instead perceive something pleasurable (passive relaxation).

1628.   It is necessary to be reasonable, but also not to be always so.

1629.   Una comprensione limitata fa danni più gravi quando spinta da affetti profondi, come l'amore possessivo di certe madri.

1630.   Quando si critica a torto, o siamo incompetenti o siamo malevoli. O ambedue. Bisognerebbe rendersi conto che, da come si criticano gli altri, anche noi siamo giudicati.

1631.   La vita è un mistero irrepetibile a cui ognuno dà la sua soluzione personale. Non ci rimane che sperare che la nostra soluzione non sia troppo sbagliata.

1632.   Se si semina solo la normalità, si finisce col raccogliere solo la mediocrità. Per questo, l'educazione deve inculcare il desiderio di eccellere. In questo senso ristretto, la normalità fa rima con la mediocrità (per lo meno in italiano).

1633.   Su ogni soggetto, ci può essere una verità oggettiva e diverse verità soggettive (opinioni personali). Per esempio, un oggetto può pesare 20 chili e questo è vero per tutti ("verità oggettiva"). La verità oggettiva può essere verificata e misurata oggettivamente e pertanto è valida per tutte le menti. Invece, l'opinione personale è il risultato di una valutazione dell'oggetto da parte di menti differenti ("verità soggettiva"). Così, lo stesso oggetto di 20 chili può essere pesante per alcuni e leggero per altri, o anche per la stessa persona in epoche diverse (per es., differente età o indebolimento fisico). Questo perché *in natura esistono oggetti di un certo peso, ma non oggetti pesanti o leggeri*. L'essere pesante o meno riflette la valutazione della mente di ciascuno (così come l'essere fragile o duro, bello o brutto, grande o piccolo, largo o stretto, freddo o caldo, pratico o inutile, caro o economico, ecc.). La valutazione è differente perché la mente di ciascuno è differente da quella degli altri. Per questo motivo, la verità oggettiva è sempre universale (valida per tutti, "verità delle misure"; per es., la durata in minuti di un'ora), e la verità soggettiva è individuale (valida per ciascuno, "verità degli aggettivi"; per es., soggettivamente un'ora può essere lunga o corta a seconda dello stato della nostra mente). L'opinione personale può essere "oggettivamente vera" in certi casi (per es., il concetto della verità oggettiva e verità soggettiva) e completamente sbagliata in altri casi. Questo può succedere perché la mente non è sufficientemente critica, non capisce abbastanza, non sa abbastanza, è troppo emotiva, o spera troppo, ecc.

1629.   A limited comprehension causes greater damage when driven by deep affections, like the possessive love of certain mothers.

1630.   When we wrongfully criticize, we are either incompetent or malevolent. Or both. We should realize that, by the way we criticize others, we are also judged.

1631.   Life is an unrepeatable mystery to which everyone gives his personal solution. We are only left with the hope that our solution is not too wrong.

1632.   If we sow only normalcy, we end up harvesting only mediocrity. For this reason, education should inculcate the desire to excel. In this narrow sense, normalcy rhymes with mediocrity (at least in Italian).

1633.   On every subject, there may be one objective truth and different subjective truths. For example, an object may weigh 20 kilograms and this is true for everybody ("objective truth"). An objective truth can be objectively verified and measured, and therefore is valid for every mind. Instead, the personal opinion is the result of the evaluation of the object by different minds ("subjective truth"). Thus, the same object weighing 20 kilograms may be heavy for some and light for others, or even for the same person at different times (e.g., different age or physical weakening). This is so because *in nature there are objects of a given weight, but not heavy or light objects*. To be heavy or light reflects the evaluation of the mind of each person (like being fragile or hard, beautiful or ugly, large or small, wide or narrow, cold or warm, practical or useless, expensive or cheap, etc.). The evaluation is different because the mind of each person is different from that of others. For this reason, the objective truth is always universal (valid for all people, "truth of the measures"; e.g., the duration of an hour in minutes), and the subjective truth is individual (valid for each person, "truth of the adjectives"; e.g., subjectively an hour may be long or short depending on the state of our mind). The personal opinion may be "objectively true" in some instances (e.g., the concept of objective truth and subjective truth) and completely wrong in others. This may occur because the mind is not sufficiently critical, does not understand enough, does not know enough, is too emotional or hopes too much, etc.

1634. Il desiderio di essere attraenti ci rende certo diversi, ma spesso anche ridicoli. Basta considerare l'abbigliamento o il trucco di alcune persone.

1635. Se improvvisamente e contemporaneamente ci apparissero davanti tutti i nostri difetti, si sarebbe così sorpresi da rifiutarci di credere di averne così tanti.

1636. La vecchiaia non è una colpa, ma è come se lo fosse.

1637. La semplicità è ben lontana dall'essere ovvia, tanto è vero che per taluni è incomprensibile.

1638. I due sessi sono caratterizzati dalle loro differenze: una donna è più femminile quando l'uomo è più maschile. Non è del tutto chiaro perché la donna dovrebbe essere più donna quando è meno femminile; o l'uomo più uomo quando è meno maschile.

1639. Per la stessa mente, la fantasia ha mille forme e la realtà percepita una sola.

1640. Invece di liberarci da quello che ci diminuisce, ci si libera da quello che non ci conviene. Si seguono le nostre inclinazioni, non i nostri interessi. O piuttosto le nostre inclinazioni dettano i nostri interessi.

1641. Le istruzioni per ogni nuovo essere sono scritte nel libro della genetica da lui ereditata. Non sono ammesse correzioni (per lo meno per ora), neanche quando vi è uno sbaglio.

1642. Le opere dei grandi rivelano la loro grandezza professionale e le loro biografie la loro umana piccolezza (e non tutta).

1643. L'amore ha bisogno di penombre per trovare espressioni delicate. Per quello, ama il chiarore della luna nel silenzio della notte.

1644. Quello che si desidera è raramente il risultato di una scelta deliberata e cosciente. Anzi, i nostri desideri possono rivelare alla nostra mente aspetti di noi stessi che ignoravamo.

1645. Il segreto della confessione è imposto dal fatto che si confessa l'inconfessabile.

1634. The desire to be attractive renders us certainly different, but often also ridiculous. It suffices to consider the attire or the make-up of some persons.

1635. If suddenly and simultaneously all our defects were to appear before us, we would be so surprised that we would refuse to believe that we have so many.

1636. Old age is not a fault, but it is as if it were so.

1637. Simplicity is far from being obvious, so much so that for some it is incomprehensible.

1638. The two sexes are characterized by their differences: a woman is more feminine when the man is more masculine. It is not entirely clear why a woman should be more of a woman when she is less feminine or a man more of a man when he is less masculine.

1639. For the same mind, imagination has a thousand forms and the perceived reality only one.

1640. Instead of getting rid of what diminishes us, we get rid of what is not convenient for us. We follow our inclinations, not our interests. Or rather, our inclinations dictate our interests.

1641. The instructions for each new being are written in the book of the genetics inherited by him. No corrections are allowed (at least for the time being), even when there is a mistake.

1642. The works of the great reveal their professional greatness and their biographies their human pettiness (and not all of it).

1643. Love needs the twilight to find delicate expressions. For this reason, it loves the glimmer of the moon in the silence of the night.

1644. What we desire is rarely the result of a deliberate and conscious choice. In fact, our desires may reveal to our mind aspects of ourselves that we ignored.

1645. The secret of confession is imposed by the fact that we confess the unmentionable.

1646. Come le altre leggi naturali, anche le leggi morali sono uno strumento dell'Ordine divino.

1647. La luce, il calore, il ciclo dell'acqua e la clorofilla sono tra gli strumenti con cui il sole dona la sua energia alla terra.

1648. Se al cuore non si comanda, spesso non si disubbidisce nemmeno, non perché siamo disciplinati, ma perché non ne siamo capaci.

1649. Il privilegio della maggior parte delle donne è prima di tutto essere madri. E il più modesto destino dell'uomo è di provvedere alla famiglia con la qualifica di padre.

1650. Se Dio proteggesse ciascuno di noi contro tutto quello che ci danneggia, si diventerebbe come i figli di certi ricchi: arroganti e viziati.

1651. In genere, si preferisce essere intrattenuti da qualcosa che non istruisce piuttosto che essere istruiti da qualcosa che non intrattiene. O se si vuole, prima di tutto, vogliamo essere intrattenuti. Se poi si impara, tanto meglio.

1652. Non si nasce duri: ci si diventa. O ci fanno diventare.

1653. La bellezza è sempre moderna. È la stranezza che ha bisogno di sempre nuove mode.

1654. Sbagliare ogni tanto può essere meglio di non cambiare mai. Un errore può portare alla sua correzione, ma il ristagno porta solo al degrado progressivo.

1655. La debolezza è forte in chi è debole.

1656. Nella scienza, si è esposti non alle opere della genialità ma a quelle della divinità.

1657. I miti sono necessari come la logica. Pertanto, non si debbono distruggere i miti se non si è capaci di sostituirli con altri. Certo, non si può essere così ingenui da illudersi di poter sostituire i miti con i ragionamenti. Se si deve scegliere, abbiamo più bisogno di fede che di comprensione.

1646. Like other natural laws, also moral laws are an instrument of the divine Order.

1647. Light, heat, the cycle of water and chlorophyll are among the means by which the sun donates its energy to the earth.

1648. If we do not command the heart, often we do not disobey it either, not because we are disciplined but because we are unable to.

1649. The privilege of most women is first of all to be mothers. And the more modest destiny of man is to provide for the family with the title of father.

1650. If God were to protect each one of us against all that damages us, we would become like the children of certain wealthy people: arrogant and spoiled.

1651. In general, we prefer to be entertained by something that does not instruct us rather than to be instructed by something that does not entertain us. Or, if you prefer, first of all, we want to be entertained. If we also learn, all the better.

1652. We are not born hard: we become so. Or they make us so.

1653. Beauty is always modern. It is strangeness that needs always new fashions.

1654. Occasionally making a mistake may be better than never change. Errors may lead to their correction, but stagnation leads only to a progressive deterioration.

1655. Weakness is strong in those who are weak.

1656. In science, we are exposed not to the works of a genius, but to those of the divinity.

1657. Myths are as necessary as logic. Therefore, one must not destroy myths if he is incapable of substituting them with others. Certainly, one can not be so naïve to delude himself of being able to substitute myths with reasoning. If we have to choose, we need to have faith more than to understand.

1658. La realtà ha le dimensioni della nostra comprensione e l'intensità dei nostri sentimenti.

1659. Non si può essere giovani e maturi allo stesso tempo. Se si è maturi, non si è giovani anche lo siamo fisicamente. La maturità doma gli impulsi del cuore attraverso l'esperienza e rende la mente prosaicamente ragionevole e ragionevolmente cauta.

1660. Col tempo, le passioni ci tormentano di meno, non perché noi si diventa più forti, ma perché le passioni diventano più deboli.

1661. Ciascuno di noi è interessante, non tanto per se stesso, ma per la varietà che contribuisce con l'essere differente.

1662. Certe persone hanno convinzioni ostinate, perché ignorano i dubbi e le obiezioni che derivano da una migliore comprensione. Inoltre, sono intolleranti, perché temono che una migliore comprensione dimostri che loro hanno torto.

1663. Una logica perfetta non fa una persona intelligente: la fa solo logica.

1664. Il senso di colpa presuppone l'esistenza non tanto di inibizioni quanto di principi.

1665. Non vogliamo sentire obiezioni alle nostre convinzioni o ai nostri interessi, soprattutto quando le obiezioni sono giustificate. Anche perché raramente riteniamo i nostri interessi ingiustificati.

1666. La mente perde interesse a quello a cui si abitua. Per questo, l'abitudine è uno stimolo potente per desiderare qualcosa di nuovo, e questo a sua volta è uno stimolo potente per mantenere la mente attiva e protesa a realizzarsi.

1667. Vi è una melanconica tristezza nel declino ineluttabile della bellezza fisica.

1668. Una sostanziale coincidenza di interessi conduce a relazioni cordiali e vantaggi reciproci. Ma la coincidenza raramente persiste invariata, e la sua diminuzione porta prima al graduale raffreddamento e poi al disaccordo.

1658. Reality has the dimensions of our comprehension and the intensity of our feelings.

1659. One can not at the same time be young and mature. If one is mature, he is not young even if he is physically so. Maturity tames the impulses of the heart through experience and renders the mind prosaically reasonable and reasonably cautious.

1660. With the passing of time, passions trouble us less, not because we become stronger, but because our passions become weaker.

1661. Each one of us is interesting, not so much in himself, but for the variety that each contributes by being different.

1662. Some people have obstinate convictions, because they ignore the doubts and objections that derive from a better understanding. Furthermore, they are intolerant, because they fear that a better understanding may prove them wrong.

1663. A perfect logic does not make a person intelligent: it makes that person only logical.

1664. The sense of guilt implies the existence not so much of inhibitions as of principles.

1665. We do not want to hear objections to our convictions or to our interests, especially when the objections are justified. Also because we rarely believe our interests to be unjustified.

1666. The mind loses interest in that which it gets used to. For this reason, habit is a powerful stimulus for desiring something new. In turn, this is a powerful stimulus to maintain the mind active and keen on developing.

1667. There is a melancholy sadness in the ineluctable fading of the beauty of the body.

1668. A substantial coincidence of interests leads to cordial relations and reciprocal advantages. But coincidence rarely persists unaltered, and its diminution leads first to a growing coolness and then to disagreement.

1669. Nell'attività giornaliera, il reagire è assai più frequente dell'agire.

1670. Se non c'è del merito, il voler essere speciali si traduce spesso nell'essere solo eccentrici.

1671. Tanto le grandi virtù come i grandi vizi sono le eccezioni; e piccole virtù e piccoli vizi la regola.

1672. Senza la conoscenza dei dettagli, si è superficiali. E senza la comprensione dei principi generali si è miopi.

1673. Nel paradosso, si enuncia quella verità che vi è nell'eccezione.

1674. Un gusto sicuro è l'amante più fedele della bellezza.

1675. Una buona educazione dovrebbe sviluppare la mente, invigorire il corpo, formare il carattere ed eccitare il desiderio di eccellere.

1676. Nel trattare con la gente è indispensabile comprendere la psicologia di ciascuno, piuttosto che quella di tutti.

1677. Il non dire nulla ci permette di non mentire, ma dichiara che non vogliamo dire o non possiamo dire la verità. In certi casi, è un silenzio generoso.

1678. Sono tanti i pensieri che non concepiremo mai e che pertanto non diraderanno le nebbie della nostra incomprensione.

1679. Chi è incapace o riluttante a migliorarsi preferisce che gli si dica una cosa piacevole (anche se contro il suo interesse) che una cosa spiacevole (anche se nel suo interesse).

1680. La mente sa che non è capace di comprendere tutto. Eppure, quando non comprende qualcosa, la mente, invece di dubitare di sé, dubita di quello che non comprende.

1681. Ci sono occasioni in cui bisogna sapere essere deboli. Per esempio, nel trattare con i deboli.

1682. Ci si ascolta con piacere perché è il nostro Io che parla. Ed inoltre dice quello che vogliamo sentire.

1669. In daily activity, to react is a great deal more frequent than to act.

1670. If there is no merit, wishing to be special often results only in being eccentric.

1671. Great virtues as well as great vices are the exceptions; and small virtues and small vices the rule.

1672. Without knowledge of details, one is superficial. And without comprehension of general principles, one is myopic.

1673. In paradox, one states whatever truth there is in the exception.

1674. An unerring taste is the most faithful lover of beauty.

1675. A good education should develop the mind, strengthen the body, mold the character and excite the desire to excel.

1676. In dealing with people it is essential to understand the psychology of each person, rather than that of all persons.

1677. Not to say anything allows us not to lie, but it declares that we do not want to or can not speak the truth. In certain instances, it is a generous silence.

1678. Many are the thoughts that we will never conceive and that therefore will not dissipate the fog of our incomprehension.

1679. Those who are unable or unwilling to improve themselves prefer to be told a pleasant thing (even if against their interest) than a disagreeable thing (even if in their interest).

1680. The mind knows that it is incapable of understanding everything. Yet, when it does not understand something, the mind, instead of doubting itself, doubts what it does not understand.

1681. There are occasions in which we need to know how to be weak. For example, in dealing with the weak.

1682. We listen to ourselves with pleasure because it is our Self that speaks. In addition, it says what we want to hear.

1683. Morendo, spesso si cambia solo il nostro tipo di anonimato.

1684. La nostra mediocrità aspira al conforto di un'uniformità anonima.

1685. L'ozio della mente la rende opaca.

1686. Non raramente, si ritiene di saperne di più quanto più grande è la nostra ignoranza, poiché si ignora quanto non si sappia.

1687. Chi ha il potere vede tutto e tutti in termini di utilità. Ma i più abili concepiscono l'utilità nel senso lato della parola (che è quello più utile).

1688. Solitudine è l'essere lontani da chi si ama.

1689. Nella danza, il ritmo dei suoni si traduce in quello dei movimenti, come se vi fossero connessioni dirette tra centri sensoriali e motori che evitano la coscienza pensante. Ne risulta un senso di piacevolezza e di abbandono.

1690. Non si nega un padre neanche ad un figlio illegittimo, ma qualcuno non esita a negare un Padre all'universo.

1691. I megalomani annoiano stancando.

1692. Che cosa costituisca l'armonia è un gran mistero. Perché certi suoni sono musicali e altri cacofonici? Sembrerebbe che la differenza dovesse farla l'effetto dei suoni sui neuroni. Il che fa anche della musica un fenomeno genetico, sia pure soggetto ad influenze acquisite.

1693. L'inaridirsi della spiritualità apre la porta all'animale che si agita irrequieto nella gabbia del nostro subconscio. Forse, questo è quello che alcuni intendono per "liberazione".

1694. La verità oggettiva è unica e universale, mentre le bugie sono personali, varie, variabili, contraddittorie, innocenti, perfide, fantasiose, pittoresche, ridicole, ecc.

1695. Le meraviglie del mondo sono apprezzate solo dalla mente umana, che è la più grande delle meraviglie.

1683. In dying, often one only changes his own kind of anonymity.

1684. Our mediocrity aspires to the comfort of an anonymous uniformity.

1685. Idleness of the mind makes it opaque.

1686. Not rarely, we believe to be more knowledgeable the greater our ignorance is, since we ignore how much we do not know.

1687. Those in power see everything and everybody in terms of usefulness. But the ablest of them conceive usefulness in the broad sense of the word (which is the most useful).

1688. Loneliness is to be far away from the beloved.

1689. In dancing, the rhythm of sounds is translated into that of movements, as if there were direct connections between sensory and motor centers that bypass the thinking consciousness. A sense of pleasantness and abandon ensues.

1690. We do not deny a father even to an illegitimate child, but some do not hesitate to deny a Father to the universe.

1691. Megalomaniacs tiresomely bore.

1692. What constitutes harmony is a great mystery. Why are certain sounds musical and others cacophonous? It would seem that the effect of sounds on neurons should make the difference. That makes music also a genetic phenomenon, even if subject to acquired influences.

1693. The drying up of spirituality opens the door to the animal that restlessly paces the cage of our subconscious. Perhaps, this is what some mean by "liberation".

1694. Objective truth is unique and universal, whereas lies are personal, varied, variable, contradictory, innocent, malicious, fanciful, picturesque, ridiculous, etc.

1695. The marvels of the world are appreciated only by the human mind, which is the greatest of marvels.

1696. Le aspirazioni di una mente hanno le dimensioni di quella.

1697. La lunga intimità con se stessi è alla base del proprio Io. Viviamo con i nostri segreti e ne conosciamo le sfumature.

1698. Le passioni profonde non risparmiano neanche le persone superficiali, perché non hanno nulla a che fare con l'intelletto.

1699. Come in un circo esiste solo quello che si svolge nel cono di luce, così le più vivide vicende umane scompaiono lentamente nell'oscurità della dimenticanza man mano che il cerchio illuminato dalla nostra memoria si sposta più avanti sotto la frusta del tempo.

1700. Ci si può permettere di essere completamente sinceri quando ci si può permettere di ignorarne le conseguenze.

1701. La natura mantiene l'equilibrio tra gli organismi attraverso servo-meccanismi che funzionano egregiamente. A noi sembrano crudeli, come se anche noi non mangiassimo polli, vitelli, agnelli, uccelli, pesci, ecc. come fanno gli altri animali.

1702. La gaiezza può ispirare una creatività semplice e spontanea.

1703. "Moderno" è solo quello che ci è contemporaneo. Non è chiaro perché il fatto di esserci contemporaneo lo debba fare anche eccellente, superiore o perfino desiderabile.

1704. Prima o poi, ci si ferma. Ma l'essere soddisfatti troppo facilmente di noi stessi ci fa fermare assai prima.

1705. La casuale mescolanza di quello che si applica a noi con quello che si applica ad altri li rende incerti circa i confini della nostra intimità.

1706. Come il vento, la mente non ha anatomia. La mente è un fermento di immagini, pensieri, desideri, gioie, sentimenti, sofferenze, contraddizioni e speranze.

1707. La varietà delle menti è dimostrata dal fatto che non c'è teoria, neanche la più strampalata, che non abbia dei seguaci devoti e convinti. Addirittura pronti a morire.

1696.   The aspirations of a mind have the dimension of that mind.

1697.   The long intimacy with oneself is at the basis of the Self. We live with our secrets and know their nuances.

1698.   Deep passions do not spare even superficial people, because passions have nothing to do with the intellect.

1699.   As in a circus only what occurs in the cone of light exists, similarly the most vivid human events slowly fade into the darkness of forgetfulness as the circle lighted by our memory moves forward under the whip of time.

1700.   We can afford to be completely sincere when we can afford to ignore the consequences thereof.

1701.   Nature maintains a balance among organisms through feed-back mechanisms that work very well. They seem cruel to us, as if we too did not eat chickens, calves, lambs, birds, fish, etc. as other animals do.

1702   Gaiety may inspire a simple and spontaneous creativity.

1703.   "Modern" is just what is contemporary to us. It is not clear why the fact of being contemporary to us should make it also excellent, superior or even desirable.

1704.   Sooner or later, we come to a stop. But to be too easily satisfied with ourselves leads to our coming to a standstill much sooner.

1705.   The casual mixture of what applies to us with that which applies to others renders them uncertain about the boundaries of our intimacy.

1706.   Like the wind, the mind has no anatomy. The mind is a ferment of images, thoughts, desires, joys, feelings, suffering, contradictions and hopes.

1707.   The variety of minds is demonstrated by the fact that there is no theory, not even the most queer, that does not have some devoted and convinced followers. Followers even ready to die.

1708. Le nostre azioni sono determinate più spesso dalle nostre irrequietezze che dalle nostre aspirazioni.

1709. Non si è ispirati dai pensieri, ma dalle convinzioni. I pensieri ci determinano nella misura in cui diventano convinzioni.

1710. Sembrerebbe logico accettare solo quello che la mente può dimostrare. Ma quello che esiste non cessa di essere solo perché la mente, per le sue limitazioni, non lo sa dimostrare.

1711. Per un bambino, il padre è importante, e la madre è essenziale.

1712. L'amore delude solo quando non ci appassiona più.

1713. La pomposità di certe cose ufficiali e formali teme le frecciate di una mordace ironia, perché scompigliano la dignità della necessaria commedia.

1714. Non sapremo mai se viviamo la vita nella maniera giusta. Se pure una maniera "giusta" esiste.

1715. Il coraggio più pericoloso è quello degli sciocchi.

1716. Il sonno è la quotidiana vacanza non tanto *della* mente, quanto *dalla* mente.

1717. Se non è illuminato, l'altruismo può solo essere un ingenuo preoccuparsi dell'altrui egoismo.

1718. Quanto più si ama meno si calcola. Anzi, si ama lo stesso anche se i conti non tornano.

1719. La transitorietà dei piaceri (per esempio, un buon pranzo) non li squalifica. Vi si oppone il ricordo piacevole e il ricorrente desiderio.

1720. La via dell'amore è pavimentata con le pietre dei desideri dei sensi.

1721. L'acqua è il veicolo universale dei processi vitali e il vino il veicolo occasionale per rallegrare la mente. Certo non si ride o si scherza allegramente solo per aver bevuto tre bicchieri d'acqua.

1708. Our actions are more often determined by our restlessness than by our aspirations.

1709. We are not inspired by thoughts, but by convictions. Our thoughts move us in the measure that they become convictions.

1710. It would seem logical to accept only what the mind can demonstrate. But what exists does not cease to be only because the mind, due to its limitations, is unable to demonstrate it.

1711. For a child, the father is important, and the mother is essential.

1712. Love disappoints only when we are no longer passionate.

1713. The pomposity of certain official and formal matters fears the taunts of a biting irony, because they upset the dignity of a necessary comedy.

1714. We will never know if we spend our life in the right way. Assuming that there is a "right" way.

1715. The most dangerous courage is that of the silly.

1716. Sleep is the daily rest not so much *of* the mind, as *from* the mind.

1717. If it is not enlightened, altruism may only be a naïve concern for the egoism of others.

1718. The more we love the less we reckon. More than that, we love all the same even if the numbers do not add up.

1719. The transitoriness of pleasures (for example, a good dinner) does not disqualify them. The pleasant remembrance and the recurrent desire oppose that.

1720. The road of love is paved with the stones of the desires of the senses.

1721. Water is the universal vehicle of vital processes and wine is the occasional vehicle to cheer up the mind. Certainly, one does not merrily laugh or joke only for having drunk three glasses of water.

1722. Il tatto consiste nel dire quello che altri vogliono sentire. Ed il garbo nel non farsene accorgere.

1723. Siamo disturbati dagli errori che abbiamo fatto e da quelli che stiamo facendo, ma per ragioni differenti. Nel primo caso ci dispiace di aver ceduto alla soluzione sbagliata, e nel secondo ci dispiace di cedere alla soluzione giusta.

1724. Si è seccati dalle attenzioni che non si vogliono e si rimane male se cessano.

1725. L'immortalità dell'anima è straordinaria dal momento che non richiede meriti speciali ed è concessa a tutti, anche a chi ha solo demeriti.

1726. Per chi non ha meriti particolari, il languore è più adatto dell'energia. Nel languore vi è per lo meno la pigra grazia dei gatti.

1727. Solo i vanitosi e quelli che hanno poco discernimento prendono se stessi sempre sul serio. Una maniera per essere seriamente ridicoli.

1728. Ci si difende più facilmente dall'odio che dall'amore.

1729. Perché si dovrebbe temere Dio piuttosto che amarlo: non è forse il nostro Creatore? A meno che non si voglia dire che la paura è più efficace dell'amore nel farci comportare bene.

1730. Non la verità, ma l'amore della verità ci impedisce di essere aridi. Si cerca appassionatamente la verità per trovare la sostanza (non l'apparenza) della nostra identità.

1731. Al contrario di tante cose, non è assurdo amare inutilmente.

1732. Solo negli affetti vi è una speranza di felicità.

1733. Se la virtù è acida, non è il risultato di una libera scelta.

1734. La vita si apprezza soprattutto al presente, anche se mediocre. Quello che di grande è stato fatto nel passato interessa solo la cultura di una minoranza selezionata. Ma la conoscenza del passato allarga gli orizzonti delle menti del presente.

1722. Tact consists in saying what listeners want to hear. And graciousness in not making them aware of it.

1723. We are disturbed by the errors that we have made as well as by those that we are making, but for different reasons. In the former case, we dislike having yielded to the wrong solution, and in the latter we dislike to yield to the right solution.

1724. We are annoyed by the attentions that we do not want and we are disappointed if they cease.

1725. The immortality of the soul is extraordinary since it does not require special merits and is given to everyone, even to those that have only demerits.

1726. For those who do not have special merits, languor is more suited than energy. At least, in languor there is the lazy grace of cats.

1727. Only the vain and the uncritical always take themselves seriously. A way of being seriously ridiculous.

1728. We defend ourselves more easily from hate than from love.

1729. Why should we fear God rather than love Him: is He not our Creator? Unless what is meant is that fear is more effective than love in making us behave well.

1730. Not truth, but the love of truth prevents us from becoming arid. We passionately pursue the truth to find the substance (not the appearance) of our identity

1731. In contrast to so many things, it is not absurd to love in vain.

1732. Only in affections can there be a hope of happiness.

1733. If virtue is acid, it is not the result of a free choice.

1734. Life is appreciated above all in the present tense, even if mediocre. Whatever greatness there has been in the past interests only the culture of a selected minority. But the knowledge of the past expands the horizons of the minds of the present.

1735. Di tanto in tanto, la mente ha bisogno di essere meravigliata. Lo richiede il suo bisogno del nuovo, del fantastico o del bello.

1736. Nella tentazione vi è spesso un insistente e persistente elemento di seduzione.

1737. Si tenta invano di rivivere le nostre emozioni ricordandole.

1738. La mancanza di comprensione reciproca rende estranei anche quelli che vivono insieme, perché non vi è sovrapposizione delle menti. Questo facilita l'antagonismo delle loro differenze.

1739. Ci si può risentire di essere l'oggetto della generosità altrui. Ce ne sentiamo diminuiti, perché né siamo altrettanto generosi né vogliamo esserlo.

1740. Se si comprendesse tutto, la gioia di vivere e la spontaneità del nostro abbandono ne sarebbero diminuite.

1741. La creatività non tollera di essere irreggimentata, e spesso prospera in epoche turbolente anche grazie ai più numerosi stimoli.

1742. Come per i giunchi, la flessibilità può essere una forma di forza.

1743. I maleducati e i grandi ricchi non si disturbano a ringraziare.

1744. Quando non si approvano i nostri desideri, quasi si crede di aver successo quando si fallisce nel realizzarli: non si è contenti, ma si può essere sollevati.

1745. Chissà perché alle sfilate di moda le modelle hanno l'espressione del viso di chi non ha digerito bene.

1746. La storia è la cronaca delle lotte dei popoli per mantenere la propria identità, cioè per sopravvivere come popoli con la propria lingua, tradizioni, religione, credenze, leggende, ecc. Ma alcuni popoli vogliono mantenere la propria identità dentro i loro confini; ed altri vogliono accrescere la propria identità aggredendoli.

1747. In tanti dei nostri sentimenti più sinceri c'è un'intima gentilezza che è difficile condividere.

1735. Once in a while, the mind needs to be marveled. This is demanded by its need for the new, the fantastic or the beautiful.

1736. In temptation there is often an insistent and persistent element of seduction.

1737. We vainly try to live again our emotions by remembering them.

1738. The lack of mutual understanding makes strangers also of those who live together, because there is no overlap of the minds. This facilitates the antagonism of their differences.

1739. We may resent being the object of the generosity of others. We feel diminished by it, because neither are we equally generous nor do we want to be.

1740. If we understood everything, the joy of living and the spontaneity of our abandon would be diminished.

1741. Creativity does not suffer to be regimented, and often prospers in eras of strife also thanks to the more numerous stimuli.

1742. As for reeds, flexibility may be a form of strength.

1743. The ill-mannered and the very rich do not bother to thank.

1744. When we do not approve of our desires, we almost feel successful when we fail to carry them through: we are not happy, but we may be relieved.

1745. God knows why at fashion shows models have the expression of the face of someone who is experiencing indigestion.

1746. History is the chronicle of the struggle of nations to maintain their identity, that is to say to survive as nations with their tongue, traditions, religion, beliefs, legends, etc. However, some nations want to maintain their identity within their borders; and others want to increase their identity by assaulting them.

1747. In many of our most sincere feelings there is an intimate gentleness which is difficult to share.

1748. E se l'infinito fosse solo un'astrazione? Solo una parola per esprimere quantità di dimensioni estremamente grandi rispetto all'uomo? Anche così, la nostra piccolezza non ne sarebbe diminuita. Inoltre, cosa vi sarebbe oltre i limiti del finito? Dopo tutto, anche il vuoto ha delle dimensioni. Come le ha il nulla.

1749. È più facile che ci perdonino di essere *talvolta* non coerenti che di essere *sempre* coerenti.

1750. L'espressione del viso riflette gli sbandamenti emotivi dell'anima. E negli attori li sostituisce. Ma gli attori più bravi possono identificarsi a tal punto con il loro personaggio da provarne le emozioni (sempre col dovuto controllo).

1751. In situazioni speciali, l'abilità può consistere nel sembrare di non averne.

1752. Un aforisma dovrebbe essere riconosciuto immediatamente come vero o falso. Se non è chiaro se sia vero o falso, non è un aforisma, ma un'affermazione da dimostrare. Se lo riconosciamo come vero, quella verità comincia ad esistere perché ne diveniamo coscienti. Per questo, è assai più facile riconoscere come vero un aforisma dopo averlo letto di quanto sia il formularlo prima di leggerlo.

1753. Si elogiano senza riserve solo i morti, anche quando non se lo meritano. Lo facciamo sinceramente per umana compassione e per rispetto a quella morte che si teme. Nell'elogio, cerchiamo l'eleganza della dizione e una magnanimità che non teme danno.

1754. La maniera più "economica" per disobbligarsi è l'ingratitudine. Per lo meno a breve scadenza.

1755. Una componente della forza è una scarsa sensibilità al proprio dolore, fisico e mentale.

1756. Essendo la realtà mentale, tutti cercano di influenzarla con mezzi diversi. Noi lo facciamo col selezionare quello con cui vogliamo intrattenere la nostra mente (romanzi, musica, quadri, poesie, ecc.). E gli altri con parole, reclami e propaganda.

1757. La nostra vanità mal sopporta l'altrui vanità.

1748. And if infinite were only an abstraction? Only a word expressing quantities of extremely large dimensions compared to man? But, even so, our smallness would not be decreased. Furthermore, what there would be beyond the limits of the finite? After all, even vacuum has dimensions. As nothingness does.

1749. It is more likely that they pardon us our being *sometimes* inconsistent than our being *always* consistent.

1750. The expression of the visage reflects the emotional vagaries of the soul. And in the actors it substitutes them. But the best actors identify themselves to such an extent with the character they play that they feel its emotions (always under due control).

1751. In special situations, ability may consist in seeming not to have any.

1752. An aphorism should be immediately recognized as true or false. If it is not clear whether it is true or false, it is not an aphorism, but a statement that needs to be proven. If we recognize it as true, that truth then begins to exist because we become conscious of it. For this reason, it is much easier to recognize as true an aphorism after having read it than to formulate it before reading it.

1753. We praise without reserve only the dead, even when they do not deserve it. We sincerely do it out of human compassion and of respect for that death which we fear. In the praise, we seek the elegance of diction and a magnanimity that does not fear damage.

1754. The "cheapest" way to get rid of one's obligations is ingratitude. At least in the short run.

1755. A component of strength is a scarce sensitiveness for our own pain, physical and mental.

1756. Reality being mental, everyone seeks to influence it with various means. We do it by selecting what we want to entertain the mind with (novels, music, paintings, poems, etc.). And others with words, advertising and propaganda.

1757. Our vanity finds it difficult to stand the vanity of others.

1758. L'ironia ci fa divertire di quello che altrimenti ci farebbe arrabbiare o infastidire.

1759. I nostri difetti aumentano la nostra capacità di comprendere, se non altro i difetti altrui.

1760. È penosamente inutile essere spiritosi se chi ascolta non ha il senso dell'umorismo. Ed è inutilmente penoso aver del senso dell'umorismo se chi parla non è spiritoso.

1761. La rassegnazione è figlia di una protratta stanchezza.

1762. Alcuni cercano di attirare l'attenzione con la stranezza, non potendolo fare con la bellezza.

1763. Sembrerebbe improbabile, ma succede anche di rimpiangere di essere stati abbastanza forti da non aver commesso un errore (che si desiderava commettere).

1764. Qualcuno si crede di essere brillante e anticonformista solo perché è confusionario e indisciplinato.

1765. Uno stimolo senza un recettore non è nulla. Certamente, non è uno stimolo.

1766. Come la maggior parte dei pesci nuota nelle trasparenze liquide del mare e non vede mai la sua superficie che riflette la luminosità dei raggi del sole, così talvolta viviamo a nostro agio nel mondo delle percezioni e dei riflessi, ignorando le sovrastanti generalizzazioni della mente e la sua ansia di chiarezza.

1767. Quanto si presuma circa se stessi lo rivela la discrepanza fra aspirazioni e realizzazioni.

1768. L'evoluzione continuerà a modificare l'uomo fisicamente e intellettualmente nelle migliaia di secoli a venire. A meno che non subentri l'involuzione.

1769. Nella solitudine, si è liberi dalle altrui preferenze e interferenze.

1770. In un sorriso affettuoso vi è un raggio di sole.

1758. Irony amuses us with that which otherwise would upset us or make us weary.

1759. Our faults enlarge our capability of understanding, if nothing else the faults of others.

1760. It is sadly useless to be witty if the listener does not have a sense of humor. And it is uselessly sad to have a sense of humor if the speaker is not witty.

1761. Resignation is the daughter of a long weariness.

1762. Some try to attract attention with strangeness, being unable to do it with beauty.

1763. It would seem improbable, but it also happens that we regret to have been strong enough not to have made a mistake (that we wished to make).

1764. Some consider themselves brilliant and unconventional only because they are muddling and undisciplined.

1765. A stimulus without a receptor is nothing. Certainly, it is not a stimulus.

1766. As most fish swim in the liquid transparence of the sea and never see its lucid surface reflecting the luminosity of the rays of the sun, similarly sometimes we comfortably dwell in the world of perceptions and reflexes, ignoring the overlying generalizations of the mind and its yearning for clarity.

1767. How much we presume about ourselves is revealed by the discrepancy between aspirations and realizations.

1768. Evolution presumably will continue to physically and mentally modify man in the thousands of centuries to come. Unless involution takes over.

1769. In solitude, one is free from others' preferences and interference.

1770. In an affectionate smile there is a ray of sun.

1771. Le diverse religioni sono tutte l'espressione di un generale istinto religioso: in tutte le religioni si onora Dio, anche se usando forme diverse di devozione. L'appartenenza ad una data religione generalmente risulta non da una scelta cosciente, ma dall'educazione ricevuta nel rispetto delle lunghe tradizioni di una stirpe. Ma non ci sono stati popoli, primitivi o civilizzati, senza dèi. Al contrario, spesso ne hanno avuti troppi.

1772. Con l'età, la mente di alcuni matura e quella di altri solo invecchia.

1773. Nella decadenza, la raffinatezza diventa una virtù, perché la fatuità diventa la regola.

1774. Nel provare un disprezzo sincero, allo stesso tempo ci si compiace della nostra superiorità (reale o immaginaria).

1775. La malinconica grazia dell'autunno non è meno attraente degli estremi rigori dell'inverno, della lieta gentilezza della primavera, o dell'ardente rigoglio dell'estate.

1776. Il fiume degli stimoli quotidiani viene filtrato dalla personalità di ciascuno: solo quello che individualmente interessa è trattenuto. Ma solo i filtri più fini trattengono le finezze.

1777. L'unica uguaglianza concessa a tutti e che nessuno vuole è quella della morte.

1778. La finezza varia in culture differenti. Va da un'ipocrita sottigliezza ad uno strano senso dell'umorismo.

1779. L'equità dovrebbe essere il confine ideale dove i differenti interessi s'incontrano. E invece spesso è il confine dove i diversi interessi si scontrano.

1780. Per farci cambiare opinione su qualcuno, basta che quello ci tratti male.

1781. La politica è una lotta di interessi: la verità vi è incidentale o accidentale.

1782. Sulla base di quello che si definisce, si viene poi definiti.

1771. Different religions are all the expression of a general religious instinct: in all religions people honor God, even though using different forms of worship. Belonging to a given religion generally results not from a conscious choice, but from the education received in the respect of the long traditions of a race. But there have been no peoples, primitive or civilized, without gods. On the contrary, they often have had too many.

1772. With aging, the mind of some matures and that of others just becomes old.

1773. In decadence, refinement becomes a virtue, because fatuity becomes the rule.

1774. In feeling a sincere contempt, at the same time we are pleased with our superiority (real or imaginary).

1775. The melancholy grace of autumn is not less attractive than the extreme rigors of winter, the joyous gentleness of spring, or the ardent luxuriance of summer.

1776. The stream of daily stimuli is filtered by the personality of each one of us: only what individually is interesting is retained. But only the finer filters retain the finesses.

1777. The only equality granted to everyone, and that nobody wants, is that of death.

1778. Cleverness varies in different cultures. It goes from a hypocritical subtlety to a strange sense of humor.

1779. Equity should be the ideal boundary where different interests meet. Instead, often it is the boundary where the different interests clash.

1780. To make us change opinion about someone, it suffices that he mistreats us.

1781. Politics is a struggle of interests: there, truth is incidental or accidental.

1782. On the basis of what we define, we are then defined.

1783. Gli interessi riconoscono solo le loro verità; e gli altrui torti. O i propri diritti e gli altrui doveri. Dopo tutto, difendiamo i nostri interessi perché i nostri interessi fedelmente difendono noi.

1784. L'amore si nutre soprattutto di se stesso. Se la persona amata sia meritevole o ricambi i sentimenti, per questa passione fa poca differenza (anche se lo fa per la propria felicità).

1785. Una notevole abilità dialettica o letteraria fa gli sbagli di una parziale comprensione più cospicui, perché li espone con più efficacia.

1786. I numeri non hanno emozioni e non ne danno (eccetto ai matematici).

1787. Non interessano le risposte alle domande a cui non siamo interessati.

1788. L'universo parla un linguaggio divino che anche noi possiamo intendere. Ci parlano il crescente splendore del sole che sorge, la sottile malinconia del crepuscolo, la silenziosa bellezza di una notte stellata, la grazia delicata della luna piena, i variabili umori del cielo, le distanze inconcepibili, la varietà infinita di corpi celesti, le loro incredibili velocità, gli esplosivi drammi delle galassie, i miracoli di grandi equilibri esatti, gli inesplicabili collassi di masse enormi, i vuoti improbabili, i silenzi eterni, gli echi di tempi da tanto perduti... La nostra piccolezza ne è così meravigliata che persino la scienza ne trae delle favole e la fisica è tormentata da dubbi.

1789. Una situazione è complessa quando è determinata da molti fattori e diventa complicata quando non li si capiscono tutti.

1790. Si fa il bene comune quando si fa bene quello che si deve fare individualmente.

1791. In biologia, la genetica è un codice delle leggi di Dio. Come in altri campi lo sono la fisica, matematica, chimica, astronomia, ecc.

1792. Per essere idealisti, bisogna essere forti e persino duri. Altrimenti si diventa ben presto disillusi.

1783. Interests recognize only their truths; and the wrongs of others. Or their rights and others' duties. After all, we defend our interests because our interests faithfully defend us.

1784. Love is based above all on itself. Whether or not the beloved is deserving or reciprocates the feeling, for this passion makes little difference (although it does for one's happiness).

1785. A remarkable dialectical or literary skill makes the mistakes of a partial comprehension more conspicuous, since it expounds them more effectively.

1786. Numbers have no emotions and do not give them (except to the mathematicians).

1787. The answers to the questions in which we are not interested do not interest us.

1788. The universe speaks a divine language that we too can understand. Speak to us the growing splendor of the rising sun, the subtle melancholy of dusk, the silent beauty of a starred night, the delicate grace of a full moon, the variable moods of the sky, the inconceivable distances, the infinite variety of celestial bodies, their staggering velocities, the explosive dramas of galaxies, the miracles of vast exact equilibria, the unaccountable collapses of enormous masses, the improbable vacuums, the eternal silences, the echoes of times long lost... Our smallness is so stunned that even science resorts to fables and physics is tormented by doubts.

1789. A situation is complex when it is determined by numerous factors, and it becomes complicated when we do not understand all of them.

1790. We do the common good when we do well that which we have to do individually.

1791. In biology, genetics is a code of the laws of God. As in other fields are physics, mathematics, chemistry, astronomy, etc.

1792. To be an idealist, one has to be strong or even tough. Otherwise very soon one becomes disillusioned.

1793. Si fa ridere quando siamo spiritosi e quando siamo seri in manicra maldestra.

1794. Le parole toccanti di certi predicatori rimuovono il velo di vapore con cui l'indifferenza e convenienza quotidiane appannano lo specchio dell'anima e ci impediscono di vedere troppo chiaramente gli egoismi del nostro Io intimo.

1795. La saggezza spicciola consiste non in una maggiore comprensione, ma nell'evitare le irritazioni della vita quotidiana.

1796. Nell'affermare che "Esse est percipi", si afferma allo stesso tempo la necessità che vi sia qualcosa da percepire al di fuori dell'essere.

1797. Tra le ferree leggi della storia vi è poco posto per quelle del cuore umano.

1798. I dubbi sono utili solo se diventano domande a cui vogliamo dare una risposta.

1799. Quando vogliamo ignorare un'emozione, per lo più lo facciamo emotivamente.

1800. La realtà di un libro, un film o un dramma risiede nelle immagini, vicende ed emozioni suscitate nella mente di chi vi è esposto. Una realtà diversa per ciascuno.

1801. L'amore è quel filtro che crea l'intimità fra due estranei.

1802. Le offese che abbiamo perdonato e dimenticato quando si amava riemergono inaspettatamente dalla memoria quando non si ama più.

1803. Le leggi divine sono ineluttabili, perché i fenomeni che regolano devono funzionare immancabilmente.

1804. La bellezza della natura non stanca perché è varia. Così, bellissime giornate di sole si alternano con la violenza paurosa di un uragano, col ritmo musicale della pioggia o con la sottile malinconia della nebbia. Per non parlare della seduzione delle stagioni.

1805. Non sempre ci si rende conto che negare una verità è già un errore.

1793. We make people laugh when we are witty or when we are serious in a maladroit manner.

1794. The touching words of certain preachers wipe out the veil of mist with which the daily indifference and convenience blur the mirror of the soul and prevent us from seeing too clearly the egoism of our inner Self.

1795. Petty wisdom consists not in a better comprehension, but in avoiding the irritations of daily life.

1796. In affirming that "Esse cst percipi", one asserts at the same time the necessity that there is something to be perceived outside the "Esse".

1797. Among the iron laws of history there is little room for those of the human heart.

1798. Doubts are useful only if they become questions to which we want to give an answer.

1799. When we want to ignore an emotion, usually we do it emotionally.

1800. The reality of a book, a film or a drama resides in the images, events and emotions elicited in the mind of those who are exposed to them. A reality different for each one.

1801. Love is a philtre that creates intimacy between two strangers.

1802. The offenses that we pardoned and forgot when we were in love unexpectedly resurrect from memory when we are no longer in love.

1803. The divine laws are ineluctable, because the phenomena that they regulate must unfailingly work.

1804. The beauty of nature does not tire us because it is varied. Thus, beautiful sunny days alternate with the frightful violence of a hurricane, with the musical rhythm of the rain or with the subtle melancholy of fog. Not to speak of the seduction of the seasons.

1805. We do not always realize that denying a truth is already an error.

1806. È molto difficile evitare di innamorarsi, ma è impossibile evitare di non esser più innamorati.

1807. Se si abolissero le contraddizioni, si rimprovererebbe alla coerenza l'insipidezza di non averne.

1808. Lo stile aggiunge un tocco di amabilità e di piacevole eleganza a quello che si fa o si dice.

1809. Il progredire dell'età ci umilia con i frequenti errori associati col lento decadere della mente. Si diviene allora penosamente coscienti che la strada è solo in discesa; e che è una strada chiusa.

1810. La libertà cessa con la schiavitù, ma anche con l'arbitrarietà, l'indisciplina, il disordine, la licenza o l'anarchia. La libertà è un diritto, ma un diritto che bisogna meritare, non abusare.

1811. La comune malinconia è come il soffuso grigiore della nebbia, mentre la depressione mentale è come l'oscurità opprimente di una notte senza luna e senza stelle. Nella prima vi è un elemento di seduzione, nella seconda solo uno di solitudine, tristezza e ansia.

1812. Attraverso modificazioni interne e riflessi, la genetica determina la condotta degli animali e dell'uomo, per quanto in quest'ultimo lo faccia anche attraverso la mente. E l'influenza della mente può talvolta prevalere sulle modificazioni interne e i riflessi.

1813. Solo la mente umana è cosciente del creato e delle sue leggi. E pertanto del suo Creatore.

1814. La professione dei vari individui non è scelta *da* loro, ma *per* loro dalle inclinazioni e doti personali. E talvolta dal caso.

1815. La bontà fa del bene soprattutto a chi ce l'ha.

1816. Naturalmente si evita la sofferenza, ma sarebbe ben triste non soffrire mai. La piattezza di una vita "tranquilla" ci priverebbe del dramma di tante indispensabili emozioni.

1817. La vita è una lotta per realizzare quanto si vale. Si può anche non lottare, ma allora si dimostra quanto non si vale.

1806. It is very difficult to avoid falling in love, but it is impossible to avoid not being in love any longer.

1807. If contradictions were to be abolished, we would reproach coherence for the insipidity of having none.

1808. Style adds a touch of lovableness and pleasing elegance to what we do or we say.

1809. The advancing age humiliates us with the frequent errors associated with the slow decay of the mind. We then become painfully aware that the road is downhill; and that it is a dead-end street.

1810. Freedom ceases with slavery, but also with arbitrariness, lack of discipline, disorder, license or anarchy. Freedom is a right, but a right that we must deserve, not abuse.

1811. Common melancholy is like the suffuse greyness of the fog, while mental depression is like the oppressing darkness of a night without moon and stars. In the former, there is an element of seduction, in the latter only one of loneliness, sadness and anxiety.

1812. By means of internal modifications and reflexes, genetics determines the behavior of animals and man, although in the latter it does so also through the mind. And the influence of the mind can sometimes overrule the internal modifications and reflexes.

1813. Only the human mind is conscious of creation and its laws. And therefore of its Creator.

1814. The profession of people is not chosen *by* them, but *for* them by their personal inclinations and gifts. And sometimes by chance.

1815. Goodness does good mostly to those who have it.

1816. Naturally we avoid suffering, but it would be rather sad never to suffer. The flatness of a "tranquil" life would deprive us of the drama of many indispensable emotions.

1817. Life is a struggle to realize our worth. We may also not struggle, but then we show how little our worth is.

1818. Il fatto che, quando piove, l'acqua delle nuvole non cada tutta insieme ma in singole gocce è un esempio della finezza e ingegnosità della leggi di natura.

1819. Se non ci fosse permesso di peccare, perderemmo non solo la virtù, ma anche la libertà: se si pecca o no deve dipendere non solo dalla nostra percezione della moralità, ma anche dalla nostra volontà.

1820. Ciascuno noi comprende qualcosa e nessuno di noi abbastanza. Per esempio, tante volte non si capisce che certe cose non hanno bisogno di essere capite, ma invece vanno sentite.

1821. Non solo non è necessario rendersi conto di quanto siamo determinati da fattori di cui non abbiamo controllo, ma, nel nostro interesse e per la nostra felicità, è assai meglio non rendersene conto.

1822. Gli oggetti esistono solo nella mente e per la mente: di fuori, ci sono non oggetti, solo molecole. Un fatto anche questo stabilito dalla mente. Gli oggetti (come tali) esistono in quanto pensati e noi si esiste finché si pensa.

1823. Senza gratitudine, si offende la nostra vanità e quella degli altri senza il minimo riserbo, come se la vanità non desse a ciascuno di noi più soddisfazioni delle nostre realizzazioni.

1824. La genetica è fissa: la varietà dei suoi prodotti è resa possibile solo dal mescolarsi dei differenti patrimoni genetici dei due genitori. È questo uno degli strumenti che conciliano la necessità dell'ordine con quella della varietà.

1825. Nella prima infanzia, le successive generazioni sono uguali nelle loro caratteristiche biologiche. Ma ben presto, i bambini di ogni nuova generazione trovano un ambiente che è differente dal punto di vista mentale e fisico da quello dei bambini della precedente generazione. A sua volta, la loro generazione modifica l'ambiente, creando le sue differenze. Non la fisiologia, ma le sue manifestazioni cambiano a contatto con un ambiente diverso. Solo quando una società primitiva non si sviluppa, le successive generazioni rimangono simili nelle loro espressioni: le modificazioni sono impedite dal rigido rispetto delle tradizioni.

1818.   The fact that, when it rains, the water of the clouds does not fall all together but in separate drops is an example of the finesse and ingenuity of the laws of nature.

1819.   If we were not allowed to sin, we would lose not only our virtue, but also our freedom: whether we sin or not must depend not only on our perception of morality, but also on our will.

1820.   Each of us understands something and none of us enough. For example, often we do not understand that some things need not to be understood, but instead need to be felt.

1821.   Not only is it not necessary to be aware of how much we are determined by factors of which we have no control, but, in our interest and for our happiness, it is much better not to be aware of them.

1822.   Objects exist only in the mind and for the mind: outside there are no objects, only molecules. Even this fact is established by the mind. Objects (as such) exist insofar as they are thought and we exist as long as we think.

1823.   Ungratefully, we offend our vanity and that of others without the slightest restraint, as if vanity did not give to all of us more satisfactions than our accomplishments.

1824.   Genetics is fixed: the variety of its products is made possible only by the mixing of the different genetic patrimonies of the two parents. This is one of the instruments that reconcile the necessity of order with that of variety.

1825.   In early infancy, all successive generations are equal in their biological characteristics. But, pretty soon, the children of each new generation find an environment that is different from a mental and physical point of view from that of the children of the preceding generation. In turn, their generation modifies the environment, creating its own differences. Not physiology, but its manifestations change in the contact with a different environment. Only when a primitive society does not undergo development, successive generations remain similar in their expressions: the modifications are prevented by the rigid respect of traditions.

1826.   È considerato bello quello che si conforma al nostro senso estetico, che è una caratteristica in gran parte genetica. Se qualcuno trova bello quello che è brutto, semplicemente non ha gusto (un errore genetico come tanti altri).

1827.   Il nostro modo di vedere cambia lentamente sotto l'influenza delle cose vedute.

1828.   Anche se si dimenticano molti dei nostri pensieri, il nostro modo di pensare cambia molto lentamente, assicurando così la continuità della nostra identità col passare del tempo.

1829.   La gente segue il suo gusto: se sia buono o cattivo se lo domandano solo pochi.

1830.   Le nostre convinzioni sono atti di fede generalmente inculcati dall'educazione, selezionati dalla nostra personalità e condizionati dalla struttura genetica del nostro cervello e del nostro corpo.

1831   Si vive sempre e solo nel presente, ma non è mai lo stesso: come l'acqua di un fiume che alla fine si perde nel mare.

1832.   Ci si sbaglia così spesso credendo di amare ancora come credendo di non amare più.

1833.   Spesso ci sentiamo schiavi dei nostri impulsi, ma bisogna rendersi conto che senza impulsi saremmo non liberi, ma svuotati.

1834.   Il futuro di ogni moda è di passare di moda.

1835.   Tutti ci riteniamo perfettamente normali, quando invece ciascuno è peculiare alla sua maniera.

1836.   La nostra memoria ha il suo epicentro nel presente e un raggio limitato. Come ogni giorno il presente si sposta in avanti, necessariamente i ricordi più periferici rimangono oltre il raggio della memoria negli oscuri territori dove vaga immemore l'Io che fu.

1837.   Affermazioni e negazioni arbitrarie si possono fare solo su cose che nessuno sa o capisce. Di qui, tante dispute filosofiche, ciascuno affermando solo la propria opinione.

1826. We consider beautiful what conforms to our aesthetic sense, which is largely a genetic characteristic. If someone finds beautiful that which is ugly, quite simply he does not have good taste (a genetic error like many others).

1827. Our way of seeing things slowly changes under the influence of the things seen.

1828. Even if we forget many of our thoughts, our way of thinking changes very slowly thus insuring the continuity of our identity with the passing of time.

1829. People follow their taste: only a few ask themselves whether it is good or bad.

1830. Our convictions are acts of faith generally inculcated by education, selected by our personality and conditioned by the genetic set-up of our brain and our body.

1831. We only and always live in the present, but it is never the same: as the water of a river that in the end vanishes in the sea.

1832. We are mistaken as often in believing to be still in love as in believing not to be in love any more.

1833. Often, we feel slaves of our drives, but we have to realize that without drives we would be not free, but emptied.

1834. The future of every fashion is to become out of fashion.

1835. All of us believe to be perfectly normal, whereas each of us is peculiar in our own way.

1836. Our memory has its epicenter in the present and a limited radius. As every day the present moves forward, necessarily the more peripheral remembrances remain beyond the radius of memory in the dark lands where forgetful wanders the Self that has been.

1837. Arbitrary assertions and denials can be made only about matters that nobody knows or understands. Hence, many philosophical disputes, everyone affirming only his opinion.

1838. Desideri d'amore: si ama teneramente quello che si desidera e si desidera ardentemente quello che si ama.

1839. Non si è grati per i pensieri che si ereditano, perché ce li lascerebbero anche se non li volessimo.

1840. La solitudine più pesante è quella creata dalla mancanza di profondi affetti.

1841. Una mente scettica presume di sé: si crede di sapere la verità nascosta in fondo alle cose. E invece ignora la verità che è presente nella sostanza delle cose.

1842. In certa musica classica, la gioia fluisce con lo stesso leggero abbandono con cui l'acqua limpida come il cristallo scorre mormorando tra i sassi levigati dei rivoli.

1843. Non si è liberi di non amare.

1844. Si prova un piacere intenso quando si è mossi fino alle lacrime da un emozione profonda e gentile, come nelle opere tragiche.

1845. La bellezza fisica dà piacere a tutti, ma non è né necessaria né sufficiente per suscitare l'amore.

1846. La sensibilità abbassa la soglia per la percezione degli stimoli. Per questo, la sensibilità rende la comprensione più duttile, sottile, penetrante, esatta ed estesa.

1847. Una delle occupazioni più impegnative della vita è l'intrattenersi. Abbiamo bisogno di fare qualcosa che ci distenda mettendoci in un modo di sentire piacevole. Il semplice non far nulla è noioso, perché non impegna né intrattiene la mente.

1848. Si investiga il mistero del sorriso di Monna Lisa sulle sue labbra, mentre lei sorride impercettibilmente con gli occhi.

1849 Nel mentire frequentemente si getta via la propria credibilità. Siccome *sanno* per esperienza che siamo bugiardi, non credono più a nulla di quello che si dice. Pertanto, non siamo creduti quando si dice la verità o (forse peggio) le necessarie plausibili bugie.

1838.   Love desires: we tenderly love what we desire and ardently desire what we love.

1839.   We are not grateful for the thoughts that we inherit, because they would leave them to us even if we did not want them.

1840.   The solitude most heavy to bear is that created by the lack of deep affections.

1841.   A skeptical mind presumes of itself: it believes to know the truth hidden at the bottom of things. And instead ignores the truth that is present in the substance of things.

1842.   In some classical music, joy flows with the same lighthearted abandon with which crystal clear water runs murmuring among the smooth stones of the streams.

1843.   We are not free not to love.

1844.   We feel an intense pleasure when we are moved to tears by a deep and gentle emotion, such as in the tragic operas.

1845.   Physical beauty gives pleasure to all, but it is neither necessary nor sufficient to elicit love.

1846.   Sensibility lowers the threshold for the perception of stimuli. For this reason, sensitivity makes comprehension more ductile, subtle, penetrating, exact and extensive.

1847.   One of the most demanding occupations of life is to entertain oneself. We need to do something that relaxes us by putting us in a pleasant mood. Simply doing nothing is boring, since it neither engages nor entertains the mind.

1848.   They investigate the mystery of the smile of Mona Lisa on her lips, while she imperceptibly smiles with her eyes.

1849.   In lying frequently, we throw our credibility away. Since they *know* from experience that we are liars, they do not believe any longer anything that we say. Therefore, we are not believed when we say the truth or (perhaps worse) the necessary plausible lies.

1850. Quando si analizza, si riconosce la necessità del bene e del male nell'economia generale; e quando si vive, naturalmente ciascuno cerca di perseguire il bene ed evitare il male. Questa due necessità (teoretica e pratica) generano la confusione di alcuni che generalizzano le proprie esperienze individuali e credono che solo il bene dovrebbe o potrebbe esistere. E la confusione di altri che credono che quello che è valido in teoria debba essere applicato in pratica e chiamano saggezza l'indifferenza sia al bene che al male.

1851. Possiamo anche predicare, ma riservandoci convenientemente il diritto di peccare. In tempi differenti, non possiamo resistere né al richiamo della virtù né alla seduzione del peccato.

1852. Si considera garbo l'uso scelto di parole delicate per coprire di un velo di grazia tante miserie umane. Purtroppo, il velo è spesso penosamente trasparente.

1853. Durante le vacanze estive, si cerca soprattutto il sole e le sue ombre.

1854. La pornografia scandalizza perché dà un volto alla nostra volgarità.

1855. L'utopia è un posto che non esiste, adatto per chi non sa quello che vuole.

1856. Gli adulti hanno bisogno di giocattoli come i bambini, ma non ne sono altrettanto facilmente divertiti.

1857. Alcuni sarebbero solo semplicemente sciocchi, se non fossero così abili nell'essere sottilmente assurdi.

1858. L'indole forgia il modo di esprimersi. In bocca ad uno scrittore, l'amore diventa letterario e gli amanti diventano poeti. Se c'è passione, è per le belle frasi.

1859. La natura della realtà (e pertanto la realtà della natura) è da trovarsi nella mente.

1860. In ogni società, le pressioni sono così intense, varie, numerose e contrastanti che il governare consiste spesso nell'affrontare crisi successive.

1850.   When we analyze, we recognize the necessity of good and evil in the general economy; and when we live, naturally we seek to obtain good and avoid evil. These two necessities (theoretical and practical) cause the confusion of some who generalize their own individual experiences and believe that only the good should or could exist. And the confusion of others who believe that what is valid in theory should be applied in practice and call wisdom the indifference both to good and evil.

1851.   We may even preach, but conveniently reserving ourselves the right to sin. At different times, we can not resist either the call of virtue or the seduction of sin.

1852.   We consider gracefulness the selective use of delicate words to cover with a veil of grace many human weaknesses. Unfortunately, the veil is often painfully transparent.

1853.   During our summer vacation, we seek mostly the sun and its shadows.

1854.   Pornography scandalizes because it gives a face to our vulgarity.

1855.   Utopia is a place that does not exist, suited for those who do not know what they want.

1856.   Adults need toys like children do, but they are not as easily entertained by them.

1857.   Some would just be plain silly, if they were not very skilled at being subtly absurd.

1858.   Our nature shapes the way we express ourselves. In the hands of a writer, love becomes literary and lovers become poets. If there is passion, it is for beautiful phrases.

1859.   The nature of reality (and therefore the reality of nature) is to be found in the mind.

1860.   In each society, pressures are so intense, varied, numerous and contrasting that governing often involves dealing with successive crises.

1861. Si può anche essere così ingenerosi da essere generosi solo per dimostrare la nostra superiorità.

1862. Essere innamorati e non volerlo essere è sempre meglio di non essere innamorati e volerlo essere.

1863. Le verità troveranno sempre sia chi le nega sia chi le accetta solo per denaturarle esagerandole.

1864. La gente si adatta alle condizioni prevalenti anche perché dopo un po' non conosce che quelle.

1865. La ragione per cui la verità è soggetta a diverse opinioni è che tutto dipende da ciascuna struttura mentale e dall'angolo con cui le singole menti vedono la verità. Per quanto riguarda la struttura, ogni mente è il risultato di numerosi fattori congeniti ed acquisiti ed è pertanto differente da tutte le altre. Ma, in generale, *ogni mente si considera normale e considera differente dalla normalità quello che è differente dalla sua normalità*. Per esempio, consideriamo spilorcio chi spende meno di noi e spendaccione che spende più di noi. Similmente, usiamo la nostra "normalità" nel considerare un individuo ambizioso o ignavo, buono o cattivo, energico o infingardo, giovane o vecchio, morale o immorale, ecc. Pertanto, la stessa persona è considerata differentemente da ogni altra persona. Per quanto riguarda l'angolo con cui si vede la verità, uno che è basso di statura considera un'altro alto (più che se stesso basso); e l'altro considera il primo basso (più che se stesso alto).

1866. Per valutare oggettivamente le verità soggettive e diminuirne la loro soggettività e arbitrarietà, si ricorre ad una valutazione statistica dei fenomeni che è valida per tutti. Per es., (in una certa popolazione) la statura più frequente è considerata normale e gli estremi definiscono chi è alto o basso. Si usano i centimetri invece delle opinioni personali. E allora si dice parlando di una persona di statura media: "È alto (o basso) *per te*". Da come una mente giudica una verità, se ne deduce quale sia la sua "normalità", cioè il suo modo di pensare: è questo che cambia nei differenti individui, non il fenomeno osservato. Naturalmente, fluttuazioni statistiche rendono la verità mobile per tutti (per es., statura media o idee morali prevalenti possono variare con successive generazioni).Una mente anormale poi non può ritenere vere che opinioni anormali.

1861.   We can also be so ungenerous to be generous only to show off our superiority.

1862.   To be in love against our will is still better than not to be in love and wanting to be so.

1863.   Truths will always find both those who deny them and those who accept them only to denature them through exaggeration.

1964.   People adapt to the prevailing conditions also because after a while they are the only ones they know.

1865.   The reason why the truth is subject to different opinions is that everything depends on each mental structure and on the angle with which each mind sees the truth. As for the structure, every mind is the result of numerous congenital and acquired factors and it is therefore different from all other minds. But, in general, *every mind considers itself normal and considers different from normality what is different from its normality*. For example, we consider stingy those who spend less than us and spendthrift those who spend more than us. Similarly, we use our "normality" in considering another person ambitious or indolent, good or bad, energetic or lazy, young or old, moral or immoral, etc. Therefore, the same person is considered differently by every other person. As for the angle with which we see the truth, one who is short considers somebody else tall (rather than himself short); and the latter considers the former short (rather than himself tall).

1866.   To objectively evaluate the subjective truths and to decrease their subjectivity and arbitrariness, we resort to a statistical evaluation of the phenomena that is valid for all minds. For example, (in a given population) the most frequent height is considered normal and the extremes define who is tall or short. We use centimeters instead of our personal opinions. We then say speaking of a person of average height: "He is tall (or short) *for you*". From the way a mind judges a truth, we deduct what is its "normality", that is to say its way of thinking: this is what changes in different persons, not the observed phenomenon. Of course, statistical fluctuations make truth mobile for all (e.g., average height or prevailing moral ideas can vary with successive generations). And an abnormal mind can not but hold true abnormal beliefs.

1867. Alcune cose (e persino alcune verità) possono non appartenere al nostro tempo, perché appartengono a tutti i tempi. Molte altre cose appartengono al nostro tempo, ma solo a quello.

1868. È più facile essere flessibili quando siamo deboli o indeboliti.

1869. La logica è un modo di pensare per mezzo del quale si stabiliscono relazioni tra pensieri e nozioni diversi e se ne traggono delle deduzioni: si ragiona su quello che si sa. In tal maniera, si aumenta la nostra conoscenza andando oltre le singole percezioni. Tuttavia, si può sbagliare anche logicamente, perché spesso si usa la logica come strumento al servizio delle nostre opinioni. Si stabiliscono relazioni logiche tra diversi pensieri, ma i pensieri o nozioni da cui diversi individui traggono le loro deduzioni non sono gli stessi.

1870. La nostra volontà ci impone una certa condotta e la nostra debolezza decide se si obbedisce o no.

1871. Vi è qualcosa di dolce nell'amore sincero e affettuoso tra due persone brutte.

1872. Le strettoie della realtà forzano anche le aspirazioni più generose ad assoggettarsi alla mediocrità dei compromessi.

1873. L'ostilità degli onesti è incompatibile non tanto con la verità quanto con l'obiettività: si dicono allora solo le verità che danneggiano gli altri. Invece, l'ostilità dei disonesti non esita a servirsi anche delle bugie e della calunnia.

1874. L'intensità della vita è proporzionale tanto al vigore della mente quanto a quello del corpo.

1875. L'elegante piacevolezza di certa musica ricorda la danza dei cerchi intersecanti creati dal ritmo delle gocce di pioggia sulla liscia e lucida superficie di uno stagno.

1876. Il linguaggio di Dio si esprime soprattutto nella bellezza. Persino l'ordine e varietà sono sottoposti a questa legge.

1877. Per essere una pecora nera, basta essere originali o addirittura non essere conformisti.

1867. Some things (and even some truths) may not belong to our time, because they belong to all times. Many other things belong to our time, but only to our time.

1868. It is easier to be flexible when we are weak or weakened.

1869. Logic is a way of thinking through which we establish relations among different thoughts or notions and we derive deductions from them: we reason on what we know. In this fashion, we increase our knowledge by progressing beyond single perceptions. However, we can also err logically, because often we use logic as a means at the service of our opinions. Logical relations among different thoughts are established, but the thoughts or notions from which different individuals derive their deductions are not the same.

1870. Our will imposes on us a given behavior and our weakness decides whether or not we obey.

1871. There is something sweet in the sincere and affectionate love between two ugly persons.

1872. The straits of reality force even the most generous aspirations to submit to the mediocrity of compromise.

1873. The hostility of the honest is incompatible not so much with truth as with objectivity: only the truths damaging to others are then said. Instead, the hostility of the dishonest does not hesitate to also use lies and slander.

1874. The intensity of life is proportional as much to the vigor of the mind as to that of the body.

1875. The elegant pleasantness of some music reminds one of the dance of the intersecting circles formed by the rhythm of the drops of rain on the smooth and lucid surface of a pond.

1876. The language of God is expressed above all in beauty. Even order and variety are subjected to this law.

1877. To be a black sheep, it suffices to be original or even not to be a conformist.

1878. Si mentirebbe di meno se non ci facessero domande indiscrete, domande che spesso non hanno il diritto di fare.

1879. Il vantaggio delle teorie oscure è che ciascuno vi legge quello che gli pare. Non essendovi nulla, vi si può leggere tutto: di qui, le interpretazioni più disparate e altrettanto confuse.

1880. Molti dei nostri impulsi sono dovuti alla necessità di mantenere constante l'ambiente interno, sia fisico che mentale.

1881. L'ipocrisia nasce dal fatto che non si può confessare tutto a tutti. Né tutti sarebbero disposti ad ascoltare confessioni, specialmente se non sono interessati al pettegolezzo.

1882. A qualcuno sembra che imparare dagli altri comporti il riconoscere di aver torto.

1883. In certe intuizioni, vi si sente la verità, anche se non è definita esattamente o non sappiamo definirla esattamente.

1884. Ci sono dei rischi nel volersi conoscere meglio: non si sa mai cosa si possa trovare scavando.

1885. La mancanza di esperienza permette alla gioventù la lieta ignoranza di una mente sgombra.

1886. Il nostro presente è fatto di percezioni, ricordi e anticipazioni. La struttura del presente è costante, ma il suo contenuto cambia continuamente: man mano che si percepiscono nuove cose, i ricordi aumentano a spese delle anticipazioni. Il che è come dire che il passato e il futuro esistono solo nel presente. Si può anche non avere un passato (amnesia) o un futuro (depressione). Ma se il presente cessa, spariscono presente, passato e futuro.

1887. Quando affermo che il bene ed il male sono inevitabili, non dico che non facciano differenza. Se così fosse, sarebbero la stessa cosa; e cesserebbe il loro antagonismo e pertanto la loro necessità. Invece, dico che non potrebbe esistere il bene se non esistesse il male. E che è naturale perseguire il primo ed cercare di evitare il secondo: questa relazione tra bene e male è un fattore essenziale nel determinare il comportamento umano.

1878.   We would lie less if they did not ask us indiscreet questions, questions that often they have no right to ask.

1879.   The advantage of obscure theories is that everybody reads in them whatever he likes. There being nothing, one can read in it anything: hence, the most disparate and equally confused interpretations.

1880.   Many of our drives are due to the necessity of maintaining constant the internal environment, both physical and mental.

1881.   Hypocrisy is due to the fact that we can not confess everything to everybody. Nor would everybody be willing to listen to confessions, especially if they are not interested in gossip.

1882.   To some it seems that learning from others involves acknowledging being wrong.

1883.   In certain intuitions, we feel the truth, even if it is not precisely defined or we do not know how to define it precisely.

1884.   There are risks in wanting to know ourselves better: we do not really know what we might dig out.

1885.   Lack of experience permits youth to have the cheerful ignorance of an uncluttered mind.

1886.   Our present is made up of perceptions, remembrances and anticipations. The structure of the present is constant, but its content changes continuously: as we perceive new things, remembrances increase at the expense of anticipations. It is like saying that the past and future exist only in the present. We may also not have a past (amnesia) or a future (depression). But if the present ceases, present, past and future disappear.

1887.   When I affirm that good and evil are inevitable, I am not saying that they make no difference. If it were so, they would be the same thing; and their antagonism and therefore their necessity would cease. Instead, I am saying that good could not exist if evil did not exist. And that it is natural to pursue the former and try to avoid the latter: this relationship between good and evil is an essential factor in determining human behavior.

1888.   La mente ha bisogno di comunicare con altre menti. Un lungo
        silenzio ininterrotto diventerebbe una prigione in cui la mente
        languirebbe nella grigia monotonia di una solitudine senza echi.

1889.   Una mente stanca è una mente sterile.

1890.   Il buon senso può criticare la filosofia a torto, perché manca di
        profondità e si ferma alle apparenze. Ma se il rigore filosofico è ben
        superiore al buon senso, non può permettersi di non averne, come
        quando non vede le trappole della logica. Le quali trappole
        consistono nell'uso inappropriato delle parole e nell'abuso della
        struttura logica di una frase per fare delle deduzioni invalide.

1891.   L'indifferenza condanna non le cose verso cui siamo indifferenti,
        ma la nostra ignavia.

1892.   Come la luce del sole dirada il grigiore della nebbia e rivela il
        paesaggio, così la luce della comprensione dissipa la confusione di
        opinioni contrastanti e rivela le coerenze della Necessità.

1893.   Spesso si trova la verità solo attraverso le conseguenze dei propri
        sbagli. Verità e sbagli che alcuni rapidamente dimenticano.

1894.   Ad un'età avanzata, un abbigliamento ridicolmente giovanile rivela
        non una mente giovane, ma una puerile (se non senile).

1895.   È un peccato che le pecore non ridano. A causa di questo, manca
        un facile termine di confronto per certi tipi di ilarità.

1896   Spesso si desidera ardentemente una cosa e poi con più calma il suo
        contrario. Naturalmente, sulla base di opposte considerazioni:
        quello che si desidera contro quello che si dovrebbe desiderare.

1897.   Si vedono più chiaramente quelli che ci sono vicini quando se ne
        è lontani per un po'.

1898.   La realtà che è nella nostra mente non ha bisogno di (e non può)
        essere confrontata con una realtà esterna, semplicemente perché la
        realtà mentale è la sola realtà che esista. Fuori della mente, vi sono
        molecole e aggregati di molecole, ma non oggetti, idee, speranze,
        emozioni, ecc.

1888.   The mind needs to interact with other minds. A prolonged uninterrupted silence would become a prison in which the mind would languish in the grey monotony of a solitude without echoes.

1889.   A tired mind is a dull mind.

1890.   Common sense may wrongly criticize philosophy, because it lacks depth and stops at appearance. But if philosophical rigor is far superior to common sense, it can not afford to be senseless, as when it does not see the traps of logic. These traps consist in the inappropriate use of words and in abuse of the logical structure of a sentence to make invalid deductions.

1891.   Indifference condemns not the objects toward which we are indifferent, but our indolence.

1892   As the light of the sun dissipates the greyness of the fog and reveals the landscape, so the light of comprehension dispels the confusion of contrasting opinions and reveals the coherence of Necessity.

1893.   Often, the truth is found only through the consequences of one's mistakes. Truth and mistakes that some people quickly forget.

1894.   At an advanced age, ridiculously juvenile clothing reveals not a youthful mind, but a childish (if not a senile) one.

1895.   It is a pity that sheep do not laugh. Because of that, a facile term of comparison for certain types of hilarity is missing.

1896.   Often we ardently desire one thing and then more quietly its opposite. Naturally, on the basis of opposite considerations: what we desire versus what we should desire.

1897.   We see more clearly those who are close to us when we are far away from them for a while.

1898.   The reality that is in our mind does not need to (and can not) be compared with an external reality, simply because the mental reality is the only reality that exists. Outside of the mind, there are molecules and aggregates of molecules, but not objects, ideas, hopes, emotions, etc.

1899. Nel labirinto della vita, il filo di Arianna è la comprensione: la comprensione dell'importanza degli affetti.

1900. La decadenza è una forma di involuzione, in genere irreversibile. Più che assenza di coraggio, vi è scoraggiamento (giustificato o meno). Si cercano i piaceri perché mancano le aspirazioni, ma più sono i piaceri e più è la tristezza di un vuoto interiore. I piaceri falliscono perché la sofferenza è senza significato.

1901. In una mente che si sviluppa, l'educazione fissa nozioni che in genere persistono per tutta una vita. Per questo, l'educazione è importante e una buona educazione lo è ancora di più.

1902. A meno che non si espanda nell'universo, non è affatto certo che la razza umana possa continuare per sempre: il suo progresso è proprio quello che la minaccia sempre di più.

1903. Cambiare si deve; migliorare o peggiorare si può.

1904. Se la realtà è mentale, quale è la differenza tra reale, ideale, immaginato, ipotetico o allucinante? Teoricamente non vi è nessuna differenza, nel senso che sono tutte diverse forme di realtà mentale. Praticamente, la differenza è grande. "Reale" è quello che si percepisce come conseguenza degli stimoli dal mondo fisico (per es., un gatto). "Ideale" è il risultato di una generalizzazione mentale (per es., la virtù). "Immaginato" è quello che la fantasia o immaginazione crea (per es., i personaggi di un romanzo). "Ipotetico" è quello che è teoricamente possibile (per es., un pericolo). "Allucinante" è quello che percepisce una mente anormale. Gli ultimi quattro casi sono indipendenti della immediata percezione di stimoli dal mondo fisico (il mondo delle molecole). Sono invece il risultato di processi mentali, normali o anormali. Ma la loro realtà è suggerita dal fatto che sia un pericolo reale che un pericolo ideale, immaginato, ipotetico o allucinante possono essere ugualmente rischiosi. Pertanto, parte della realtà dipende da percezioni sensoriali dall'esterno e parte da processi mentali.

1905. Le intuizioni confuse si riconoscono dall'uso di parole o concetti incomprensibili. Ma alcuni fanno finta di capire le intuizioni oscure per paura di essere considerati poco intelligenti: hanno paura, perché non capiscono che c'è ben poco da capire.

1899.　In the labyrinth of life, the thread of Ariadne is comprehension: the comprehension of the importance of affections.

1900.　Decadence is a form of involution, generally irreversible. More than lack of courage, there is discouragement (justified or not). Pleasures are sought because aspirations are lacking, but the more the pleasures, the more the sadness of an inner vacuum. Pleasures fail because suffering has no meaning.

1901.　In a developing mind, education fixes notions that generally persist for a whole life. Because of this, education is important and a good education is even more so.

1902.　Unless it expands in the universe, it is not certain at all that the human race can continue for ever: its very progress threatens it more and more.

1903.　Change we must; improve or get worse we may.

1904.　If reality is mental, what is the difference between real, ideal, imagined, hypothetical and hallucinatory? Theoretically the difference is none, since there are all different forms of mental reality. Practically, the difference is great. "Real" is what is perceived as a consequence of stimuli from the physical word (e.g., a cat). "Ideal" is the result of a mental generalization (e.g., virtue). "Imagined" is what fancy or imagination creates (e.g., the characters of a novel). "Hypothetical" is theoretically possible (e.g., a danger). "Hallucinatory" is what an abnormal mind perceives. The last four cases are independent from the immediate perception of the stimuli from the physical world (the world of molecules). They are instead the result of mental processes, normal or abnormal. But their reality is suggested by the fact that both a real danger or an ideal, imagined, hypothetical or hallucinatory danger may be equally hazardous. Therefore, part of reality depends on sensorial perceptions from outside and part depend on mental processes.

1905.　Obscure intuitions are recognized by the use of incomprehensible words or concepts. But some simulate understanding them out of fear of being considered unintelligent: they are afraid, because they do not understand that there is rather little to understand.

1906. Prima o poi, tutte le menti raggiungono i limiti della loro comprensione che coincidono con i confini della loro realtà.

1907. Per alcuni, la vita è un ballo in maschera in cui impersonano il carattere che hanno scelto: alla fine, lo diventano.

1908. È più facile essere genuini nell'ostilità che nell'amicizia.

1909. Il ritmo della luce è creato dal gioco delle ombre.

1910. Si persegue con ardore la giustizia che si confà con il nostro carattere e convinzioni. In nome di quella giustizia, qualcuno arriva ad uccidere gli avversari, e solo perché non la pensano come lui.

1911. Vi sono mode in ogni campo e non solo nell'abbigliamento, perché ci sarà sempre chi ha idee "nuove". Questa inflessibile necessità di varietà talvolta risulta in prodotti ben tristi.

1912. Le vicende storiche seguono una determinata necessità: la necessità di ottenere quello che uno ha la forza di ottenere. Quando sono abbastanza forti, i nobili si ribellano ai re, la borghesia ai nobili, il proletariato alla borghesia. Ogni volta, è necessario creare una teoria che giustifichi gli interessi o dei re, o del popolo, o di una classe sociale, ecc.: la teoria viene usata per stabilire che si ha diritto a quello che la forza può ottenere. Una teoria prevale finché gli opposti interessi diventano più forti e giustificano una nuova teoria. Spesso le teorie si servono del supporto morale della "giustizia" contro gli abusi di coloro che sono al potere in quel momento. Si tratta essenzialmente di uno scontro di forze per eliminare gli svantaggi della sudditanza e ottenere i vantaggi del potere: per questa ragione, il fenomeno è obbligatoriamente ciclico. Fatta di interessi, teorie e lotte, la storia dipana il suo dramma senza fine, spesso intessuto di crudeltà selvaggia.

1913. Essere liberi significa che si può fare quello che ci pare (lecito o illecito), ma anche che siamo giuridicamente e moralmente responsabili di quello che si fa. Delitti e peccati nascono dalla infrazione delle rispettive leggi giuridiche e morali.

1914. Quando cominciamo a fare sbagli con l'avanzare dell'età, in un certo senso si entra nell'adolescenza delle senescenza.

1906.   Sooner or later, every mind reaches the limits of its comprehension which coincide with the confines of its reality.

1907.   For some, life is a masked ball in which they personify the character that they have chosen: eventually, they become it.

1908.   It is easier to be genuine in hostility than in friendship.

1909.   The rhythm of light is created by play of the shadows.

1910.   People pursue ardently the justice that suits their personality and convictions. In the name of that justice, some even kill their adversaries, and only because they have different convictions.

1911.   There are fashions in every field (and not only in clothing), because there will always be those who have "new" ideas. This inflexible necessity of variety sometimes results in rather sad products.

1912.   Historical vicissitudes follow a definite necessity: the necessity to obtain what one has the force to obtain. When strong enough, the nobles rebel against the kings, the bourgeoisie against the nobles, the proletariat against the bourgeoisie. Each time, it becomes necessary to develop a theory that justifies the interests either of kings, or of the people, or of a social class, etc.: the theory is meant to establish that one has the right to what force can obtain. A theory prevails until opposing interests become stronger and justify another theory. Often theories seek the moral support of "justice" against the abuses of those in power at the moment. Essentially, it is a clash of forces to eliminate the disadvantages of subjection and to obtain the advantages of power: for this reason, the phenomenon is obligatorily cyclical. Made up of interests, theories and struggles, history unfolds its endless drama, often interwoven with savage cruelty.

1913.   To be free means that we can do what we please (licit or illicit), but also that we are legally and morally responsible for what we do. Crimes and sins are infractions of the respective juridical and moral laws.

1914.   When we start making mistakes due to the advancing age, in a sense we enter into the adolescence of senescence.

1915. L'eleganza è fatta per essere gustata. Se educa, educa la nostra sensibilità.

1916. Per piacere ai più, non occorre che qualcosa sia bello o vero: basta che sia fuori del comune e pertanto piacevolmente stimolante. Questa è la base della maggior parte delle mode.

1917. Si nega a Dio quello che si concede alla nostra debolezza. Per esempio, la nostra anima.

1918. Seduti in platea, si assiste al passaggio dall'evoluzione alla progressiva involuzione della nostra mente sul palcoscenico della vita sotto l'implacabile regia di un tempo che non conosce sosta.

1919. Differenti menti pensano pensieri simili in epoche differenti, ma raramente con gli stessi significati, nello stesso contesto o con le stesse conclusioni.

1920. Si è inconcludenti quando non si raggiungono conclusioni o quando se ne raggiungono troppe.

1921. L'attrattiva dell'altrui gioventù è soprattutto fisica e quella della nostra è soprattutto emotiva. Per questo, ad ogni età, la gioventù più attraente è (o è stata) la nostra.

1922. Nelle meraviglie della natura vi è l'ombra della grandezza di Dio.

1923. Ci si sente vivi con le emozioni e ancor di più con le passioni.

1924. L'invidia non perdona neanche quando è perdonata. Il perdono la esaspera, perché non vuol essere diminuita.

1925. Le avversità ci fanno crescere solo quando le superiamo.

1926. La ricerca della verità esige la libertà assoluta da tutto quello che non è la verità. La verità è così forte da dover essere accettata che piaccia o non piaccia. Certamente, è più forte di tutte le falsità messe insieme.

1927. Quello che si fa nella vita è misurato tanto dalla qualità delle nostre domande quanto dalla qualità delle nostre risposte.

1915. Elegance is meant to be enjoyed. If it educates, it educates our sensitivity.

1916. To please most people, it is not necessary that something be beautiful or true: it suffices that it be uncommon and therefore pleasantly stimulating. This is the basis of most fashions.

1917. We refuse God what we concede to our weakness. For example, our soul.

1918. Seated in the stalls, we witness the passage from evolution to progressive involution of our mind on the stage of life under the implacable direction of a time that knows no respite.

1919. Different minds think similar thoughts in different eras, but rarely with the same meaning, in the same context or with the same conclusions.

1920. We are inconclusive when we do not reach a conclusion or when we reach too many of them.

1921. The attractiveness of others' youth is above all physical and that of our youth is above all emotive. For this reason, at any age, the most attractive youth is (or has been) ours.

1922. In nature's marvels there is the shadow of the greatness of God.

1923. We feel alive with emotions and even more so with passions.

1924. Envy does not pardon even when it is pardoned. Pardon exasperates it, because it does not want to be diminished.

1925. Adversities make us grow only if we overcome them.

1926. The search for truth demands absolute freedom from anything that is not the truth. Truth is so strong that it has to be accepted whether it pleases or not. Certainly, it is stronger than all falsehoods bound together.

1927. Our performance in life is gauged by the quality of our questions as much as by the quality of our answers.

1928. I peccati tendono ad essere più intimi e meno astratti delle virtù.

1929. Come gli insetti, siamo attratti da quello che luccica: le città sarebbero assai meno attraenti e forse anche meno popolate se si proibissero le insegne al neon, colorate e intermittenti.

1930. Secondo il caso, la mente deve essere lucida, acuta e all'erta; o pastosa, rilassata e non-pensante.

1931. La forza poco si cura della moderazione. A meno che non lo imponga l'abilità (per aumentare la forza).

1932. Per riconoscere i propri limiti, bisogna averne la capacità.

1933. Si ha diritto solo al rispetto che si merita, non a quello che si pretende. Darsi importanza diminuisce il rispetto degli altri. Per lo meno, di quelli che capiscono.

1934. L'immaginazione divina non ha limiti, e l'immaginazione umana ne è il pallido riflesso come la penombra della luce lunare.

1935. La mente opera secondo le caratteristiche dell'età. La vecchiaia, a causa dell'esperienza e ridotta emotività, è in grado di pensare in maniera più sistematica e distaccata. Ma c'è il pericolo che perda la capacità di immedesimarsi nella maniera di pensare e di sentire di menti giovani.

1936. Il negare una verità diminuisce noi, non la verità.

1937. La gelosia verso chi si ama è un'ossessione di possesso. Non si tollera che l'oggetto della nostra gelosia cresca, perché così sembra sfuggirci. Pertanto, chi è geloso in amore è geloso anche in altri campi.

1938. La politica persegue interessi e la scienza cerca la verità. Per questo, in politica, la verità è perseguita nelle scienze politiche; e nella scienza, gli interessi sono perseguiti nella politica della scienza.

1939. Senza la mente, non vi sarebbero né domande né risposte. Di fatto, non vi sarebbe nulla.

1928.   Sins tend to be more intimate and less abstract than virtues.

1929.   Like insects, we are attracted by what sparkles: the cities would be far less attractive and perhaps even less populated if the colored and intermittent neon lights were prohibited.

1930.   Depending on the situation, the mind has be lucid, sharp and alert; or doughy, relaxed and unthinking.

1931.   Force has little regard for moderation. Unless the latter is imposed by ability (to increase force).

1932.   To recognize one's own limits, one must have the capacity thereof.

1933.   We have a right only to the respect that we deserve, not to the respect that we demand. To be presumptuous decreases the respect of others. At least, of those who are not fooled.

1934.   The divine imagination is boundless, and human imagination is its pale reflection like the twilight of the moon light.

1935.   The mind works according to the characteristics of each age. Old age, due to experience and reduced emotivity, can think in a more systematic and detached manner. But there is the danger that it might lose the capability of identifying itself with the manner of thinking and feeling of young minds.

1936.   To deny a truth decreases us, not the truth.

1937.   Jealousy towards a beloved one is an obsession of possession. We do not tolerate that the object of our jealousy should grow, because that person then seems to escape us. Therefore, those who are jealous in love are jealous also in other fields.

1938.   Politics pursues interests and science seeks the truth. For this reason, in politics, truth is pursued in political science; and in science, interests are pursued in the politics of science.

1939.   Without the mind, there would be neither questions nor answers. Actually, there would be nothing.

1940. Il silenzio è la conveniente tomba di tante colpe. E il loro complice segreto.

1941. Siamo troppo immersi nella vita per domandarci in che cosa consista. Si vivono le nostre emozioni e passioni nell'ignoranza del nostro destino. Solo raramente ci si domanda il significato di quello che si fa, perché in genere si agisce sotto l'influenza di impulsi istintivi. Ma forse è così perché non è nel nostro interesse capire troppo.

1942. Si perdona ai nostri figli, persino quando non si correggono. Come è possibile che si possa amare più di Dio?

1943. La tolleranza è uno strumento con cui la ragione modera (con una certa riluttanza) la nostra istintiva antipatia verso quello che è differente da quello che ci piace.

1944. In giorni diversi, si possono percepire gli stessi stimoli dall'esterno e dall'interno, ma la loro realtà nella mente può essere ben diversa a seconda del nostro modo di sentire.

1945. L'altrui acutezza dà l'impressione di privarci delle nostre difese: ci sembra che renda la nostra mente trasparente.

1946. La filosofia educa la mente; quando non la confonde.

1947. I desideri sono la sorgente di molte delle nostre emozioni e i desideri insoddisfatti di emozioni più forti.

1948. Mode e tendenze sono opportunità offerte a differenti virtù e difetti per prevalere temporaneamente sulla scena umana.

1949. Quello che è convenzionale ha il torto di essere ovvio, ma non quello di essere inutile.

1950. I differenti recettori aggiungono differenti caratteristiche alle percezioni. Pertanto, lo stesso oggetto è differente a seconda del numero e la qualità dei recettori di chi percepisce. E dell'acutezza e della struttura funzionale della mente che analizza ed interpreta segnali provenienti dai recettori. Per questo, la realtà non è mai identica per menti diverse, e le opinioni divergono.

1940.   Silence is the convenient tomb of many faults. And their secret accomplice.

1941.   We are too immersed in life to ask ourselves of what it consists. We live our emotions and passions in the ignorance of our destiny. Only rarely we ask ourselves the meaning of what we do, because generally we act under the influence of instinctive drives. But perhaps it is so because it is in our interest not to understand too much.

1942.   We pardon our children, even if they do not redress their ways. How could it be possible that we might love more than God?

1943.   Tolerance is an instrument by means of which our reason moderates (with some reluctance) our instinctive antagonism toward what is different from what we like.

1944.   In different days, we may perceive the same stimuli from outside and inside, but their reality in our mind may be very different depending on our mood.

1945.   The keenness of others seems to deprive us of our defenses: we feel as if it renders our mind transparent.

1946.   Philosophy educates the mind; when it does not confuse it.

1947.   Desires are the source of many of our emotions and unsatisfied desires of stronger emotions.

1948.   Fashions and trends are the opportunities offered to different virtues and faults to temporarily prevail on the human stage.

1949.   What is conventional has the fault of being obvious, but not that of being useless.

1950.   Different receptors add different characteristics to perceptions. Therefore, the same object is different depending on the number and quality of the receptors of the perceiver. And of the sharpness and functional structure of the mind that analyzes and interprets the signals coming from the receptors. For this reason, the reality is never identical in different minds, and opinions diverge.

1951. Quello che è incantevole è in genere alogico.

1952. La distinzione tra la luce ed il calore del sole è fatta solo dalla mente. Fisicamente, gradazioni di uno stesso fenomeno sono percepite dalla mente attraverso recettori differenti.

1953. Nuove menti causano cambiamenti solo per il fatto di essere nuove. E nel processo, chi ha merito viene separato da chi non ne ha.

1954. La forza di un dramma risiede nell'intensità dei suoi contrasti. I lampi, i tuoni, le minacciose nuvole nere e gli scrosci violenti di pioggia di un temporale che termina un periodo di siccità hanno una più vivida intensità emotiva quanto più lunga e devastante è stata la siccità. Diventano la risoluzione fisica della precedente tesa ansietà.

1955. Una comprensione incompleta può portare ad una incomprensione completa.

1956. Quando gli occhi sono inespressivi, la bellezza fisica è condivisa con gli animali (o con le bambole dallo sguardo vitreo).

1957. Per "giustizia" spesso intendiamo l'ottenere quello che non abbiamo, e raramente il dare quello che gli altri vorrebbero da noi. Nel primo caso ci si sente virtuosi, e nel secondo si diventa irragionevoli. Probabilmente, si considera perfetta la giustizia che non interferisce con i nostri interessi. Non per nulla, l'amore della vera giustizia è un puro amore platonico, e non un'intensa passione.

1958. Si onora Dio sia con la semplicità dell'anima che con la straordinaria bellezza delle grandi opere umane.

1959. Se è vero che la verità non conosce mode, quando mai le mode hanno cercato la verità?

1960. Col passare del tempo, il nostro Io man mano comprende tutti i nostri Io delle nostre età precedenti. Si vedono allora le nostre successive identità come attraverso un telescopio alla rovescia.

1961. L'intelligenza è importante per la mente solo se si rende conto che da sola varrebbe ben poco.

1951. What is charming is generally alogical.

1952. The distinction between the light and the heat of the sun is made only by the mind. Physically, different aspects of the same phenomenon are perceived by the mind through different receptors.

1953. New minds cause changes just because they are new. And in the process, those who have merit are separated from those who do not.

1954. The force of a drama resides in the intensity of its contrasts. The lightening, thunder, threatening black clouds and violent rain showers of a storm that terminates a period of drought have a more vivid emotional intensity the longer and more devastating the drought has been. They become the physical resolution of the preceding tense anxiety.

1955. An incomplete comprehension can lead to a complete incomprehension.

1956. When the eyes are inexpressive, physical beauty is shared with the animals (or with dolls with a glassy stare).

1957. Often by "justice" we mean obtaining what we do not have, and rarely giving what others would want from us. In the former case, we feel righteous, and in the latter case we refuse to reason. Probably, the justice that we consider perfect is the one that does not interfere with our interests. Not by hazard, the love of true justice is a pure Platonic love and not an intense passion.

1958. We honor God with simplicity of the soul as well as with the extraordinary beauty of the great human works.

1959. If it is true that truth ignores fashions, when have fashions ever sought the truth?

1960. With the passing of time, our Self progressively includes all our Selves of our preceding ages. We then see our successive identities as through a reversed telescope.

1961. Intelligence is important for the mind only if intelligence is aware that alone it would not be worthy of much.

1962. Per crescere un po' basta solo essere un po' meno meschini.

1963. La felicità si trova nell'abbandono ai propri sentimenti, anche quelli che ci sono incomprensibili.

1964. In una società di sole persone rigorosamente virtuose vi sarebbero tante asprezze e poca generosità. La diversa importanza attribuita da differenti individui a differenti virtù (per esempio, religiosità e valore militare) porterebbe a profonde tensioni. E alla erosione delle virtù.

1965. Il significato e l'importanza di quello che si legge varia considerevolmente a seconda del lettore.

1966. Essere innamorati non è che sognare.

1967. Qualche volta si convince non perché abbiamo ragione, ma perché gli altri non sanno trovare argomenti più convincenti.

1968. Per essere efficace, la vanità deve essere coerente e ferma.

1969. Non si insegna se non si stimola una mente a pensare.

1970. L'arte di essere diplomatici consiste nel non dire la verità senza dire delle bugie.

1971. Le contraddizioni sono l'espressione obbligatoria del passaggio da uno stato mentale e emotivo ad uno opposto. Senza le contraddizioni, sarebbe ben difficile avere drammi.

1972. Per mantenersi umili, bisogna fare delle cose umili: l'apprendistato dell'anima verso l'inafferrabile perfezione.

1973. Suo malgrado, l'avarizia è generosa: risparmia per gli eredi.

1974. Solo una naturale semplicità è immune ai successi di una sua profonda umiltà.

1975. Si trova noioso quello che non interessa. Ma non diciamo che non siamo interessati, perché non suona bene: diciamo che la cosa non è interessante, perché suona meglio.

1962. To grow a little, it only suffices to be a little less petty.

1963. We find happiness in the abandon to our feelings, even those that we do not comprehend.

1964. In a society of only rigorously virtuous persons, there would be much sourness and little generosity. The different importance attributed by different individuals to different virtues (e.g., religiousness and military valor) would lead to deep tensions. And to the erosion of virtues.

1965. The meaning and importance of what one reads considerably varies depending on the reader.

1966. To be in love is but to dream.

1967. Sometimes one is convincing not because he is right, but because others can not find more convincing arguments.

1068. To be effective, vanity must be coherent and firm.

1969. We do not teach unless we stimulate a mind to think.

1970. The art of being diplomatic consists in not saying the truth without saying lies.

1971. Contradictions are the obligatory expression of the passage from a mental and emotive state to an opposite one. Without contradictions, it would be rather difficult to have dramas.

1972. To stay humble, one must do humble deeds: the training of the soul toward the elusive perfection.

1973. In spite of itself, avarice is generous: it saves for the heirs.

1974. Only a natural simplicity is immune to the successes of its profound humility.

1975. We find boring what does not interest us. But we do not say that we are not interested, because it does not sound good: we say that the thing is not interesting, because it sounds better.

1976. Il presente è come il raggio di un faro che gradualmente illumina il semicerchio della vita: un mobile sprazzo di luce circondato dall'oscurità di un'eternità di cui si ignora l'insondabile profondità e di cui si teme la vastità del silenzio.

1977. In qualsiasi maniera si allevino i figli, ci saranno sempre dei problemi, perché la personalità e convinzioni dei due genitori e dei figli sono differenti. Ma lo scopo dell'educazione dovrebbe essere uno solo: il vantaggio dei figli (e non l'amor proprio dei genitori).

1978. È giusto che ad una mente superficiale interessino solo le cose superficiali. Come le altre menti, non ha certo l'obbligo di avere interessi che le sono estranei.

1979. Non raramente, si critica quello che non coincide con le nostre idee (giuste o sbagliate) e solo perché non coincide.

1980. Le menti pratiche sopravvalutano il costo della bellezza perché ne sottovalutano il valore.

1981. Essere liberi significa anche potersi comportare come imbecilli.

1982. La gente abusa delle opportunità con entusiasmo ottuso piuttosto che usarle con sottile accortezza a loro vantaggio. Ma forse l'entusiasmo è più energico di quanto l'accortezza sia sottile.

1983. La mente costruisce gli oggetti non soltanto combinando le percezioni derivanti da stimoli diversi attraverso recettori diversi, ma anche attribuendo loro speciali valori (estetici, affettivi, morali, ecc.). Questi valori sono esclusivamente mentali (non dipendendo dalle percezioni) e sono inoltre variabili a seconda delle persone e delle circostanze. Solo per la mente, l'oro è più prezioso del piombo; ed è ancora più prezioso per la mente di un avaro. E il pane è più prezioso dell'oro per uno che non mangia da una settimana.

1984. La noia risulta non tanto dalla mancanza di interessi quanto dalla mancanza delle conseguenti emozioni.

1985. Si capisce che è necessario non capire tutto solo quando si è capito abbastanza.

1976. The present is like the beam of a lighthouse that gradually illuminates the semicircle of life: a mobile flash of light surrounded by the darkness of an eternity of which we ignore the unfathomable depth and of which we fear the vastness of silence.

1977. No matter how we educate our children, there will always be problems, since the personality and beliefs of the two parents and of the children are different. But the aim of education should be only one: the advantage of the children (and not the pride of the parents).

1978. It is right that a superficial mind should be interested only in superficial things. As other minds, it certainly has no obligation of having interests that are extraneous to itself.

1979. Not rarely, we criticize what does not coincide with our ideas (right or wrong) and only because it does not coincide.

1980. Practical minds overestimate the cost of beauty because they underestimate its value.

1981. To be free also means that one can behave like an imbecile.

1982. People often abuse opportunities with obtuse enthusiasm rather than using them with subtle perspicacity to their advantage. But perhaps enthusiasm is more energetic than perspicacity is subtle.

1983. The mind forms objects not only by combining the perceptions deriving from different stimuli through different receptors, but also by attributing them special values (aesthetic, affective, moral, etc.). These values are exclusively mental (not depending on perceptions) and furthermore are variable according to the circumstances. Only for the mind, gold is more precious than lead; and it is even more precious for the mind of a miser. And bread is more precious than gold for someone who has not eaten for one week.

1984. Boredom results not so much from the lack of interests as from the lack of the consequent emotions.

1985. We understand that it is necessary not to understand everything only when we have understood enough.

1986. Lo spazio (vicino e lontano, destra e sinistra, sopra e sotto, ecc.) è relativo a dove la nostra mente ed il suo corpo si trovano in quel momento. Similmente, il tempo (passato e futuro, presto o tardi, lungo o corto, ecc.) è relativo a quello che la mente sta pensando in quel momento. Pertanto, in termini specifici, lo spazio e il tempo cambiano a seconda del punto di riferimento (la mente). Per es., se siamo in Europa, l'America è lontana, e se si va in America è l'Europa ad essere lontana (anche se Europa ed America sono esattamente dove erano). Similmente, quello che si pensava non è più il presente, ma il passato; e alle dieci di sera è tardi se la mente è stanca ed è presto se la mente si diverte ad un ricevimento.

1987. Ci si libera dalle cose che non si capiscono con l'impazienza di una ignoranza che non vuol essere disturbata.

1988. I sentimenti più delicati hanno spesso una sfumatura di poesia.

1989. L'esprimersi semplicemente può essere più spesso il risultato di chiarezza di idee che di semplicità di mente.

1990. La forza di carattere spesso comporta durezza verso se stessi. Se ne incarica l'autodisciplina.

1991. L'anima si abbandona sconsideratamente alle emozioni per trovarsi poi dominata dalla passioni.

1992. L'evoluzione di alcuni pittori con l'età (per es., Michelangelo) si riflette nel fatto che la bellezza non è più espressa nelle forme levigate del corpo, ma in una forza interiore intensa. Si rappresenta non più la perfezione del corpo, ma i drammi dello spirito.

1993. Per un po' di felicità, talvolta si chiede solo che ci sia permesso di sognare.

1994. La forza della tradizione consiste nel fatto che è instillata in ogni nuova generazione quando la mente di questa viene plasmata dall'educazione e ancora non pensa indipendentemente. Pertanto, la tradizione imprime un'impronta nella mente che condiziona la sua maniera di pensare e di sentire, ed è trasmessa come un'eredità obbligata. Se un bambino cresce sotto l'influenza di una tradizione diversa, assorbe i valori di quella.

1986. In general terms, space (near or far away, right and left, above and below, etc.) is what irradiates from where our mind and its body happen to be at the moment. Similarly, time (past and future, early or late, long or short, etc.) is what irradiates from that which our mind is thinking at the moment. Therefore, in specific terms, space and time change according to the reference point (the mind). For example, if we are in Europe, America is far away, and if we go to America, it is Europe that is far away (even if Europe and America are exactly where they were). Similarly, what we were thinking is no longer the present, but the past; and at 10 PM it is late if the mind is tired and early if the mind is enjoying itself at a party.

1987. We get rid of things that we do not understand with the impatience of an ignorance that does not want to be disturbed.

1988. The most delicate feelings have often a nuance of poetry.

1989. To express oneself simply may be more often the result of clarity of ideas than of simplicity of mind.

1990. Strength of character often involves hardness toward oneself. Self-discipline sees to it.

1991. The soul recklessly gives itself up to emotions to then find itself dominated by passions.

1992. The evolution of some painters with age (e.g., Michelangelo) is reflected in the fact that beauty is no longer expressed in the smooth forms of the body, but in an intense inner strength. They no longer represent the perfection of the body, but the dramas of the spirit.

1993. For a little happiness, sometimes we only ask to be allowed to dream.

1994. The force of the tradition consists in the fact that it is instilled in each new generation when its mind is being molded by education and does not think independently yet. Therefore, tradition makes an imprint in the mind that conditions the way of thinking and feeling, and is transmitted as an obligatory heritage. If a child grows under the influence of a different tradition, it absorbs the values thereof.

1995. È nuovo quello che la mente percepisce per la prima volta cd è vecchio quello che la mente sa già. È per questo che inevitabilmente il nuovo diventa vecchio.

1996. Più felici si è, tanto meno si ragiona; e tanto meno ci importa di ragionare.

1997. La mente è più completa quanto più sono le caratteristiche che include, come la sensibilità, interesse, curiosità, riflessione, perspicacia, attenzione, energia, capacità d'analisi, tenacia, emotività, sveltezza, flessibilità, passione, ecc. Forse, l'intelligenza è la somma di queste e altre qualità.

1998. Per essere riconosciuti, bisogna essere apprezzati. Per essere apprezzati, bisogna essere capiti. E per essere capiti, ci vuole chi ci capisca o, meglio ancora, abbia interesse a capirci. E lì comincia una delle difficoltà.

1999. La fisiologia determina la maggior parte delle azioni umane e la filosofia ne influenza alcune. Ovverosia, la filosofia propone e la fisiologia dispone.

2000. Come gli abeti sulle montagne, l'anima umana è protesa verso le vette e la luce del sole.

1995.   It is new what the mind perceives for the first time and it is old what the mind already knows. For this reason, the new inevitably becomes old.

1996.   The happier we are, the less we reason; and the less we care to reason.

1997.   The mind is more complete the more numerous are the characteristics that it includes, such as sensitivity, interest, curiosity, reflection, perspicacity, attention, energy, capability of analysis, tenacity, emotivity, alertness, flexibility, passion, etc. Perhaps, intelligence is the sum of these and other qualities.

1998.   To be recognized, one needs to be appreciated. To be appreciated, one needs to be understood. And to be understood, one needs those who understand him or, better yet, have an interest in understanding him. And here begins one of the difficulties.

1999.   Physiology determines most human actions and philosophy influences some of them. That is to say, philosophy proposes and physiology disposes.

2000.   As the firs on the mountains, the human soul yearns for the peaks and the light of the sun.

CONCLUSIONI

È chiaro che una mente opera secondo la sua struttura funzionale. In tutti, la struttura funzionale comprende le stesse componenti, perché altrimenti sarebbe impossibile comunicare con gli altri. Ma, in menti differenti, le varie componenti hanno uno sviluppo differente. Per esempio, taluni hanno una totale indifferenza verso quello che è bello e altri ne possono fare una ragione di vita. Similmente per la parte logica della mente. Anche se l'intensità del desiderio di conoscere e capire e la capacità di soddisfarlo variano da individuo a individuo, tutti abbiamo tale desiderio.

Se non si può impedire alla mente di ragionare, quali ne sono i vantaggi e gli svantaggi? La mente indaga comunque, anche se non ci sono vantaggi apparenti, perché per la mente il ragionare è come per il corpo l'alimentarsi: una necessità fisiologica inderogabile.

Ma i vantaggi ci sono. Il primo è per l'appunto quello di soddisfare un bisogno fisiologico: si evita il digiuno della mente. Inoltre, esiste anche il piacere di capire. E, se si capisce, è probabile che si facciano meno errori e si migliori la qualità delle nostre azioni.

Il pericolo (e pertanto uno svantaggio) è che si capisca molto, ma non abbastanza. In tal caso, gli errori possono essere più gravi, perché non siamo protetti dai necessari dubbi: *l'arroganza di quello che si sa non tiene conto della vastità di quello che si ignora.*

Inoltre, indagando, ci sono i pericoli connessi con lo scoprire i meccanismi necessari per un ordinato sviluppo della vita. Scoprendoli, ci si crede allora di avere in un certo senso superato quell'Ordine, per essere divenuti coscienti dei meccanismi che lo determinano. Possiamo essere così sciocchi da credere che la nostra acutezza svuoti l'Ordine dei suoi misteri e pertanto lo ridimensioni. E invece, la nostra acutezza dovrebbe sentirsi affascinata dalla straordinaria complessità, necessità e bellezza dell'Ordine. Questo è un esempio di come si possa capire di meno quando ci si crede di capire di più.

Ne deriva che neanche la verità può permettersi di non essere saggia, intendendo per saggezza la comprensione del fatto che nella vita di ciascuno vi saranno sempre vizi e virtù, ordine e disordine, idealismo e scetticismo, purezza e corruzione, bontà e cattiveria, generosità e invidia, ecc. In altre parole, nella vita vi sarà sempre il bene ed il male, il loro conflitto e la necessità inderogabile di voler far prevalere il bene. *Si può anche non essere virtuosi, ma non ci si può permettere di non volerlo essere.*

Ne deriva altresì la superiorità degli affetti sulle arroganze dell'intelletto. Si può vivere una vita normale con sentimenti normali, ma sarebbe una vita ben triste quella in cui invece di affetti si avessero solo pensieri. Questo sembra essere il significato dell'adagio "Primum vivere, deinde philosophari".

Ma allora è inutile cercare di capire? Certamente no, se non altro perché vi si trova piacere. Inoltre, se il capire per taluni è un lusso inutile, per altri è una necessità di cui non ci si può privare. Ma se non si capisce abbastanza, allora il capire può essere non tanto inutile quanto dannoso. In altre parole, *non si capisce abbastanza se non si capiscono le limitazioni del capire.* Inoltre, quello che si capisce non ha una sufficiente profondità se non è analizzato con senso critico. Quindi, *è necessario essere coscienti sia della nostra ignoranza sia della qualità, significato e limiti della nostra comprensione.*

Solo con la semplicità degli affetti o con una sufficiente profondità di comprensione si apprezza quello spettacolo meraviglioso che è la natura e lo straordinario dono della vita. E ancor più si apprezza l'umanità che vi è nella divinità di Dio.

In fondo, sia gli affetti che la comprensione dovrebbero essere il ponte che congiunge la creazione col suo Creatore. Gli affetti si servono della fede che è essenzialmente un intuitivo atto di fiducia: questo mezzo di comunicazione con Dio è concesso a tutti. La comprensione si serve della mente che è il più grande dono di Dio: nell'indagare le meraviglie della creazione e scoprirne la loro straordinaria natura, anche la mente innalza il suo magnificat al Creatore.

Sia gli affetti che l'intelletto confluiscono poi nell'umiltà: i primi istintivamente e il secondo sotto l'influenza di quello che scopre. *L'umiltà non è la negazione dei propri meriti, ma la coscienza di quelli di Dio.* Con gli affetti si ama Dio e con la mente si scopre quanto sia degno di essere amato.

CONCLUSIONS

It is clear that the mind operates according to its functional structure. In everyone, the functional structure includes the same components, since otherwise it would be impossible to communicate with others. But in different minds, the different components are developed to a different degree. For example, some have a total indifference toward beauty and others may make of it the center of their life. Similarly for the logical part of the mind. Even if the intensity of the desire of knowing and of understanding and the capacity of satisfy it vary from individual to individual, all of us have such a desire.

If we can not prevent the mind from reasoning, what are the advantages and disadvantages thereof? The mind investigates anyhow, even if there are no apparent advantages, because reasoning for the mind is like food for the body: an absolute physiological necessity.

But the advantages are there. The first is precisely that of satisfying a physiological need: avoiding the starvation of the mind. Furthermore, there is the pleasure of understanding. And, if we understand, it is probable that we make fewer mistakes and that we improve the quality of our actions.

The danger (and therefore a disadvantage) is that we understand much, but not enough. In that case, the mistakes can be more serious, because we are not protected by the necessary doubts: *the arrogance of what we know does not take into account the vastness of what we ignore.*

Furthermore, by investigating, there are the dangers connected with the discovery of the mechanisms necessary for an orderly development of life. In discovering them, we then believe of having in a certain sense surpassed that Order, by having become aware of the mechanisms that determine it. We may be so silly as to believe that our sharpness empties the Order of its mysteries and therefore reappraises it. Instead, our sharpness should feel fascinated by the extraordinary complexity, necessity and beauty of the Order. This is an example of how we may understand less when we believe that we understand more.

It follows that not even virtue can afford to not to be wise, meaning by wisdom the understanding of the fact that in the life of each of us there will always be vices and virtues, order and disorder, idealism and skepticism, purity and corruption, goodness and malice, generosity and envy, etc. In other words, in life there will always be good and evil, their conflict and the absolute necessity of our wanting good to prevail. *We may even not be virtuous, but we can not afford not wanting to be so.*

It also follows that affections are superior to the arrogance of the intellect. One can live a normal life with normal feelings, but it would be a very sad life that in which instead of feelings one had only thoughts. This seems to be the meaning of the adage: "Primum vivere, deinde philosophari".

But then is it useless to try and understand? Certainly not, if nothing else because we find pleasure in it. Furthermore, if for some people understanding is a useless luxury, for others it is a necessity which they can not do without. But if we do not understand enough, then understanding may be not so much useless as it may be dangerous. In other words, *we do not understand enough if we do not understand the limitations of understanding.* In addition, what we understand has no sufficient depth if it is not critically analyzed. Therefore, *it is necessary to be conscious both of our ignorance and of the quality, meaning and limitations of our comprehension.*

Only with the simplicity of affections or with a sufficient depth of understanding we appreciate that marvelous spectacle that is nature and the extraordinary gift of life. And even more we appreciate the humanity that there is in the divinity of God.

In the end, both affections and comprehension should be the bridge that connects the creation with its Creator. Affections use faith which is essentially an intuitive act of confidence: this means of communication is conceded to everyone. Comprehension uses the mind which is the greatest gift of God: in investigating the marvels of creation and in discovering its extraordinary nature, also the mind elevates its Magnificat to our Creator.

Both affections and the intellect meet in humility, the former instinctively and the latter under the influence of what it discovers. *Humility is not the negation of one's merits, but the awareness of those of God.* With affections we love God and with the mind we discover how much He deserves to be loved.

APPENDICE

APPENDIX

APPENDICE

Uno dei pregi degli aforismi è il fatto di essere concisi. Il rovescio della medaglia è che gli aforismi definiscono il succo di un pensiero, ma non ne elaborano la definizione. Per questa ragione, riporto qui qualche esempio di trattazione di concetti a cui alcuni degli aforismi si riferiscono. Alcuni di questi brani (Spazio; Movimento; Tempo; l'Io; Natura della Realtà) sono tratti dal Diario di un Fisiologo del Cuore dove questi concetti sono elaborati in maggior dettaglio. Altri (Relazione tra Tempo, Spazio e Movimento; L'Arte; Dio) sono stati sviluppati più tardi.

Si tratta solo di esempi isolati, ma, se non altro, possono essere utili per intravedere il sottofondo filosofico che è alla base degli aforismi. Quelli tratti dal Diario sono presentati solo in inglese dal momento che il testo italiano è disponibile nel Diario. Devo avvertire che ho fatto delle piccole modificazioni per evitare ripetizioni o migliorare la comprensione di un concetto, ma la sostanza della traduzione è la stessa del testo originale italiano. I saggi scritti dopo la pubblicazione del Diario sono presentati in italiano ed inglese.

APPENDIX

One advantage of the aphorisms is that they are concise. One unavoidable limitation is that the aphorisms define the essence of a thought, but they do no elaborate the definition thereof. For this reason, I include here some examples of the treatment of concepts to which some of the aphorisms refer. Some of these excerpts (Space; Movement; Time; the Self; Nature of Reality) are taken from the Diario di un Fisiologo del Cuore (Diary of a Physiologist of the Heart) where these concepts are elaborated in more detail. Others (Relation among Time, Space and Movement; Art; God) have been developed at a later date.

These are only isolated examples, but, if nothing else, they can be useful to catch a glimpse of the philosophical background that is at the basis of the aphorisms. Those from the Diary are presented only in English, since the Italian text is available in the Diary. Please note that I have made minor modifications to avoid repetitions or improve the understanding of a concept, but the substance of the translation is the same as that of the original Italian text. The essays written after the publication of the Diary are presented in Italian and English.

BRANI SCELTI
SU ALCUNI SOGGETTI

SELECTED EXCERPTS
ON A FEW TOPICS

6 February 1991
SPACE
Our reality is three dimensional and therefore is placed in space. This raises the question as to *what space is*.

Physical basis of space
From a physical point of view, the place occupied by a molecule can not be occupied by another one. So that, if there is an aggregate of molecules (forming a body), these molecules must occupy a certain space that is not available for other bodies. Space then is generally created by the presence of molecules of the same or different kind. Nevertheless, there can be space even when there are no molecules (as in a vacuum). Therefore, the mind concludes that space from a physical point of view becomes that which is occupied or could be occupied by molecules.

The mental characteristics of space
From the point of view of the mind, space is mainly the result of our ability of see. If we look around, we see some objects near and others distant (with respect to us). Therefore, we deduce that the objects are arranged in space [***actually, the objects are arranged in our visual field; better yet, the objects are arranged in the images perceived by our mind***] and occupy it. They have a certain dimension and position.

Dimensions. Space (large or small) has the dimensions that we attribute to it: space is big or small in relation to human dimensions. For example, a room of a house is considered small in comparison to a great hall of a royal palace; for us, a lizard is small and an elephant is large.

In addition, the size of space is relative to the dimensions to which a given Self is accustomed. Someone who lives in a cottage in the country finds enormous an eight story buildings that he sees in a town. In turn, the inhabitants of that town are amazed by the enormousness of the skyscrapers that they see in a metropolis. This shows that the concept of space is not an exception to the rule that *everything is measured with the meter of our dimensions, physical and mental.*

That dimensions depend on our perception of images is shown by the fact that the *same* object can be large or small. If an object occupies a small fraction of the visual field [and therefore of the image perceived by the mind], its image is small. This could be due to the fact that the object is indeed small (e.g., a tiny pin) or that is far away (e.g., a container ship at the horizon). On the basis of what I know about the relative physical size of objects, if I see at a distance a car which appears as small as a scale model,

I conclude that it is a real car (and not a scale model) and that it seems small because it is distant. This conclusion is confirmed by the fact that the objects near the car also appear small. The large space that separates me from the car and the other objects causes their images to be small on my retina (fovea). Of course, I conclude that a car is a scale model if it is near and small, while other objects have their usual dimensions.

Furthermore, *the dimension of the space that one perceives is a function of his visual field or of his visual acuity.* If the visual field becomes narrower, the space that can be perceived immediately decreases, although it suffices only to turn the head to see what could not be seen because of the narrowing of the visual field. If one is markedly myopic, not much space is perceived beyond a certain range. If astigmatism is present, the perceived space may be distorted.

If one closes his eyes or the light is switched off in a room without windows, the perception of objects disappears and with it the conventional space: it could be said that one only *sees* the darkness. Still, it is possible to perceive our body (for example, the position of our hands), since for that we do not need eyesight. If we fall asleep, space entirely disappears [we do not see anything, not even darkness], unless we dream.

Position. Space acquires for us concreteness also in other respects. *The position of things in space is a function of their position with respect to us.* We say that a thing is in front of us, or to the right or to the left, but clearly this is in relation not only to the position of the observer, but also to his orientation. If, while standing on the same spot, one turns around, what was to his left is now located to his right. If one lies on the floor, what was below him is now above him.

Mental basis of space

Physically, objects have a measurable size (e.g., in centimeters, meters, etc.) and the dimensions of objects in the same category vary within a relatively narrow range (for example, books, armchairs, bottles, pens, etc.). Usually, we take as "normal" size, the size of objects as perceived at close range, like that of the objects in a room or in the garage of our house.

However, it is not their absolute size that defines space. *Space is created by the perception (obligatory and not arbitrary) of different images according to the position of the objects with respect to us.* The same chair appears smaller at the end of a large hall than at the end of a small room. In a furnished room, we are aware that some objects are closer to us than others, not only because those nearer to us are perceived relatively bigger, but because they can mask part of the objects that are placed behind them.

The perception of the different dimensions of objects creates the perception of depth of field (that is, of space). Since more distant objects create a smaller image on the retina, the different dimensions of images tell us how large the space is between ourselves and the object that we perceive. It is for this reason that the same object (for example, a train) is small (in the perception of our mind) when it is far away from us. We know that the moon is far away, because its size is perceived as that of a soccer ball and yet we know that the measurable dimensions of the moon are enormously greater. Were the moon to shift to an orbit closer to earth, we would become aware of the smaller space between the moon and us by the increase in its perceived size.

However, if one were to change in suitable proportion the distance and the size of an object, one would be unable to perceive the change in space. If we were to look at a chair of an usual dimension near us and a large chair far away from us, they might appear of the same size if the larger chair is placed at a suitable distance. If the chairs were the **only** point of reference (e.g., seeing only the chairs through a narrow hole) it might be impossible for us to tell which chair is close and which is far away: we would be unable to determine their difference in size and to locate them in space (near or far away). Taking a picture would not help, because the images in the photos would be similar to those perceived directly by the retina: the pictures of the chairs would have the same size.

Perspective

The change in size of objects at a greater distance from us is the basis for perspective. Even for the same object, the perception of the dimensions of its parts varies with the distance from our eye. If a train is motionless in the station and we are near the locomotive, the cars appear to us gradually smaller as we move our glance toward the end of the train. It is for this reason that we say that the cars are more distant than the locomotive (from us and for us). If another person is near the end of the train, it is the locomotive that seems smaller than the cars: therefore, the locomotive is thought to be more distant (from him and for him).

The comprehension of the fact that space is created by the different dimensions of objects (in our mind) according to their distance with respect to the eye is the basis of the creation of space (through perspective) in painting. The perception of space (that is, of depth of field) is created by the painter on the flat surface of a painting, where all the painted objects are at the same distance from the viewer. The depth of field is created by painting the objects up front larger and those more distant gradually smaller.

Furthermore, perspective requires parts of the same object to have different dimensions in relation to the viewer: the part of an object that is nearer to the observer appears bigger. If a house presents itself to me at an angle, this angle appears to me bigger than the rest of the house. For painters then, perspective is the art of painting on a flat surface an object or a scene in the same way as the object or the original scene are commonly perceived by the eye, thereby simulating three dimensional space on a flat surface.

Perceiving structures

In this regard, it should be noted that on the retina objects at a different distance are recorded on the same plane. The objects then can be perceived by the mind as placed in space when their dimension and perspective (dimensions of parts of the same object) are different. The perception of space can be obtained when looking either at the original scene or at a painting on a flat surface (or at a photo).

The perception of space does not occur at the retina where the images are not recorded "in relief" but only in different dimensions: it occurs when the signals are deciphered centrally. It is centrally that it is decided that an automobile is distant on the basis that its image is small with respect to other objects that are near us. Naturally, the interpretation of where objects are located in space requires that perception be normal. If one has drunk too much wine and "sees double", he may not be able to locate with much precision the objects around himself.

Different means of perceiving space

As far as our body is concerned, we can monitor its position through internal receptors: at all times, we can determine whether we are sitting or lying down, prone or supine, and where our limbs are. Except, of course, when we lose consciousness, as in sleep, fainting or coma, again indicating the role of the mind in the perception of space.

The idea of space is also obtained from acoustic stimuli: if we hear the whistle of a train or the siren of a fire truck, we can determine whether the train or the truck are far away or close by.

Even the sense of smell can suggest space like when, walking in the street, one smells a fine scent (for example, that of "cacciucco" or of another fish soup) that becomes ever stronger as we approach the source and then decreases as we move further away. With closed eyes, we can locate things with the sense of touch.

However, it is clear that these (and other) forms of perception of space are by far inferior to that obtained with eyesight. This is why the space of a blind person is devoid of much content and is limited to the perceptions through other senses (e.g., tactile perception of the sidewalk by means of a walking stick).

Conclusions

From a physical point of view, space results from the fact that molecules forming an object have a certain volume and can not occupy the place of other molecules in the system of physical aggregates that we call bodies (a concept formulated by the mind). For the mind, space is the result of the fact that the mind perceives different objects in different places with respect to the Self and that the perception of the dimensions of a given object varies according to its distance from the receptor organ (the eye). Although the rays reflected by the various bodies are received on a flat surface (the fovea of the retina), the dimension and form (perspective) of objects perceived by the mind are a function of their distance from us.

We deduce from this that a space exists in which objects are differently located, some nearer to and others more distant from us. Necessarily, space (like time) depends on the mind in different respects: in its definition and comprehension, in its dimensions and in its perception. And in the final analysis, space depends on the mind in its essence, which resides in mental reality of our consciousness.

14 April 1990
MOVEMENT
If objects occupy a certain space, they can change their position. This raises the question as to what movement is.

The physical aspect: displacement
From a physical point of view, movement is the relative displacement of aggregates of molecules. Physically, movement requires that an object occupies successively different positions in space.

In general, this is permitted by the fact that the cohesion of the molecules of some aggregates (gasses and fluids) is not as strong as that of others (solids). In particular, the molecules of water and air are easily displaced by solid bodies. Displacement occurs also in a vacuum where there are no molecules to oppose the movement of a body that enters it.

That objects shift or can shift position can be experimentally demonstrated. For example, I can predict (and verify) that if I let an iron fall from the height of my head on one of my feet, I will feel pain for the very reason that the iron has moved from where I held it to where my foot is.

Displacement and perception of displacement
Naturally, objects that move in air or water are not aware that they are in movement. The same thing can be said of the wind or of the waves that break on a beach. *The physical phenomenon is present, but does not exist as such (that is as movement) if not for us who are aware of the displacement of bodies relative to one another.*

Only we perceive that objects move as when we see a car running in the street or a ball rolling on a tilted surface (or the iron falling on the foot.) But neither the car nor the ball would be able to determine whether they move or not, nor can they ask themselves the question. *For displacement to become movement, sense organs that register the displacement are needed as well as the perception by the mind of the related sensations.* [For example, there are volcanos in very distant planets that eject material to height of kilometers: that movement does not exist until someone demonstrate it. For that reason, that person becomes the discoverer of the volcano and of its eruption]. The fact is that the mind is the reference point without which there can not be movement. This raises the question of what is movement for the mind.

Forms of movement
For the mind, movement is a concept (or a notion) or it is the perception of displacement. If it is a concept (displacement of an object

with respect to another) or a <u>notion</u> (the earth turns on itself), the movement consists of the idea of what a displacement is: in the mind, concept and notion are static. If then a notion changes (the sun does not revolve around the earth), it is only to be replaced by another notion (the earth revolves around the sun), which in itself (as notion) is likewise static. What has changed is not the displacement (since sun and earth behave as always), but only what we think of the movement of sun and of earth.

Movement perceived by different senses

In contrast to concepts and notions, perceived movement consists of the fact that each of the perceived images is a little different from the preceding. The images that we perceive are different because either an object assumes a different relation with other objects or its dimensions become different with respect to those in the preceding images. In either case, the object is perceived in successive different positions in space.

Movement can also be perceived indirectly through other senses. If, in the dark, one leans his hand on a door and the latter opens, he knows that the door moves even if he does not see anything: he perceives the movement of his arm even in the dark. Similarly, if in the darkness of the night we hear the noise of footsteps and the noise becomes progressively stronger, we deduce that someone is drawing near. It is so because we know that the same noise increases in intensity as its origin becomes closer to the ear: to someone who is somewhat deaf we speak near his ear.

Generally, all stimuli grow in intensity as they approach their receptor. Thus, the image of an object increases in size, noise becomes louder, a scent stronger, a hot object hotter, pressure on the skin greater, and so forth. These are also perceptions of movement, but they are less precise than the visual one.

Stationary and changing images

In any case, here I deal with movement perceived as a change of images. Let us suppose that I am observing the wheel of a bicycle leaning against a tree and that successive perceptions of the wheel with respect to the tree are not different from the first perception. I conclude that the wheel does not move. If I observe a bicycle race, the wheel (or the bicycle, or the racer) shifts with respect to the trees or to the spectators, so that it is differently perceived: now I see the wheel at the level of the left knee of one spectator and soon after I see it at the level of the right knee of the same spectator. Then at the level of other spectators or of the next tree. Furthermore, the images of the wheel spokes are fused, because the spokes move rapidly. I conclude that the wheel is moving.

If the wheel becomes bigger than before, I conclude that it draws closer to me, and when it becomes smaller that it goes away from me. *The wheel draws near to or goes away from me because my mind is the reference point: it is only in the mind that the images change (or can change).*

Simulated movement

Exploiting this manner of perception, in drawings one seeks to give an impression of movement by representing multiple contours of an object, as we would perceive it were the object to move rapidly (for example, the hands of a pianist playing a rapid movement). Or by representing in successive sketches the object progressively bigger to give the impression that it draws near, or progressively smaller to give the converse impression.

If, in a station, we are in a train next to another train and suddenly the images out of the window move, we conclude that our train has started to move. But in reality, sometimes it is the train on the other track that is moving. We are confused by the fact that in both cases the images that we see change, because either our train or the other moves. Only when our window moves with respect to the platform of the station we know that it is our train that moves.

Similarly, if at night colored bulbs illuminate in sequence (as some Christmas decorations do), an illusion of movement along the string of bulbs is created because images appear in succession in different places with respect to background: yet, neither the colored bulbs (or their lights) nor the background move.

Deduced movement

Clearly, *movement exists only when someone perceives displacement* (that is, successive images of an object in successive positions). If on an uninhabited mountain a rock falls for two kilometers, but there is no one at that moment to see its fall, for whom has the rock fallen? Who can affirm it? That movement could be deduced only indirectly, if one knows that mountain well and the rock has a considerable bulk: only he could infer (seeing the new position of the rock) that the rock has moved.

If in one step or in successive steps, if pushed or spontaneously, if quickly or slowly, not even he would know. That is, of that movement he does not know anything: he deduces that it must have occurred because he remembers that rock in a higher position. The deduction is still based on the comparison between different images, between the image perceived of the rock in the new position and that preserved in the memory. If one is mistaken in what he remembers, then the movement might not have occurred at all.

[One could object that the movement of the rock might be recorded by a movie camera even if nobody is there, and then, later, one might watch the rock falling. Of course, if nobody watches the film, no one can affirm the movement of the rock. And watching the film, one does not see the rock falling, but a film of the rock falling: when, where and how might not be readily apparent. One sees not the movement, but a recording of it. In any case, even in the film, movement results from a comparison of images.]

Direction of movement

Not only movement consists of images that change in the mind of the perceiver, but the direction of movement is relative to the one perceiving it. When the images become bigger, I conclude that the object draws near (to me) and when the images become smaller that it goes away (from me). Now, in an absolute sense the object does shift position and I am aware of it, since the shift is perceived by means of images that change in dimensions or position. But the object in itself neither draws near nor moves away: it gets nearer or further away only with respect of the perceiver.

It is not even necessary that in order to draw nearer or go away an object should change the direction of displacement even for the same person. In fact, if I see someone who draws near at night in a deserted place and I grow fearful, I may start running so that the person (who perhaps is absorbed in his own worries and continues to walk at the same pace without being aware of anything) does not draw near anymore. On the contrary, he moves away (even if he continues to move exactly in the same direction as before) and his image becomes progressively smaller (for me).

Furthermore, if a car draws near to me, at the same time it moves away from someone who the car has just passed. The car at the same time draws near (me) and moves away (from the other person): in reality, the car simply shifts position and the displacement is perceived differently on the basis of the relative position of the visual stimulus (the car) and of the receptor (the eye of the observer). For the driver of the car, the car neither draws near nor moves away: simply it shifts position. Or if it draws near, it draws near to where he wants to go (so thinks the driver), even if he moves away from the pedestrian that observes him.

Speed of movement

If the images change rapidly, I conclude that the object moves quickly. But, *whether movement is considered fast or slow depends on the dimensions to which the perceiving mind is accustomed.* If the eye of the observer is accustomed to movements characterized by a slow change of images (for example, a farmer accustomed to see wagons drawn by oxen in the country), the movement of a car will appear uncommonly fast. Whereas for someone living in a city and accustomed to consider normal the speed of movement of cars, the movement of an airplane that takes off will appear particularly fast.

Movement as mental perception of physical displacement

Is movement then a purely mental phenomenon? The perception of the displacement and the awareness of movement are certainly and only mental. The question is whether movement exists outside of the perception of images on our part. As I said above, the relative displacement of objects exists, independently of our perceptions. This can be experimentally proven. If I stop suddenly in the middle of the street with closed eyes, I do not see the bus that draws near. But that the bus moves all the same even if I do not see it, I will learn after few seconds, unless the bus has good brakes. Therefore, objects shift position under different forces and often the force of gravity guarantees it.

But the real problem is not whether from a physical point of view objects shift position (they do), but rather of what movement consists and for whom. To start with, what movement consists of is a question and questions can be asked only by thinking entities. Therefore, for objects that shift position, movement does not exist, because this is a concept and objects do not have concepts.

The question then becomes what is the movement FOR US. Because it can happen that objects can shift position and we do not know anything about it; and they may not shift position while we believe that they move. This indicates that displacement and movement are two different things.

Movement with assumed or non-existent displacement

Here we return to the initial definition that movement is either perceived through the senses or is a mental notion or concept (that may or may not be correct). For example, if a stone strikes the head of somebody, there are all the indications (from pain to blood) that the stone has changed position coming in contact with the head with sufficient kinetic energy to do damage. But if no one has seen the stone move, we deal only with a deduction and not with a fact.

The deduction is generally correct, but it could also be mistaken: it could be that we did not see an obstacle because it was dark and we struck the head against the stone (that never changed position). Something has moved (either the stone or the head) but we do not know what was moving because we have not perceived the relative displacement of the objects in question.

Similarly, if in the dark of the night the whistle of a train becomes rapidly stronger, I know that a train is approaching. But this event could be easily simulated by increasing the intensity of the whistle without the train moving or even without the train being there at all. These are the "tricks" that are used in the theater or in film making, in which the movement is "created" by manipulating images (as the background that changes or the rising and falling of painted waves) and sounds (as progressively intensifying the sound of the trot of horses to suggest their drawing near).

These manipulations exploit that manner in which the displacement normally is perceived and their perception simulates the movement in our mind. They suggest a non-existing displacement through perceptions that commonly are associated with movement. In abnormal states of mind (as when a person has hallucinations), one perceives moving images without there being either external stimuli or shifts in position of objects. Here, the movement still consists of the fact that certain images (without sensory input) become different in our mind with respect to others (that also are not caused by sensory input).

We can decide if we perceive a stimulus from outside or from within the mind by means of proof (like, for example, stretching out a hand and perceiving the object that is shifting position). In this manner, we determine whether the perceptions originate from the stimulation of senses (like eye, ear or touch) by external stimuli or within the mind, "upstream" of the systems of reception of stimuli.

The danger of hallucinations consists in the fact that they simulate perceptions originating from real stimuli but in the absence of such stimuli. Thus, to avoid a train that does not exist, one can fall in a precipice that does exist.

Displacement, obligatoriness of perceptions and movement

If movement exists only as perception of different images of the same object, the images are not arbitrary (unless one is mentally sick or has hallucinations). *They are successively different for an object that shifts position because the object moves with respect to us.* But it is we (and not the object) who are aware that the object moves and that it moves because it shifts position with respect to us. If an object shifts with respect to another object and we do not see either one, for whom does movement exist?

Measuring movement

It is true that is possible to obtain objective proof of displacement and regulate it. For example, it is possible to determine that a car moves at 90 kilometers per hour by looking at the speedometer, or to continuously record the speed of any vehicle. That the car moves quickly can be seen from the rapidity with which the images from outside the window change or from the position of the hand on the speedometer.

Of the changing images, I have already written. About the speedometer, one could mention that if it does not function well (that too happens) the speed that it indicates has no meaning. Furthermore, what the speedometer indicates could have no meaning because it could be simulated. In motion pictures, in order to suggest an increasing speed and make people shiver with excitement, they show the hand of the speedometer progressively increasing, whereas in reality the car could be standing still. In any case, the speedometer is not the movement, but a measure of it.

The difference is seen clearly in the case, for example, that the car is still and the speedometer registers 90 kilometers per hour only because it is broken. But even when it works, the speedometer hand may be standing still on the number 90 (the kilometers per hour) while the automobile moves rapidly. Furthermore, the speedometer must be perceived by the mind, recognized as a speedometer, and interpreted correctly (kilometers or miles and not another unity of measure) to have any meaning.

Displacement with assumed or non-existing movement

It could be objected: the earth turns even if we do not perceive its displacement. The answer is that *the earth turns (displacement), but because we move at the same speed of every other object on earth, there is no movement relative to us.* Therefore, the revolving of the earth around itself is not perceived and is a notion learned in school. If they did not teach this to us, we would not believe it. [Similarly, a person traveling in a space craft at an enormous speed may not perceive the movement of the space craft at all, whereas he perceives the movement of the objects within the spacecraft because their images vary in his mind].

For centuries, the entire humanity believed that the sun revolved around the earth (causing day and night) and not the contrary. This because the images of the sun move with respect to us. Because the image of the sun appears in the morning at the horizon, during the day in the middle of the sky and in the evening at the other side of the horizon, it is deduced that the sun revolves around the earth. In reality, the deduction should be made that the sun turns with respect to us, given that its different positions are perceived by us, not by the earth. [Of course, this follows from the fact that movement consists in the perception of successively different images by our mind].

If today we know otherwise, it is not because the sequence of the images has changed or the illusion of the movement of the sun is not there any longer, but because scientific investigations prove that the earth turns on itself and around the sun.

But the movement of the earth for us consists of what we read in books about the movement of the earth. Where this is not taught, people still believe that the sun turns around the earth. Therefore, the movement of the earth exists not as perception, but as a concept that we learned and in which we believe on the basis of indirect proof (that is, that does not come immediately from the senses).

Nay, we say that the earth turns around itself in spite of our perceptions. We say it only because we realize that we can not see the displacement of the earth around itself since we move in unison with the rest of earthly things. In addition, we believe that the movement of the sun is only apparent on the basis of scientific observations. If we know that a non-perceived movement exists, it is through indirect proof. Therefore, the non-perceived movement consists of a mental notion that we assimilate to that concept of movement that we have developed through direct perception.

Even if displacement of objects can be perceived, still movement does not exist for a non-perceiving mind: because of its nature, movement requires consciousness. If we are asleep, no movement exists even if there is displacement, including that of our own body.

We know through experience and experimentation that bodies can shift position with respect to one another. But if we do not see the displacement (or we see only its result) for us there is no movement, even if we deduce that there has been movement (and we could be mistaken). *If there is no movement for a perceiving entity capable of appreciating its existence, it is certainly not there for inanimate structures.*

Characterization of movement by different changes in images

In each case, movement is deduced on the basis of our experience. We say that a body moves when the dimension of an object changes (it becomes bigger or smaller) or its image (even if of the same dimension) shifts in relation to the image of other objects. Or when all objects of an image change simultaneously and in the same fixed relation: then, I know that I am the one who moves.

If I draw near, objects before me become gradually bigger and objects at the periphery of the visual field gradually disappear. If an object changes dimensions with respect to others that do not change, I deduce that only that object moves (for example, a train that draws near). If the dimension of an object does not change, but its position shifts with respect to other objects, I conclude that it shifts on a direction parallel to my retina.

Essential role of changes in images in the perception of movement

The dimensions of a train do not change when it moves and therefore in absolute terms the train moves unaltered in its dimensions with respect to other objects. But neither the train nor any other object are aware that the train moves: they neither receive nor perceive changing images.

Movement consists in the perception by the mind of images showing shifting positions of an object with respect to us. *For the sensation of displacement it is necessary that there is a suitable receptor and for its perception a structure that appreciates the meaning of the change in the stimuli.* It is for this reason that inanimate objects shift position, but they do not perceive movement: they do not know that they move because they are incapable of perceiving movement.

To become aware of movement, it is necessary to become aware of the peculiarities that are associated with displacement (like modifications of the size of images or of the relation among images). If the images of a train that move were to be perceived unaltered, for us it would be impossible to conclude that the train is in movement. In fact, if a far away train moves at a slow speed because of work on the tracks, we may be convinced that the train is standing still.

If a balloon in the sky were moving away from us and at the same time were to be inflated to suitably larger dimensions, it might be impossible for us to determine whether the balloon is moving away. Reciprocally, if a large balloon approaching us were to be suitably deflated so that the size of its imagine on the retina (and in the mind) were to be unchanging, we would conclude that the balloon is stationary. Therefore, movement starts to exist when the images change dimension on the retina and these images are perceived in a certain manner (progressively bigger or smaller) by the mind.

The perceiving mind could be that of a cow that lifts its head from the pasture to look at the train that passes by, but still a mind. The difference as far as the cow is concerned is that the perceived movement probably has simpler connotations: is unlikely that the cow considers whether the movement of a train is more rapid than that of another train, or what the nature of movement is.

It is for these characteristics that there can be displacement and not be perceived (therefore not becoming movement) and perception of movement with no displacement of objects.

Misjudged movement

If it is true that movement is perceived as displacement of objects, the displacement exists outside the mind. Movement exists exclusively in our mind, but the mind perceives a phenomenon (displacement of an object) that does not originate in the mind. There is nothing arbitrary or subjective in the perception of movement. If I see a car drawing near, it is because in fact it draws near to me. It is simple to prove that: it suffices to step into the street in front of the approaching car.

Displacement exists as movement when it is perceived and it exists correctly when it is perceived correctly. This is demonstrated by the fact that one can step into the street and be run over by a car if one has drunk too much alcohol, or if he is completely absorbed mentally and is not aware that the car is drawing near, or if he is in a great hurry that drives him to underestimate the speed of displacement of the car.

The car changes position in any case, but either I am not aware that it moves or I incorrectly assess its displacement. But images are not perceived independently of stimuli that originate outside the mind. This is demonstrated by the possible occurrence of an accident or by objective proof of displacement (like measurements with instruments).

Even more importantly, if in our mind movement consists only of images that become different, there must be something that originates the images and something that explains how the images change when there is movement.

The physical basis of the changes in images due to displacement

The awareness that images change is exclusively mental, but we know that it has a physical basis. If an object draws near, it occupies a bigger section of the visual field. The image of a car at a distance of one kilometer occupies a small fraction of the visual field that includes many other objects (street, houses, street-lamps, people, etc.) and the car is seen as small as a toy. If the car draws near, the image becomes larger with respect to other things, because (even if the dimensions of the car are unaffected) *the image occupies a bigger fraction of the visual field.* When it arrives in front of me, the image may occupy all my visual field and I may see only the car.

This is the basis of the our perceiving progressively bigger images. *This is not a subjective phenomenon, because if we take photos of the car as it draws near, exactly the same result is obtained.* The car occupies a gradually bigger fraction of the surface of the photographic film as it draws near. If we move together with the object, the dimension of its image on the retina (and on a photographic film) remains the same and we do not perceive movement if we only see that object.

If I am on a station platform, I see the train that arrives, but if I am on the train and I look at the photo of cultural interest placed above the seats in front of me, nothing moves, even if the train moves at 120 kilometers/hour (and with it my eyes and the photos in front of me). The photos do not move (in relation to me), because their distance from my eyes is fixed and therefore the size of their image does not change. If I stand up to go in the corridor, I perceive movement with respect to the photos, but only at the speed at which I displace myself.

Even if I do not look out of the window and I keep my eyes shut, I can figure that the train moves. But this is a notion as any other one (such as 2 + 2 = 4 or that Budapest is the capital of Hungary) which has nothing to do with movement. The notion is abstract in the sense that I know from past experience that trains move (I saw them moving either by seeing them pass in a station or looking out of the window).

I may know that the train moves from the noise of the wheels, the jolting or the whistle of the train, but these are indirect signs that can be simulated (they are simulated in motion pictures) without the train moving. But if it is night and the car is well-sprung, the signs (direct: changing images; and indirect: noise and springing) are missing so that I do not know whether the train is moving or not (another example of displacement with no perceived movement), to the point that I need to look outside the window to ascertain it.

Conclusions

Movement of objects exists only for perceiving minds and consists us either in an immediate perception with well defined characteristics or in a static mental notion (both being conditioned by the peculiarities of our mind).

Generally, movement is the perception of displacement and, as a perception, it can only be purely mental. If there is no perception of displacement there is no movement (except possibly as a notion) even if displacement is there. But the fact that movement is perceived implies that there is something to be perceived. The perception is not arbitrary because the images are evoked by external stimuli and are not created by the mind independently of the stimuli. In addition, when the images become progressively bigger (which is correctly interpreted as the drawing near to us of an object), the object does not become bigger, but it does become closer: only its image grows in size on the retina because of the diminishing distance of the object from us. But the image (for example, of a train) increases in size in relation to a static receptor (the eye of someone standing still) and not for a pole along the rail tracks.

It has also to be considered that *in the mind images do not move: instead, they become different. The perception of movement does not imply that there is a movement in the mind, only a sequence of different images.* Similarly, the perception of sound does not imply the existence of a noise in the cells that perceive sound. And so on and so forth for the perceptions of other senses.

2 February 1991

TIME

The nature of Time

The sequence of things is not instantaneous. If we go on foot to buy the newspaper, we need a certain time. If we go by bicycle, we need less time, and by car even less. If we move more rapidly, we do it in less time. Therefore, if the distance does not change, Time is the variable that measures the speed of the movement of things. But if we read the newspaper sitting on an armchair, the movement is zero and the Time passes all the same. Then, *in what Time consists? What passes?*

Time and consciousness

Here we need to consider in what consists the difference between Time and the consciousness of Time. It would seem that time passes even if we are not aware of it, but if we are never aware of it, the non-perceived time will never exist. If we realize that time must have passed, in such case time exists only in so far as we become aware that time must have passed and only as past time.

Lifting the eyes from the newspaper and looking at the clock, we may happen to say phrases like: "What? It is already eight o' clock?" In such a case, we compare the time that we believe has passed in our mind with that measured from the hands of the clock. If there is an apparent discrepancy between what we think the time is and that marked by the clock, we trust the clock. We conclude then that (for example) we read for two hours, that is to say in the mind the non-perceived time becomes an entity (a notion) of two hours.

The measurement of Time

This demonstrates that by experience we know that the mind, for most varied reasons, does not keep an accurate account of time. *The mind uses points of reference, like the clock or the light of the sun, because it knows that these change at a constant pace and therefore are an "objective" measure of the passing of the time.* In actuality, they are a measure of our transit on this earth or, if you will, of the flux of our perceptions and of our thoughts (which is the same thing).

Even so, the clock too is not necessarily always exact. If the clock marks eight but in reality it is seven, we believe the time that we read on the clock until we realize that the time was wrong. As for the light of the sun, looking out of the window we become aware that is dawn, or full day or night. When we see the sunset, we conclude that this day has also gone. In this case, the apparent motion of the sun gives us a measure of the passing of a certain time (a day).

The necessity of a perceiving mind

But it is us who conclude that another day has passed (that is, a series of events of our life or a certain period during which we have perceived the light of the sun). The day has passed *for us who have received and elaborated different messages in succession (a process that we call time)*, for us whose life is made of a finite number of days. We who are permitted to think a certain number of thoughts and feel a certain number of emotions, a process of which our life consists. The sun does not know if a day has passed, all the more so since for the sun the cycle of 24 hours does not exist: the sun always shines in an eternal "day" to which the confines of the night have not been imposed. Nor the day exists for the earth that, revolving continually, exposes gradually a new part of its surface to the sun without a point of departure or of arrival.

Dawn is what one sees at six o' clock of the morning in Viareggio [Italy] and at six o' clock in the morning (but six hours later) if he is in New York. For the earth (if it could be aware of it), dawn is always there, eternal, on some part of its surface, and it moves continually and gradually. For the earth, at the same time, the sundown is always there, eternal, on some part of his surface, and it move continually and gradually. In fact, if one were to fly in an airplane in the correct direction and at the necessary speed, he would see always and only the dawn (or always and only the sundown, or always and only any other hour of the day). But then, where does the "new" day start for the earth? This admitting that the earth can ask itself the question and elaborate a response. The day starts when and where someone sees dawn and therefore it starts at different times depending on the position on earth of the person who sees the dawn. And a new day simply does not exist if one happens to be on the north pole in a scientific expedition.

If the clock stops or if the earth were to stop, would we be disorientated in time? Apparently not, since also where the day lasts six months or there are no clocks, people are aware that time passes all the same and they eat or sleep when the time comes for eating or sleeping. These processes do not depend on the time, but on the necessities of metabolism and of recovery of the body. From this, we conclude that both the clock and the sun are points of reference that we use to "objectively" measure a sequence of events ("He arrived two hours ago", "It happened three days ago"). But, we perceive the passing of time also if what we use to measure it does not "function" (although then the evaluation of time becomes less precise).

In fact, *both the clock and the apparent movement of the sun do not measure anything: they only offer us images that change at constant speed and that can be read in a certain manner.* If on the clock the long hand is on 12 and the short on 6, we say that it is six o' clock (if PM or AM requires additional information). But the last to become aware that it is six o' clock or any other time is the very clock. The clock not only can not read what it marks, but does not have even the conception of time. And likewise for the sun. For them, yesterday, today, and tomorrow do not exist.

The Self and the past, present and future

We then return to the original question: what it is that passes? The answer can not be but: **we**. That is, the Self. The past is what the Self has lived, the present what the Self lives and the future what the Self will live. Or, *the past is what the mind remembers, the present what the mind perceives and the future that what mind anticipates. In this manner, the mind creates the Time and measures it.* For a baby who is born today, the time is all future, and for a person that in the same day has his ninetieth birthday time almost all past. Therefore, in the same day, time can be all to come or all gone according to the age of the individual, because so it is for the mind that conceives it. The mind, that like a meteor, dashes for a certain number of years on the earth, illuminating it.

But in reality the future is not what the Self will live and the past is not what the Self has lived. For the newborn not only does neither past nor future exist, but not even the present, because his immature mind still does not think and therefore it does not have yet either the conception or the perception of Time. If the ninety year old man is affected by loss of memory or by marked cerebral arteriosclerosis, the past does not exist any more (and sometimes not even the present, not to speak of the future). That is to say, Time (being a mental phenomenon) requires a mind that functions normally. Therefore, the past becomes what the Self remembers, the present what the Self experiences and the future what the Self anticipates. It is for this reason that time has no meaning for the newborn where the Self is not there yet and in the ninety year old person where the Self may not be there anymore.

Anticipation, perception and remembrance

Time is a creature of the mind and consists of the consciousness that anticipations of the future ("What is there for supper?") are realized in what we experience (eating the supper) to then become a memory ("The supper was good"). In other words, the passing of Time identifies with the characteristics of that which we think. If we anticipate something, that belongs to the future; if we perceive something, that belongs to the present;

and if we remember something, that belongs to the past. *It is this transition in the mind from anticipation, to perception and to remembering that constitutes the passing of Time.*

It is because of this that for us "tomorrow" inevitably will become "today" to then become "yesterday." Yet, here we are speaking exactly of the same day. It is not the day that changes, but his relation to the Self. Its relation to the Self changes because the Self can recognize the difference among things that are anticipated, perceived and remembered.

One can also confuse what he anticipates or remembers with what he perceives: if this happens occasionally, we say that he made a mistake; if continually, then we say that he is disorientated with regard to Time. The present is what the Self, in his voyage from the nothingness to the eternity, perceives in a given moment on this earth. Because anticipations become first perceptions and then memories, the present is the bridge that the future crosses to become the past.

Even if nothing changes in the external stimuli, the Self perceives that the same image is present in the mind <u>without change</u>. If the mind becomes aware that the image does not change, it becomes aware that Time passes since the fixity of the image is made of successive perceptions of the same stimuli. If the consciousness of successive perceptions is not there, Time does not pass unless the mind <u>later on</u> deduces it from other clues.

Accounting of Time

Therefore, *the Self conceives and measures Time according to the changes in the characteristics of its thoughts.* But the mind does not keep an accurate account of how its successive perceptions change. Often, we have to ask others what the exact date is. If one ends up in a desert island, he is forced to make incisions on a tree to keep track of the days that pass. If on that island he is delirious for a few days due to high fever, he loses the awareness of the passing of the days and those days (2 or 3 or 5?) will never exist. Generally, to measure Time we use objects that move over a fixed distance at a constant speed: the movement of these objects then becomes a measure of time. These objects can be the clock for the hours and the sun for the days.

But the clock is not Time and does not mark Time (otherwise Time would not pass for those who do not have a clock). Similarly, the light of the sun marks only the movement of the earth around itself and it does so because we perceive the light in cycles of 24 hours (but time also passes when the day lasts six months).

It is we who read Time in the movement of the clock and in that apparent of the sun, that is to say, we take them as a measure of the passing of our life. The sentence "Tempus fugit" inscribed on some clock does not have anything to do with the clock or his hands, that, in themselves, do not fly anywhere. What flies rapidly is not what the clock marks (which on the contrary moves at a constant and relatively slow speed): what flies is the Time of our mind, because our mind only lasts a certain number of years. Or rather *what flies is the relentlessly fleeting present that becomes past with the continuous change of our perceptions, so that there is a continuous transformation of perceptions into memories.*

But also what we use as a measure of time can change. Since there are different types of Selves with different traditions, the measure of Time can be done similarly, but with different points of reference. This is the basis of the different calendars: not a real difference in the sense that a given year is the same year for all, even if in one calendar that year is 1682 and in another is 2894. What we perceive is similar and therefore it make us participants of the same epoch. What is different is the point of reference which is a purely human choice. A choice based on subjective convictions, justified only by our ignorance of the date of birth of the earth (although in such case the number that identifies the years would be too large). If Time is calculated and measured in a mistaken manner (because of an imprecise knowledge of physical phenomena on which the measurement is based), the calendar then requires periodic retouches.

It is because Time is the transition in the characteristics of what we think that what for us now is the future (for example, the year 2000) it will be the past for those that will live in the year 2001 and beyond. As for us it is the "past" what was the "future" for the preceding generations.

Non-perceived Time

If the passing of time is based on the change of the nature of the thoughts of the Self, *there can not be time if there are no thoughts.* In such case a discrepancy is created between the time of our mind and, for example, the movement of the earth. If we sleep a long time, we are surprised that (when we wake up) it is "already" day. But even normally, when we wake up we need to look at the clock to learn how long we slept. If we sleep for two nights and two days in succession, we will never know that we slept two nights (instead of one) even looking at the clock, unless there are other points of reference like the date on the clock (if correct) or on the newspaper (if it not that of the previous day). A patient that awakens from coma does not know if one day has passed, or one month or one year or more.

We know that things continue also while we sleep (for example, the earth turns, digestion continues, the heart beats), but this continuation can not be defined "Time" in an objective sense. We know that things continue while we sleep (as we can easily verify in case of insomnia), but this is still a mental notion of ours. To avert voids in our accounting of Time, we introduce in the mind the notion of a period of time equal to that of our sleep. That period did not exist for us since we had no consciousness of it, nor for the earth nor for the bowel nor for the heart exactly for the same reason.

The period of sleep exists only as an instant thought that we have when we wake up (and we are conscious again). A thought that defines and measures the time passed as any other past event (for example: "Last night I sleep eight hours" and "I have been in Viareggio for a month"). When we wake up, we deduce from various clues that the time of which we have not had consciousness must have passed all the same. *The time passed while asleep is a thought of our mind when it is awake and it exists only there.* In fact, if the mind is not conscious of having slept for eight hours, that time does not exist unless it is demonstrated, like one needs to demonstrate the existence of a satellite of Jupiter. If the mind does not wake up from sleep because life has ceased, for that mind the time spent sleeping will never exist. Nor Time in general will exist anymore.

Aging, Time and Genetics

It could be objected that if one falls asleep when he is ten years old and wakes up when he is ninety years old, he has certainly aged. And in fact he grows old every day for those who take care of him (and think the future, present and past), but as far as the patient is concerned, Time does not pass at all: if he wakes up, he does not have the slightest idea of how long he has slept unless they tell it to him. And if they tell him, we deal not so much with Time as with a notion that concerns Time, like another notion can concern what happened to a cottage that one has on the mountains. In a such case, 80 years of sleep become a thought acquired in an instant. The realization that his body has aged tells the patient that he has slept a long time, but also this realization is but a thought acquired in a moment. A thought that does not change characteristics if the sleep has lasted 10, 20, 30, 40 or 50 years.

Aging is an approximate measure of the passing of Time (there are those who precociously grow old and the converse) but it *is not due to the passing of Time (that is, to a mental notion) but to genetics*. Thus, aging can take only hours for some kind of insect and certainly varies considerably from species to species. If anything, it is the contrary: aging tells us that a given organism must have lived a certain period of time, if we know what the normal life span of that species is. But if we do not know the life span of a species, aging does not tell us anything as to how long that organism has lived.

Variability in the flow of Time

But *also when we are awake there is not a continuous and uniform consciousness of Time*. In other words, we do not continuously classify things on the base of anticipation, perception and memory. Nor there are mental signals every second to account of the sequence of our mental activity. If the mind is not actively engaged by external stimuli is likely that Time passes more slowly.

It is for this reason that in a monotonous situation (stimuli that do not change), Time never passes. The images in the brain are "constant": there are no anticipations and what we perceive is too similar to what we have perceived. That is, missing is a tangible transfer from anticipation (that does no occur in a monotonous situation) to perception and from this to remembrance. Since perceptions are unchanging, there is no consciousness of a flow among things desired, perceived and saved in the memory. This is perhaps this basis of boredom of routine work (like for some bureaucrats, although naturally not for all). If there is an anticipation, it is that of going home at the end of the day of work and this anticipation (that never seems to come true) renders still slower the flow of Time in the mind.

On the contrary, if the mind is actively busy with a continuous flow of vivacious and pleasant external stimuli simply *"lives" (that is, it is occupied by a flow of sensations, not reflections) and "forgets Time" (that is, it is not aware of the change of the characteristics of its own thoughts).* The pleasant perceptions of the moment completely occupy the mind: in the midst of laughter, there is no room for, nor interest in, thinking. The consciousness of the past or of the anticipations is suspended. We do not care about past or future (or about what usually worries us). As a consequence, in the enjoyment and in the euphoria of a masked ball (especially if we drink excellent champagne), looking at the watch many wonder: "How is it possible that it already three o' clock in the morning?"

But also if the mind is absorbed in its own thoughts, the consciousness of Time is suspended. We do not perceive when we are absorbed in thinking. The consciousness of Time is resumed when outside stimuli are perceived ("It is already night") or thoughts resume again their temporal characteristics (for example, anticipation: "It might be a good idea to have supper"). This means that when the consciousness of Time is suspended, necessarily Time has periods of absolute "vacuum". These interruptions in Time can be deduced from indirect clues. In that case, they are perceived as interruptions (which is what is perceived of the time not perceived) by the mind now conscious of Time. If instead the interruptions are not perceived at all, then they are lost for ever. Therefore, *Time, being a mental phenomenon, it exists when there is the consciousness of it, direct (perception) or indirect (deduction from other clues)*.

Characteristics of Time

Since Time is the flowing of thoughts and is the product of the human mind, *the qualities that we attribute to time (long or short) are in relation to our structures.* It is agreed that a century is a long time because the life span of mankind in general is less. We say that a tortoise is slow because it needs more time than us for cover a certain distance. Or that a hare is fast for the opposite reason. If (as a consequence of some discovery) human life were to be prolonged to 1000 years, our conception of time (long or short) would be deeply altered.

Mental state and Time

Furthermore, *time depends on our mental state.* Since Time is a mental phenomenon, it is influenced by that which influences the function of the mind. If we are intensively waiting something for which we care much (like seeing again a person dear to us after months of absence), time never passes and looking at the watch we are surprised that the hands should move so slowly. This because we intensely (and impatiently) desire to see our anticipation become a perception. If we intensely fear a test, it seems to us that time on the one hand never passes and on the other that it passes inexorably (to the point that we fear the passing of time in itself). If one is happy or enjoys himself, he does not certainly count the minutes. Therefore, the state of our mind influences how we perceive Time.

Meaninglessness of Time outside the mind

By affirming that Time is a mental phenomenon I do not deny that there is an unfolding of things in space and that this unfolding takes a definite time (defined by us) also when we are not aware of it in our mind. Indeed, the earth turns around the sun and we know how to objectively measure both the distances covered and the number of days employed for a complete cycle. We know on the basis of scientific proof that the earth turns also when we sleep, but from the point of view of Time the earth would turn in vain if its movement were not perceived, measured and translated in thoughts with different characteristics.

If the human mind and his transitoriness were not there, what meaning would have days, months, years or centuries? For whom? What meaning does the first day of the year have on Mars? What meaning would past, present and future have without the point of reference of the Self? The earth would turn for nothing and for nobody, with the only exception of God. But above all it would turn outside Time. Only we, with all our limitations and faults, introduce Time on this beautiful earth in so far as we are rational and mortal, we the witnesses of God.

10 January 1991
THE SELF
The problem
If I walk in the street, I perceive the light of the sun, the color and smell of flowers, the music of a radio, the rhythmic movements of my legs, while my feelings determine my mood and my thoughts entertain my mind. These are physical and mental experiences that only I have and that make me a distinctive, nay, an unique human being. The same is true for each one of us.

If so then, *what is the Self?* To raise this question already requires the ability to think. An inanimate object does not ask this question (because it does not ask any question) and even less could it find an answer.

The role of the mind
The ability to think is already part of the response: the first essential ingredient of the Self is the mind. We observe the world and therefore also ourselves who are a part of the world. As we are aware that a street is wide or a bench is green, we are equally aware of the characteristics of our spirit and of our body. But the Self is not only the mind and its thoughts or the consciousness that we think.

The Self includes that of which each one of us is made. It has its own identity, because the characteristics of which it is made up are different and distinguishable for each individual. The characteristics of each Self include its thoughts, convictions, natural dispositions, emotions and body as they are perceived by the mind.

Speaking of a person, we can say that he is violent or tranquil, short or tall, active or passive, with brown or black eyes, etc. Likewise, each one recognizes in himself certain characteristics like being tall, fat, with a good culture, melancholy, indolent, fussy, muscular, energetic, etc., as the case may be.

The perception that we have of ourselves allows us to recognize ourselves even if the Self changes in its content (although not in its fundamental characteristics). This is so because the Self changes gradually as a function of the external environment (school, experiences, trips, contacts with people, readings, etc) or of the internal environment (the passing of time associated with growth, maturity and finally old age, as dictated by the laws of genetics).

The normal Self
To be normal, the Self requires a normal mind, because it is there that the perception of ourselves is formed and therefore the consciousness

of our being and of our individuality (that is to say the Self).

If one becomes mad, he completely loses his identity for himself (the altered Self does not have any more the ability to perceive himself in his new "version") and in part also for others ("I do not recognize him any more: he was such an acute man and now he is only like a vegetative relict"). Others recognize the physical part of that Self, but the individual in question not even that. This shows the role of the mind in the essence of the Self: in the mad person the Self is gone, and what survives of it is in the mind of others.

For normal people, clearly *the Self is the way the mind perceives itself and its body.* For example, one may believe to be handsome or particularly smart, even if for others he is neither. His Self is made up of his self-perception and therefore that is the Self. If there is a discrepancy in the perception of the Self by himself and by others, then the Self is different for his mind and for that of others: one may consider himself handsome and others may consider him just vain.

Conscious and subconscious components

It happens that each of us does a thing out of character, a thing that we would not expect from what we know of our own Self. A perfectly cold and self-controlled person may be surprised at having been moved and at having done something generous; and a generous person for having done something cold and calculating. It is possible that both say to themselves: "What happened to me?" or "I do not recognize myself" or "This is not me".

This happens because the Self knows itself, but in not depth. *We know only what we officially think and want to think of ourselves. In general, we confirm our Self by doing those things that are in accord with our idea of ourselves.* If we consider ourselves honest, we refuse to do a dishonest thing.

But *there exists a subconscious, that is a sphere of feelings, interests and tendencies that we want to ignore because they are different from or opposed to what we think of being* (or we desire to be) or to what we believe in. Without being conscious of it (but sometimes consciously), we suppress those feelings and tendencies that we do not approve of: we do not want them to be part of the official Self. We refuse to recognize them, but this does not mean that they cease to exist. Simply, what we want to ignore is transferred to other sectors of the brain where we efface (at least officially) their memory and therefore the consciousness that they exist.

Because we refuse to think about them, these tendencies take refuge in the subconscious, in that dark cellar of the mind in which rarely we descend to take a look. When we do that (by analyzing ourselves), there we see the things that we do not love (or that we fear) and that we have driven back there, piled up in disorder among indefinite shades in dark and sometimes frightening antra.

If these things are not "visible", it does not mean that they are inactive: seething in the background of the subconscious, they disturb the normal function of the mind. They often cause those psychic and emotional disorders (for example, anxious states) that go under the generic name of neuroses. In simpler cases, these hidden strains are expressed in nightmares. This happens probably because the inhibitory control of consciousness decreases during sleep. These disturbances sometimes cease when, through a psychiatric analysis, we become aware that they are related to the tensions caused by the suppression of a part of the Self.

The official Self

These hidden tendencies are in general (but not always) weaker than those which we recognize to be part of the own conscious Self. Therefore, it is relatively easy to officially refuse admitting their existence (even if in the long run we become aware that they exist inside us, confined to the "subconscious"). When and if we become aware that inside us there were tendencies, interests and feelings that did not reach the conscious mind and therefore were not consciously perceived and recognized as such, we realize that these tendencies, interests and feelings caused emotions of which we did not understand the origin.

In fact, it can be stated that *every tendency is present in everyone (but not with the same intensity), and some reject some tendencies and others reject other tendencies.* For this reason, one can be either honest or dishonest, but in general (whether the former or the latter) imperfectly so.

This is the same as saying that the Self consists of what we think of ourselves and of what we ignore of ourselves. Or, if one prefers, *the Self consists of what we want to think of ourselves and of what we want to ignore of ourselves.* This is the result of the fact that *we have a conception of our own Self dictated by what we would like to be and not by what we actually are.* Necessarily, if all tendencies are present in everyone, each one must suppress a part of himself to conform to what the strongest tendency imposes. But the fact that in each of us there are all the tendencies and that some prevail in characterizing the official Self is the result of our human nature and also of the education that we received.

When sudden or exceptional circumstances temporarily result in the loss of control of the dominant tendencies in the official Self, we react in an unexpected manner, dictated by the instinctive forces that are in us and are officially ignored under normal conditions. Through these unexpected reactions, we come to better know our Self, in that we catch a glimpse of the things that exist beyond the confines of what we believe characterize us.

The physical component

In normal individuals, *the Self includes the physical part of the body in so far as it is perceived by the mind and depending on how it is perceived by the mind.* We identify ourselves with what we perceive of ourselves, including our body.

We know that our body has certain characteristics and, if I see an image in a mirror, I can decide whether it is me or somebody else. In other words, I recognize myself: the image that I perceive is identical to one that I remember of myself. If they show me a photo taken at the time when I was in elementary school, pointing out a boy (if I recognize myself from certain physical characteristics), I say "This is me" (more exactly "This was me").

On the contrary, a savage who has never seen his image reflected on a mirror or on the surface of water, has a more limited perception of his Self. He knows some parts of himself (like his feet and his hands) but he has indirect data concerning his face. So that, if he shown a photo of his face he will say: "Who is this?"

Physiological conditioning factors

The Self changes continually according to the degree of development. It suffices to consider that in the embryo the Self can not be but in an embryonic state. In fact, until the new organism starts to think and therefore becomes conscious of himself through the experiences of the senses and first reasoning endeavors (and this requires years after birth), the new organism exists (as a Self) only for others.

Once the new organism becomes aware of itself, its Self grows a little every day. *The Self changes every day, not in his essential characteristics* (determined by genetics: aggressiveness, energy, timidity, etc), *but in his content* (and therefore in certain attitudes), *in his accessory characters* (such as in the manner of expressing himself resulting from education) *or in his external appearance* (because of the growth, maturation and involution).

It is only because each time the change affects only a small part of the Self and because change is relatively slow, that the identity of the Self is not threatened. Each day a few things, but not all, change. Furthermore, as things gradually change, they are incorporated in the Self (or abandoned by the Self), so that each additional new thing changes the Self relatively little. But if the Self is compared over a long stretch of time, the accumulated modifications can be considerable. The Self of an adolescent is deeply different from that of the same individual when he was a child.

The adolescent is different from a child in the attitude toward toys, in affections, in social relations, in his interests, in sports, in the consciousness of having a different body and different thoughts, etc. To the point that if a child were to remain unconscious for 4 or 5 years and he were to wake up as an adolescent, there would be so many differences that he would have problems in identifying his Self with that when he was a child. Also, such an adolescent would be more of a "child" (that is more immature) since during the years of unconsciousness he would have missed the experiences and the gradual changes induced by them.

Pathological conditioning factors

If the body decreases (e.g., due to an amputation) or becomes damaged (like the disfiguring of the face caused by an accident or a fire), our Self becomes deeply altered. The perception of the Self becomes so painful that life may be completely transformed or even be no longer desirable.

In addition, the Self is altered by *illnesses of the body (and more so of the mind)*. If there is hypothyroidism, the vivacity of ideation is reduced; if there is cerebral arteriosclerosis, several processes (from memory and attention to learning) are compromised; if there is diminution of the function of the adrenal cortex, a deep asthenia transforms an energetic person into an always tired one. Not to speak of such diseases as schizophrenia.

The influence of the bodily components on the Self is marked even without illnesses, since the Self is influenced by functional changes induced by a complex series of factors. If one is mentally exhausted for having worked too much, the Self is sad and discouraged; if one is in top shape, the Self is cheerful and exhilarated. This is to say that the physical and functional status of the brain influences the mind and therefore the way the mind perceives the Self.

Dependence on emotions

Extraordinary events of life can also change the Self not so much in its fundamental identity as in the values of which it is made up. Persons who had a big shock (like, for example, the loss of a very close relative) may see life in a different manner and attach a drastically different importance to things.

Not only, but if the lost person was an integral part of the Self (because that person was the object of much affection and intimately shared experiences), the Self can not but be mutilated. Or, rather, a single emotion, because of its intensity, predominates over the other activities of the mind to the point that it entirely occupies it and paralyzes other functions.

Environmental factors

The continuous relation with the environment changes the Self either because it increases its knowledge or because it changes its attitudes. The experience that is acquired with years can not but alter the Self: it would be without influence only if the Self did not learn anything. Instead, experience (for example) can decrease impetuosity or stubbornness and increase reflection and determination, or reduce a painful timidity.

Not by chance, one hears people saying that somebody with time has become more mature (mentally) or more balanced (or harder or stingier). In any case, there is a change in our way of thinking and in what we conceive our Self to be. Because the circle of things that one thinks and learns becomes wider, the Self and its perception of itself increases.

Genetic control

It must be added that *the control of genetics on the Self is such that the different internal and external factors alter the Self within the boundaries of the inherited structure.*

Generosity may be embittered and restrained by the ingratitude of others and meanness by the negative consequences of its own actions. But it is unlikely that a generous person becomes mean and a mean person becomes generous on the basis of their experiences. Instead, it is more likely that a generous person is confirmed in his beliefs when his behavior is appreciated and a mean person when his behavior appears justified by the behavior of others. What may change instead is the more flexible and skillful use of generosity and of meanness to protect them from external assaults. The Self maintains its fundamental characteristics altering only what could damage it.

The eventual decay

With the decline associated with old age, the Self gradually shrinks in all its aspects, from affections to knowledge, from memory to hopes, from energy to the interest toward the happenings that stir on the stage of the world, from the vigor of the body to that of the mind. Then, the diminishing conscious perception of the mind and body by the fading mind leads to the fading of the Self into a gradual nothingness. The separation from the things of the world and the gradual weakening of the Self is the prelude to the final departure.

Conclusions

The Self is the perception of the mind and body by the mind. With the passing of time, the Self progressively grows, mature by restructuring and then inevitably decays. The consciousness of the relentlessness of this cycle pushes the Self to realize itself in the time that is available to it.

19 April 1960
THE NATURE OF REALITY

The physical world and perception

The universe is without colors, sounds, odors, flavors, etc. This simple truth does not seem to be clear to everyone. But it is clear that, for example, the red light exists only in our brain [actually not even in the brain, only in the mind]: before reaching it, it is either a certain wavelength (or an equivalent physical phenomenon) that exercises a certain stimulus in the eye or an electric signal that propagates along the optic nerve, or the liberation of certain neuromediators. The wavelength of what will become a red light in our brain in itself is neither red nor green nor yellow, nor are so the action potentials that transmit the information in the optic nerves or the neurotrasmittors at the synapses.

The same considerations are valid for sounds: so much so that *frequencies that are too high or too low are not perceived by the ear and therefore do not exist for us (that is to say, that in an absolute sense do not exist as sound)*. This happens despite the fact that the nature of too high or too low frequency waves is not different from that of the waves that cause audible sounds. If one is completely deaf, he does not perceive even the wavelengths that normally are audible and the world becomes completely silent. Likewise *for the blind, the physical world becomes as it actually is, namely, dark and without light.*

Outside us, there are no eternal harmonies in musical terms, only the extraordinary harmony (i.e., order) that results from fixed laws that regulate the movement and the relations among enormous inanimate masses. But also this harmony can be appreciated only by something that is aware of it, i.e. our mind.

Stimuli and perceptions

Does then the world exist (with colors, sounds, odors, flavors, etc.) only in our mind? Certainly, *colors, sounds, odors and flavors exist only in our mind and therefore the world as we know it is created by the way we perceive it.* If all the brains were to become different, the world as we perceive it would become different.

Nevertheless, analyzing the mechanism of perception, we immediately realize that we can not create a chair only by thinking it, or make a green light become red. *Only when it is perceived, an object starts to exist, but the perception does not create the stimuli that become an object with particular characteristics in our mind.* These stimuli are independent from the mind and pre-exist to the perception. In fact, *we can only perceive what is already there at the moment of perception.*

Relation between physical world and perception

What then is the identity between the physical world and our perception of the physical world? There is no identity in this sense. A lighted bulb is neither hot nor bright nor fragile. It is a source of radiations, some visible and some invisible (including heat). Its brittleness is relative to those who perceive it (it is not fragile for an ant or for a butterfly). If the perceiver is blind, the bulb is only hot; if one has lost thermal sensitivity, the bulb is only bright; if one has lost the tactile sensitivity, the bulb does not have either consistency or form at the touch. If one has lost all three manners of perception, the bulb is nothing.

Similarities and differences in the reality of different minds

If the physical world is perceived by our brain as a different entity, does the physical world vary with each person, since it provides stimuli that are changed in different sensations and perceptions by different brains?

It does not vary substantially in the direct perceptions because the receiving structure (the human brain in the case in question) is extraordinarily similar (although not equal) in each person. For example, if a bulb is alight, it will be perceived bright and hot (although with different nuances) by all normally constituted observers. That part of the physical world (the world external to the mind) all persons come to know through sensations and perceptions initiated by stimuli that act on our receptors.

But not all of us similarly appreciate the external world, because, thanks to instruments that man develops, we know that things exist that we do not perceive with the senses. These instruments allow us of investigate and measure also what does not directly excite our receptors. *This experimentation considerably enlarges our knowledge of the physical world and increases the reality of those who study and investigate.*

Even so, the things that we do not perceive by means of our senses only exist if our mind becomes aware of them through proof obtained by means of special tools and procedures. These things exist not as direct perceptions, but as **concepts or notions** acquired through conclusions derived from experimental results. What our senses or our experiments still ignore does not exist if not in the general and non-specific category of our ignorance. *Even if we know that we do not know everything, what we still ignore does not have either face or identity.*

Communication between minds

The possibility of interchanging ideas, analogous notions, analogous perceptions is due to the analogous manner in which a stimulus is perceived by individual human brains and to the creation of agreed signals such as language and writing.

When the processes of perception, reflection and ideation are inferior to those statistically more common, the individual is deemed rough and ignorant. If these processes are superior to those statistically more common (even if they deviate from the norm), the individual is considered a genius. Is these processes are inferior to those statistically more common and in addition they deviate from the norm, the individual is considered mad. Because of this common property of deviating from the norm (in opposite directions), often genius and madness are viewed as being close (sometimes equally incomprehensible).

In effect, genius and madness are close in that they are at two extremities of an interrupted circle: between these two poles, along the circle, normality is interposed and rests.

20 April 1960
Reality and degree of knowledge
If the similarity in the structure and function of different brains allow a similar perception of the physical world by different individuals, *the very fact that the degree of knowledge varies from individual to individual means that the conception of the world has common general characteristics for all of us only in the more elementary aspects.* For example, for all of us the night is dark or the sun is bright or the mountains are tall. But for each of us, natural inclinations, education, degree of intellectual development, specialization, etc., give different relevance and meaning to things.

The world of each of us includes characteristics that we share with all and peculiarities that make our reality a highly personal reality. Hence derive on the one hand the uniformity that allows communicating among different individuals and on the other hand the diversity that results in personal opinions and ideas. What is personal in our conception of the world is still communicable to others, but it is recognized as personal and it may be accepted by some and not by others according to their conception of the world.

8 February 1991
Relation between the physical world and reality
There is a physical world that we know to exist in a certain manner. We do not know everything and, on the contrary, we still ignores much. But what we know tells us that in nature there are no light, sounds, odors, flavors, consistency, heat, etc. We know that instead there are atoms and

molecules (*with these words I mean here and elsewhere the different physical particles whose exact definition is not important in the present context*), wavelengths, oscillatory movements (regular or completely irregular), etc.

This means that there is no mental reality to compare with a physical reality. *The mental reality has well defined superior characteristics that do not exist in the physical world. The world as we know it through our senses is an unique and extraordinary reality of our mind that simply does not exist as such before having been perceived.*

We know that if we perceive a perfume or a melody there must be a source outside our mind. But outside our mind there are no perfumes or melodies: only oscillations of molecules or other physical phenomena.

[Outside the mind we would in vain look for what makes up much of our reality and most of that reality that matters for us. Only in the mind there are desires, hope, despair, creativity, pleasure, exhaustion, idealism, faith, beauty, illusions, love, hunger, anxiety, hatred, compassion, resignation, courage, hypocrisy, generosity, indifference, envy, equanimity, affection, etc.]

Obligatoriness of perceptions

We are aware that there exists a physical world external to the mind in the sense that the mind can not arbitrarily perceive what it wishes (even if sometimes someone does just that). If something is an automobile, the mind perceives it as an automobile. But if the mind does not perceive that particular aggregate of molecules, that aggregate will never become an automobile.

We know that in order to see something it is necessary that the rays of the sun reflected by the object strike the retina and that nervous impulses arrive to the brain. But *what we see is the result of our ability of transform stimuli in different perceptions*. Thus, we see an automobile red and another blue even if in reality physically they are neither red nor blue, but they only emit stimuli of different wavelengths. In these perceptions there is nothing arbitrary, but the perception of colors is the result of the ability of the mind of translating a certain wavelength into a certain color.

Physical reality and mental reality?

It follows that our reality not only is different from the physical world, but is a reality unique to the living organisms and in particular to man. *Our reality is the reality* and we in vain would look for a color or a sound in nature outside our mind (or the mind of certain animals). We would find only the physical bases of color or sound, but certainly neither color nor sound. [Similarly there are not objects in the physical world, only different aggregates of molecules that are perceived as different objects].

We can record the signals that are at the basis of color and sound in an "objective" way, for example the characteristics of a sound by means of an oscilloscope. But then the sound becomes a graphic oscillation of a certain frequency: this oscillation is mute, namely, it is not a sound. It is an image that we perceive with the eye, but that does not stimulate the structures of the ear.

The physical world in the absence of the mind

Since they are incapable of translating stimuli into sensations, perceptions and thoughts, a brush or a tree do not perceive nor appreciate a symphony, the aria of an opera, the grey-rose tint of dawn, the heat of the desert, the whiteness of the snow, the perfume of a flower, the gracefulness of a pup or the delicacy of a bud. These are things that exist only in human reality.

Furthermore, a brush or a tree do not even know that they do not perceive things that could be perceived. They do not know that there are things that they ignore, that is, they do not perceive and they do not reason. They have neither perceptions nor primordial thoughts and even less the ability of use primordial thoughts to create and derive others that bring to self-consciousness. This is so because things do not have receptors that can initiate impulses and a system capable of elaborating them.

Dichotomy of realities?

However, still *it would seem that there is a dichotomy between mental reality and the physical world*. One could grant that human reality is different and in many respects superior to a purely physical world. But in doing so, one still recognizes that there is the mind and the physical world external to the mind.

It is true that *in being aware that the mental reality perceives the physical world and transforms it, we have established already a fundamental relation between the two entities*. We have established that the physical world is the source of stimuli for a substantial part of the mental reality and that therefore the mental reality (although richer) depends on the physical world in many respects. But still it would be difficult to compare a physical entity outside the mind with one inside the mind.

But *this dichotomy does not exist because the comparison between the two entities can be made only in the mind and by the mind. From the* **cognitive** *point of view, also the physical world exist only in the mind. In fact, of the physical world we know only what we have learned with our* *mind and in this the physical world consists*. We investigate the physical world not only with our senses, but also with means independent of our senses (nobody has ever seen an electron or a molecule of glucose, and yet nobody doubts their existence). With the scientific method, we obtain proof about the physical nature of light or of sound, the composition of food, the nature of the heat, bonds among atomic particles, between molecules, etc.

This means that physical phenomena that are at the basis of light or sound or heat or odors become **concepts** that can be verified experimentally to ascertain their correctness. *With the discoveries of science, the physical world acquires a different reality in our mind*: for example, one has only to consider how in the Middle Age [or in many contemporary primitive societies] the physical world was not only smaller but also different (superstitions and beliefs).

The physical world grows quantitatively and qualitatively as the knowledge of the mind becomes larger and better, but it has no intrinsic reality outside the mind because it does not know itself. Molecules exist, but they do not know that they exist. Only the mind knows which is their role in the reality of the mind (they are at the origin of the perceived stimuli). *There are no two realities (mental and physical), but a [**human**] mental reality that recognizes that a physical world exists. The physical world does not recognize anything*.

[The human mind does not deny the existence of matter, because the mind can demonstrate the source of its perceptions and even what it can not directly perceive. In addition, the human mind discovers the laws that regulate the behavior of the physical world (e.g., gravity): there could be no physical laws, if matter did not exist. On the basis of these laws, mankind can (for example) launch spaceships that overcome the force of gravity.

However, what reality would have a symphony in the absence of the human mind? The written musical notes could be on a shelf of a library, unknown (and therefore unborn) for centuries. Even a recording would be useless in the absence of the human mind (rabbits or zebras would not be much interested).Notes and sounds in themselves do not make any music. A symphony is not a symphony even for a human mind, if it is a coarse one. The symphony can acquire the reality of a symphony only in the mind of listeners who can appreciate music. And it can be a beautiful reality only if it meets our aesthetic sense and its approval The fact of the matter is that *the reality of a symphony consists of human emotions, not of molecules of notes and vibrations of sounds*. Similarly, what a computer, a car, a table, a chair, a fork, a needle, etc. would be in the absence of a human mind? Only meaningless aggregates of molecules. However, even that is an overestimation: only the human mind can makes such a statement. If there were no human minds left, those object would not be meaningless aggregates of molecules: they would be nothing, except for the mind of God. The reality that would disappear would be the **human reality**.

This means that matter needs the human mind in order to be recognized as such, since matter is made of unthinking molecules. However, the unthinking molecules are not created by the mind: when objects made up of molecules are perceived, they are perceived not only according to the characteristics of the mind, but also according to their physical entity. One can perceive the red color of a rose only if one can perceive the red color, but that this does not mean that one can perceive a red carnation instead of the red rose.

From a more general point of view, it should not be forgotten that *when people speak of the mind they automatically refer to the **human** mind and its characteristics. Inevitably, everything is seen from the cornerstone of our humanity.* For us, the reality can be only the one that exists in **our** mind. Nevertheless, a zebra only too well knows that a lion is a lion, even if that particular lion is not being perceived by any human mind.]

The mind knows that it receives "obligatory" stimuli from the world external to the mind and that these stimuli are translated in perceptions and thoughts. But *physically being (without the consciousness of being) prevents the attainment of the stage of reality* [as far as our human mind is concerned]. Can we imagine two stones discussing their "reality"? *Reality is mental not only because our mind characterizes it in an unique fashion, but because reality needs the mind in order to exist, namely, it needs the capacity of thinking.* [We are because we think and feel and as long as we think and feel].

As to the "objective" knowledge of the physical world by the mind, not only it is impossible but would be useless if, to have only one reality, the molecules of things were to physically enter our brain: the very molecules of the brain do not enter our thoughts, even if they cause them. Therefore, even if the molecules of the physical world were to enter our brain, they still would not be in the mind nor they would acquire reality. On the contrary, they would destroy the mind, as it happens when an extraneous body (for example, the bullet of a pistol) enters the brain.

Brain, mind and reality

The very molecules of the brain are not the mind, but rather the mind is one of the functions of the brain. The essence of a thing consists of the fact that specific stimuli emanating from that thing are intercepted and interpreted by organs in charge of that function (receptors and brain). If through experimentation we learn more about that thing, its reality grows in the mind.

Under normal conditions, things enter the mind because the sensory organs explore the physical world and receive stimuli that are characteristic of things (and are perceived as form, consistence, color, temperature, etc.) through specialized receptors. These stimuli are transformed into sensations in a way that is characteristic of the different biological structures. These sensations coming from different sensory organs reach simultaneously the brain through separate paths (eye, ear, touch, etc.) And they are unified by the brain in the perception of given objects.

[If we are asleep, the aggregates of molecules, the sensory organs and the brain are still there, but in the absence of a perceiving or thinking mind the reality disappears. And if we dream, there is only the reality of the dreams. Of course, if we sleep, reality continues for other perceiving minds, although it is *their* reality, which is likely to different from ours.]

Relation between sensorial and non-sensorial perceptions

The concepts on the nature of the physical world that we have acquired through the senses can be compared with the concepts acquired through the experiment. We can then affirm that sounds exist inside us as sonorous sensations and perceptions, but they are initiated by vibrations originating from the physical world and acting on the ear.

That it is so is shown by the fact that if one becomes completely deaf, the physical world does not change, but the mental world becomes silent.[The physical phenomena (vibrations) are still there, but they cease to be stimuli because the receptor is no longer working.] From this point of view, the mental reality becomes like that of the physical world. In the process, the external world is revealed for what it is: without sounds. A conclusion that is reached only because in our mind it is clear what constitutes the mental reality, the physical world and their relation.

The physical world progressively changes, not necessarily in itself (although this too happens), but in our comprehension. Our knowledge of the physical world becomes ever more profound as we progress technically. Scientific progress allows us to explore unknown areas (like the depths of oceans or of space) or what is inaccessible to the senses.

Conclusions

The [human] mind creates a reality with unique (but not arbitrary) characteristics by perceiving in an unique manner stimuli that originate from outside the mind (both from its own body and from other bodies). In addition, the mind clarifies and transforms in mental notions the essence of the physical world and of its phenomena through the experiment. Finally, the mind establishes through which biological processes the physical world is perceived and transformed in mental reality.

In fact, we must realize that *the physical world does not exist for the physical world*. The sun and all the firmament are nothing for a table or a carpet. A table or a carpet are nothing for the sun and the firmament. And all these things are nothing for themselves: neither they perceive other objects nor they perceive themselves. Things do not ceases to exist as aggregates of molecules because they are not perceived: in fact, they can not be perceived unless they are already there. But if they are not perceived, they do not exist for anybody as objects with definite characteristics (form, color, consistence, fabric, etc). and they can not start to exist unless somebody perceives them.

This means that these inanimate things are there ready to be perceived as objects: each time a mind is created and develops sufficiently, these things acquire life according to the characteristics of the mind that perceives them. Furthermore, *their reality in the mind necessarily varies with the mind that perceives them*. The firmament certainly has different dimensions and meaning for an astronomer with respect to a lizard, but also with respect to a carpenter.

The converse consequence is that *reality ceases to exist when the mind ceases to exist or even to think*. If there were no minds any more, there could not be any mental reality any more. Nor there could be a physical world because there would not be anybody who can perceive it as such. Atoms and molecules would continue to be exactly as before, but which molecules there would be or how they would be aggregated would no more make any difference: a closet, a pencil, a computer or a withered branch would have the same meaning and the same use, that is none. The mind knows that these things would immediately cease to be objects (for want of a mind that so characterizes them) and with the time they would also cease being things due to the separation of the molecules.

But above all, without the mind the problem of reality and of physical world would no longer exist, because no longer there would someone who could raise the problem. So to speak, *without the mind things would be in a vacuum of reality*: the sun would rise each morning over the desert created by the absence of the mind. Empty would its glory be because there would not be anybody who could even recognize it as sun. In fact, without a mind, all its enormous energy would not produce even the light of a candle.

8 Maggio 1999

LA RELAZIONE TRA TEMPO, SPAZIO E MOVIMENTO

La necessità della coscienza

L'Io cosciente crea il presente. Il presente richiede che la mente sia cosciente, perché consiste nell'integrazione di un flusso di particolari sensazioni, percezioni, sentimenti, emozioni e pensieri. Il presente è fatto di percezioni che provengono dall'interno e dall'esterno e raggiungono la coscienza. Quello che proviene dall'interno è relativo ad un particolare Io, alla sua struttura mentale e alle sue precedenti vicende; e quello che proviene dall'esterno è relativo ad un particolare ambiente in cui l'Io si trova e crea lo Spazio.

Il ruolo del presente

Il presente è definito dal fatto che l'Io percepisce i vari stimoli e si percepisce. Nel presente, l'Io può non percepire il mondo fisico e invece ricordare (percepisce i ricordi) o anticipare (percepisce le anticipazioni). Siccome quello che si percepisce dall'interno e dall'esterno (e come lo si percepisce) è peculiare a ciascun individuo, il presente è unico per ciascun individuo, per quanto in genere viene vissuto senza essere definito. Ma *il presente è in continua evoluzione dal momento che l'influsso continuo di nuove percezioni interne ed esterne trasferisce quelle precedenti nella memoria (cioè nel passato), creando in questo processo il Tempo.*

La mente riferisce al presente simultaneamente non solo quello che percepisce, ricorda o anticipa (Tempo), ma anche la posizione degli oggetti (Spazio) ed il loro spostamento (Movimento). *Il Tempo, lo Spazio ed il Movimento hanno in comune la necessità che la mente sia cosciente e che si renda conto del modificarsi o meno delle particolari sensazioni, percezioni, sentimenti, emozioni e pensieri.* Se la mente non è cosciente (per es., sonno), Tempo, Spazio e Movimento cessano di esistere finché la mente non torna ad essere cosciente.

Somiglianze e differenze tra Tempo e Movimento

In particolare, la percezione delle immagini del mondo fisico da parte della mente creano lo Spazio e la successione di immagini differenti il Movimento. *Il Tempo è creato dalla coscienza del passaggio dal percepire al ricordare.* Pertanto, il Tempo è necessariamente legato al Movimento, dal momento che la percezione del Movimento comporta una successione continua di immagini differenti (le nuove percezioni trasferendo nel passato quelle precedenti).

Ma il Tempo esiste anche in assenza di Movimento di oggetti, in quanto sensazioni, percezioni, sentimenti, emozioni e pensieri vengono continuamente trasferiti dal presente al passato: *questo variare mentale ("Movimento interno") si verifica sempre anche se non vi è Movimento nello Spazio, perché la coscienza comporta necessariamente il fluire dei pensieri.* Se penso sdraiato su un sofà con gli occhi chiusi, mi rendo conto che il Tempo passa anche se tutto è stazionario, perché pensieri successivi vengono trasferiti dal presente (dove sono concepiti) al passato (dove sono ricordati). *Tuttavia, se sono assorbito nel pensare posso non essere cosciente del passare del tempo, finché non mi rendo conto che stavo pensando per un po'.*

Ma anche nel caso dell'assenza del Movimento esterno (oggetti stazionari), vi è la coscienza che le immagini non variano. *Per concludere che non vi è movimento di un oggetto bisogna comparare successive immagini di quell'oggetto e trovarle identiche.* Nel percepire inalterate le immagini ripetute di un oggetto stazionario, ci si rende conto che, anche se identiche, successive immagini vengono trasferite dalla percezione alla memoria, un processo di cui è fatto il Tempo. Anzi, *si può concludere che un oggetto è stazionario solo se si percepisce la sua immagine inalterata nel Tempo.* Se vediamo una persona per un breve istante (per es., dal finestrino di un treno che viaggia a forte velocità) non sappiamo se quella persona si muove o no, perché non abbiamo percepito altre immagini di quella persona con le quali comparare l'immagine percepita.

Più spesso, solo una parte degli oggetti percepiti è stazionaria. La coscienza che l'immagine di un oggetto persiste invariata (mentre altre percezioni simultaneamente variano, per es., il cadere di una foglia, l'abbaiare di un cane o la musica della radio) ci fa coscienti di che cosa è stazionario e di che cosa varia; e simultaneamente del passare del Tempo.

Pertanto, il Tempo comporta il trasferimento dalle percezioni alla memoria, purché si sia coscienti di quel trasferimento. Nel caso del Movimento nello Spazio, se un oggetto viene successivamente percepito in una differente posizione nello Spazio, si conclude che l'oggetto è in Movimento; se invece le successive percezioni sono identiche, si conclude che l'oggetto è stazionario.

Il Tempo è la coscienza che le immagini passano dall'essere percepite all'essere ricordate, il Movimento è la coscienza che le immagini successive non sono identiche e la mancanza di Movimento che le successive immagini sono inalterate. Ma sia il Movimento che la sua assenza sono legati al Tempo in quanto sia il Movimento che il Tempo richiedono che la mente sia cosciente del passaggio dalla percezione al ricordo.

*Il Movimento è la **coscienza** del variare delle immagini, perché in realtà si percepiscono immagini successive che (come per il Tempo) sono connesse solo dalla memoria.* Se un automobile si sposta dal punto A al punto B, quando percepisco l'immagine al punto B, l'immagine percepita al punto A non esiste più se non come ricordo: dal loro confronto nella mente nasce il Movimento. Se non si ricorda l'immagine dell'automobile al punto A, si sa che l'automobile è ferma al punto B (percezione spaziale), ma non si sa da dove si è spostata o perfino se si è spostata. *Il Tempo condivide col Movimento (o la sua mancanza) la necessità di comparare quello che si percepisce con quello che si ricorda. Non vi può essere né Tempo né Movimento se si dimentica immediatamente quello che si percepisce (o, nel Movimento, se non si percepisce quello che si ricorda).*

La percezione di immagini che si succedono si verifica sia nel Movimento che nel Tempo. Le immagini possono variare a velocità diversa, ma ancora Movimento e Tempo sono associati. Quanto più è veloce il movimento tanto più è veloce il trasferimento delle immagini dalla percezione al ricordo. In tutti e due i casi, semplicemente si ha coscienza che le immagini si succedono più rapidamente. Di fatto, la velocità è il rapporto tra distanza e tempo necessario a coprirla: se la distanza è costante, la velocità del movimento è una funzione inversa del tempo richiesto.

Se invece una percezione non varia (l'automobile rimane ferma al punto B), la coscienza che altre percezioni variano (ma non quella dell'automobile), mi fa concludere che l'automobile non si muove. Il Tempo passa perché sono cosciente del variare delle percezioni, interne (per es., posizione degli arti, pensieri, emozioni, ecc.) ed esterne (visive, auditive, tattili, termiche, ecc.). Ma sono anche cosciente che non vi è movimento di un particolare oggetto perché viene percepito inalterato: solo la frazione dell'immagine mentale relativa a quell'oggetto rimane inalterata.

Naturalmente, se giro lo sguardo su lunghi scaffali di libri, mi rendo conto che le immagini successive sono differenti non perché i libri si muovono, ma perché mia testa si muove. La mia conclusione è basata sul fatto che, se il libri si muovessero, percepirei gli *stessi* libri in posizioni successivamente diverse; invece, se giro la testa, percepisco immagini di libri *differenti* e allo stesso tempo il movimento del mio collo. Pertanto, si ha movimento quando le immagini cambiano sia perché l'oggetto percepito si muove (immagini diverse dello stesso oggetto) sia perché la struttura percepente si muove (immagini diverse di oggetti differenti). Questo è possibile perché il movimento è un fenomeno mentale.

La coscienza del variare delle percezioni consiste nel fatto che l'immagine percepita viene confrontata con le immagini precedenti che mi ricordo. Se non vi è coscienza del variare delle percezioni, perché non vi è nessuna percezione (per es., sonno o svenimento) non vi può essere né Spazio, né Movimento, né Tempo. Similmente, non vi può essere coscienza del Tempo (passato) o del Movimento se non ricordo più le percezioni immediatamente precedenti a quelle che ricevo (amnesia), per quanto posso ancora essere cosciente dello Spazio (che però non riconosco) ed avere (nuove) anticipazioni. Pertanto, **lo Spazio consiste della percezione di immagini, il Movimento nel confronto di successive immagini, e il Tempo nella transizione dalle anticipazioni alle percezioni e al ricordo.** Spazio e Movimento possono essere percepiti anche da altri sensi (per es., tatto), ma meno precisamente o comprensivamente.

Direzioni del Tempo e del Movimento

Dal punto di vista del Tempo, la successione delle immagini percepite ha una sola direzione (dal presente al passato, dalla percezione al ricordo) ed è irreversibile. Anche per il futuro, le immagini che si anticipano possono solo muoversi verso la percezione di fatto. I Movimenti (essendo la coscienza del modificarsi delle immagini nello Spazio) possono avere tutte le direzioni rispetto all'Io percepente. Tuttavia, come per il tempo, un dato movimento non è reversibile (eccetto quando la direzione della proiezione di un film viene invertita), dal momento che consiste in una determinata successione di immagini, una successione che non può cambiare: solo la direzione di movimenti successivi può essere invertita.

Per esempio, se vado da Viareggio a Lucca e torno il giorno dopo, il Movimento mi riporta al punto di partenza (ritorno alle immagini originarie, inversione della direzione del Movimento), ma né il giorno passato né il Movimento del viaggio d'andata ritornano più; né il movimento può cambiare direzione. Se il movimento percepito in una certa maniera e immagazzinato nella memoria potesse cambiare direzione, si diventerebbe completamente confusi. Per aver significato e utilità, la memoria deve essere una registrazione accurata di quello che successivamente si verifica nella mente.

Per quanto riguarda il Movimento, le immagini che si sono succedute in un certo ordine mentre andavo a Lucca, si presentano in ordine inverso quando ritorno a Viareggio. Il particolare ordine con cui le immagini si succedono (per es., il nome delle stazioni) mi rende cosciente della direzione del Movimento e pertanto se si tratta del viaggio di andata o di quello di ritorno. Ma è la direzione di **due** Movimenti (andata e ritorno) che è opposta, non la direzione dello stesso Movimento. Similmente, sia all'andata che al ritorno, il Tempo è creato dalla coscienza che le immagini percepite sono sostituite da altre (passaggio unidirezionale dal presente al passato), per quanto non necessariamente alla stessa velocità durante il viaggio d'andata e di ritorno.

Se il treno si ferma in una stazione intermedia per mezz'ora per ragioni tecniche, mi rendo conto che non c'è Movimento perché l'immagine del treno non cambia nello Spazio. Ma mi rendo conto che il Tempo passa lo stesso perché mi rendo conto che l'immagine che percepisco è uguale a quelle percepite prima (e mi aspetterei che dovessero cambiare se il treno si muovesse). Inoltre, mentre l'immagine del treno rimane invariata, altre cambiano (gente che si muove, o treni che transitano in un altri binari).

Se mi addormento sul treno, e mi sveglio a Lucca, ne deduco che deve esserci stato Movimento, dal momento che l'immagine che percepisco (stazione di Lucca) è differente da quello che avevo prima di addormentarmi (stazione di Viareggio). Mi rendo conto anche che deve essere passato del Tempo dal momento che il trasferimento da Viareggio a Lucca non può essere stato istantaneo: è questa una deduzione che confermo e quantifico guardando l'orologio della stazione di Lucca. Naturalmente, non so nulla del Movimento e del Tempo che non ho percepito mentre dormivo. Per esempio, non so che il treno si è fermato per mezz'ora o a quali stazioni intermedie si sia fermato o quando.

L'ordine nel Tempo: cronologia

Quale che sia la direzione del Movimento (cioè il particolare ordine con cui le immagini sono percepite dalla mente), *quel movimento viene inserito in un punto ben definito nella successione ordinata e irreversibile delle immagini che ricordo (e che chiamo passato, Tempo). Questo punto di inserzione è all'immediato passaggio dal presente (percezione) al passato (ricordo) e quel punto di inserzione si sposta sempre di più nel passato man mano che nuove percezioni vengono aggiunte alla memoria.* È in questa maniera che il passato acquista "profondità di campo" e si stabilisce nella mente la cronologia dei ricordi. È in questa maniera che "il tempo passa" man mano che le percezioni immagazzinate nella memoria retrocedono progressivamente, spinte implacabilmente dalle nuove percezioni, finché quelle più vecchie vengono sospinte nell'irrealtà dell'oblio. In questa maniera, si invecchia nella mente sotto il peso crescente di una sempre più lunga cronologia.

Il processo temporale è irreversibile, perché non si può trasferire un ricordo dal passato al presente o al futuro: si può rievocare un avvenimento (ricordo), ma non percepirlo di nuovo (sensazione). Non si può neanche modificare la sua inserzione in un particolare punto del passato (cioè della memoria) senza denaturare il Tempo e divenire disorientati alterandone l'ordine. Se si ritorna in un posto visitato nel passato, lo si percepisce di nuovo, ma non si riporta il passato (la prima visita) nel presente:

semplicemente si aggiunge al passato la nuova visita e si ricorda poi che si è visitato quel posto due volte.

Movimento percepito e Movimento ricordato

Bisogna qui distinguere tra Movimento percepito e Movimento ricordato. Il Movimento *percepito* richiede la coscienza del modificarsi delle immagini provenienti dallo Spazio: appartiene al presente, perché si ha coscienza del trasferimento delle immagini dalla percezione al ricordo. *Quando si confronta un'immagine percepita con le precedenti immagini che si ricordano, il Movimento è percepito perché il confronto tra le immagini è fatto nel presente.*

Invece, *il Movimento **ricordato** non è il confronto di successive immagini spaziali percepite, ma una nozione (per es., viaggio a Lucca) inserita in un punto particolare nella successione dei ricordi che costituisce il passato (Tempo).* Quello che si ricorda, può essere percepito solo come ricordo (dove la maggior parte dei dettagli sono spariti), e non come una vivida percezione attuale.

Naturalmente, *è necessario che gli avvenimenti siano ricordati nello stesso ordine in cui sono accaduti. La cronologia è il ricordarsi correttamente la successione degli eventi immagazzinati nella memoria.* È per questo che ritornando da Lucca a Viareggio, sono cosciente che ritorno alle immagini originarie, ma un giorno dopo. Il viaggio d'andata è inserito nella successione del Tempo nella mente in un certo punto delle cronologia personale e il viaggio di ritorno è inserito nei ricordi del giorno successivo.

Anche se il giorno dopo si ritorna alle immagini originarie (per es., la stazione di Viareggio), in realtà vi sono molti cambiamenti che fanno le immagini differenti da quelle originarie. Per es., il giorno dopo può essere più freddo, o piove, o sono stanco o arrivo più tardi di quando sono partito, o ho avuto esperienze diverse, ecc.

In altre parole, si ritorna allo stesso luogo fisicamente, ma non allo stesso punto della nostra vita mentale. *L'Io che ritorna allo stesso posto non è lo stesso: il che è come dire che non si ritorna neanche allo stesso posto dal momento che chi lo percepisce è cambiato.* Per essere lo stesso Io, la mente (e pertanto il Tempo) avrebbe dovuto fermarsi al giorno precedente: in tal caso, il viaggio non esisterebbe per noi. Ma se il viaggio non esistesse, non ci sarebbe nulla con cui comparare il posto e pertanto anche in questo caso non potremmo concludere che il posto è lo stesso: lo stesso di che cosa? Si deve aggiungere che un posto è tale quale ciascuna mente lo percepisce. Per questo, lo stesso posto non solo è differente per menti differenti, ma è differente anche per la stessa mente man mano che quella matura ed ha nuove esperienze.

Ma la mente non si ferma se non quando perde la coscienza (ma in tal caso non ha coscienza che si è fermata) . Se la mente ricorda quello che è accaduto in un certo giorno, è differente dalla mente del giorno prima, dal momento che il giorno precedente la mente non aveva ancora avuto esperienza di quello che ora ricorda. *L'esistenza dell'Io è resa possibile da quello che ordinatamente ricordiamo. Basta considerare le conseguenze di una perdita totale di memoria: si diventa estranei a se stessi e bisogna ricominciare da zero.*

La mente non solo esiste, ma cresce (diventando pertanto ancora più differente) come funzione dell'età, quando impara da quello di cui ha esperienza e che ricorda, e quando crea il nuovo. E decade quando si riduce nella sua capacità di aver esperienze, ragionare, ricordare, sentire e creare. In un giorno, l'Io può cambiare poco (per quanto non necessariamente), ma *ciascun giorno aggiungiamo le nostre esperienze (fisiche, mentali ed emotive) alla nostra mente*: in questo processo consiste in gran parte la vita.

Si percepisce il Movimento anche se si ha una debole memoria, ma, se la memoria è debole, più tardi sia il Movimento che il Tempo diventano incerti ("Sono andato a Lucca due o tre settimane fa? O non ci sono andato per nulla?"). Pertanto, il Movimento ricordato dipende interamente dalla memoria (e non più dalla percezione), e diventa una nozione che è integrata in quell'ordinata successione dei ricordi che chiamiamo Tempo.

Considerazioni simili si possono fare per quanto riguarda lo Spazio. Nella mia mente, posso evocare dalla memoria l'immagine della piazza di San Pietro a Roma (Spazio ricordato), ma mi rendo conto quanto il mio ricordo sia differente da una percezione reale (Spazio percepito).

La relazione con l'Io

Naturalmente, Spazio, Movimento e Tempo sono relativi all'Io: andare via o ritornare, andare forte o piano, andare a destra o a sinistra, su o giù, presto o tardi, ecc. hanno significato solo in relazione all'Io. Inoltre, le percezioni in tempi successivi non sono mai le stesse per la mente anche se quello che è percepito è assolutamente lo stesso, dal momento che le percezioni incessantemente e progressivamente diventano ricordi (e i ricordi sono differenti dalle percezioni).

Questa è in realtà la base del *panta rei*, nel senso che quello che cambia continuamente è la mente ed il suo contenuto. Un fiume non cambia come fiume da un'ora all'altra (le carte geografiche non sarebbero possibili), e anche l'acqua che vi scorre rimane acqua: è vero che le molecole d'acqua non sono le stesse, ma tutte sono fatte di H_2O e sono indistinguibili: è per questo che le singole molecole dell'acqua cambiano, ma l'acqua non cambia.

Ma certamente cambia il contenuto della mente dell'osservatore, nel senso che la mente passa dalla percezione del fiume al ricordo delle precedenti percezioni. Quello che la mente ha percepito prima non esiste se non come ricordo ed è differente da quello che percepisce al momento, nella stessa maniera in cui tutti i ricordi sono differenti dalle percezioni di fatto.

Pertanto, a rigore, non è che non mi posso bagnare due volte nello stesso fiume, ma che *l'Io che si bagna nel fiume due volte non è lo stesso Io*: la prima volta l'Io percepiva il fiume, e la seconda volta l'Io ricorda la precedente esperienza e pertanto riconosce il fiume che percepisce di nuovo. E la differenza nell'Io può essere considerevole se, per esempio, la prima volta l'Io ha rischiato di affogare.

Conclusioni

Quando una nuova mente umana percepisce il mondo fisico per la prima volta crea lo Spazio. Immediatamente, segue la creazione del Tempo nel senso che le immagini dello spazio passano dalla percezione al ricordo. Segue la creazione del Movimento quando le successive immagini dello stesso oggetto diventano differenti. Naturalmente, questi processi non sono istantanei, dal momento che dipendono dal grado di sviluppo della coscienza. Ma *in questa maniera una nuova (e differente) realtà umana è creata che si svilupperà con il maturare di quella mente, e alla fine scomparirà con quella.*

Per ciascuna mente, il Movimento è dunque il variare delle immagini dallo Spazio, variare che può esistere solo nel Tempo (passaggio delle immagini dalla percezione al ricordo). Si potrebbe anche dire che *lo Spazio è un cono di percezione che può essere di varie dimensioni (da una stanza al firmamento); il Tempo è la percezione **nel presente** di immagini (presente), di ricordi (passato) e di anticipazioni (futuro); il Movimento è la coscienza che l'immagine dell'oggetto che percepiamo diventa gradualmente differente da quelle che abbiamo percepita prima.*

Se si chiudono gli occhi, lo Spazio sparisce e si vede il nulla. Tuttavia, si possono ancora sentire, per esempio, gli uccelli che cantano ed il fruscio delle foglie. Questi suoni si sviluppano in sequenza e pertanto comportano successive percezioni che sono tipiche del Tempo. Se si chiudono anche gli orecchi, si sente il nulla. In tal caso, si presume che lo Spazio esista, ma non ha che i dettagli percepiti attraverso il tasto. Se non si tocca nulla, non rimangono che le percezioni dal proprio corpo. In tal caso, le percezioni diventano piuttosto simili: l'uniformità del nulla. Spazio, Tempo e Movimento diventano vuoti di contenuto e rimangono solo come concetti.

8 May 1999

RELATION AMONG TIME, SPACE AND MOVEMENT

The necessity of consciousness

The conscious Self creates the present. The present requires that the mind be conscious, because it consists in the integration of a flow of distinctive sensations, perceptions, feelings, emotions and thoughts. The present is made of perceptions that originate from inside and from outside of the mind and reach the consciousness. What originates from inside of the mind is relative to a particular Self, to its mental structure and to its previous vicissitudes; and what originates from outside is relative to a particular surrounding in which the Self happens to be and creates Space.

The role of the present

The present is defined by the fact that the Self perceives different stimuli and perceives itself. In the present, the Self may not perceive the physical world and instead it may remember (perceives the remembrances) or it may anticipate (perceives the anticipations). Because what one perceives from inside and outside (and the way one perceives it) is peculiar to each person, the present is unique for each person, although in general the present is lived without being defined. But *the present is in continuous evolution since the continuous inflow of new perceptions from inside and outside transfers the preceding perceptions in the memory (that is, to the past), creating in this process Time.*

The mind simultaneously refers to the present not only what it perceives, remembers or anticipates (Time), but also the position of the objects (Space) and their displacement (Movement). *Time, Space and Movement have in common the necessity that the mind be conscious and aware of whether or not there is a change in the particular sensations, perceptions, feelings, emotions and thoughts.* If the mind is not conscious (e.g., sleep), Time, Space and Movement stop existing until the mind becomes again conscious.

Similarities and differences between Time and Movement

In particular, the perception of the images from the physical world by the mind creates Space and the sequence of different images creates Movement. *Time is created by the consciousness of the passage from perceiving to remembering.* Therefore, Time is necessarily linked to Movement, since the perception of Movement involves a continuous sequence of different images (the new perceptions transferring to the past the preceding ones).

However, Time also exists in absence of Movement of objects, since sensations, perceptions, feelings, emotions and thoughts are continually transferred from the present to the past: *this mental change ("internal Movement") always occurs even if there is no Movement in Space, because consciousness necessarily involves a flow of thoughts.* If, recumbent on a couch, I think with the eyes closed, I can be aware that Time passes even if everything is motionless, because successive thoughts are transferred from the present (where they are conceived) to the past (where they are remembered). *However, if I am absorbed in thinking I may not be aware of the passing of time, until I realize that I have been thinking for a while.*

Even in the absence of external Movement (motionless objects), there is the consciousness that images do not change. *In order to conclude that there is no movement of an object, one needs to compare successive images of that object and conclude that they are identical.* In perceiving unaltered repeated images of a static object, we become aware that, even if identical, successive images are transferred from perception to memory, a process of which Time is made. Nay, *we can conclude that an object is static only if we perceive its image unaltered in Time.* If we see a person for a fleeting moment (e.g., from the window of a fast-travelling train) we do not know whether that person is moving or not, because we did not perceive other images of that person with which to compare the perceived image.

More often, only a part of the perceived objects are motionless. The consciousness that the image of an object persists unchanged (while other perceptions simultaneously change, e.g., the falling of a leave, the barking of a dog or the music of the radio) makes us conscious of what is stationary and of what changes; and simultaneously of the passing of Time.

Therefore, Time involves the transfer of perceptions to memory, as long as we are aware of that transfer. In the case of Movement in Space, if an object is successively perceived in different positions in space, we conclude that the object is in movement; if instead the successive perceptions are identical, we conclude that the object is static.

Time is the consciousness that the images change from being perceived to being remembered, Movement is the consciousness that successive images are not identical and the lack of Movement that the successive images are unaltered. However, both Movement and its absence are linked to Time in so far as both Movement and Time require that the mind be conscious of the transition from perception to memory.

*Movement is the **consciousness** that images change, because in reality we perceive successive images that (like for Time) are connected* *only by the memory.* If an automobile moves from the point A to point B, when I perceive the image at point B, the image perceived at point A does not exist anymore if not as a remembrance: from their comparison in the mind, Movement is born. If we do not remember the image of the automobile at the point A, we know that the automobile is standing at point B (spatial perception), but we do not know from where it has moved or even if it has moved. *Time shares with Movement (or its lack) the necessity of comparing what we perceive with what we remember. There can be neither Time nor Movement if one immediately forgets what he perceives (or, in Movement, one does not perceive what he remembers).*

Perception of successive images occurs both in Movement and Time. Images can change at a different pace, but still Movement and Time are linked. The faster the movement the speedier the transfer of images from perception to memory. In both cases, simply we are aware that images succeed each other more rapidly. Speed is the ratio of distance over the time necessary to cover it: if distance is constant, speed of movement is an inverse function of the time needed.

Instead, if a perception of an object does not change (the automobile remains motionless at point B), the consciousness that other perceptions change (but not that of the automobile) makes me conclude that the automobile does not move. Time passes because I am conscious of the changing of perceptions, internal (e.g., position of the limbs, thoughts, emotions, etc.) and external (visual, acoustic, tactile, thermal, etc.). But I am also conscious that there is no movement of a particular object because it is perceived unaltered: only that fraction of the mental image related to that object remains unaltered.

Of course, if I scan with my eyes long shelves of books, I realize that the successive images are different not because the books move, but because I move my head. My conclusion is based on the fact that, if the books were to move, I would perceive the *same* books in successive different positions; instead, if I turn my head, I perceive images of *different* books as well as the movement of my neck. Therefore, there is movement when the images become different either because the perceived object moves (different images of the same object) or the perceiving structure moves (different images of different objects). This is possible because movement is a mental phenomenon.

The consciousness of the changing of perceptions consists in the fact that the perceived image is compared with the preceding images that I remember. If there is no consciousness of the changing of perceptions because there are no perceptions (e.g., sleep or a fainting fit) there can not be Space, Movement or Time. Similarly, there can not be consciousness of

Time (past) or Movement if I do not remember any longer the perceptions immediately preceding that which I receive (amnesia), although I can still be conscious of Space (which however I do not recognize) and have (new) anticipations. Therefore, **Space consists in the perception of images, Movement in the comparison of successive images, and Time in the transition from anticipation to perception to remembrance.** Space and Movement can be perceived also by other senses (e.g., touch), but far less precisely or comprehensively.

Directions of Time and of Movement

From the point of view of Time, the sequence of images perceived has an only direction (from the present to the past, from perception to memory) and it is irreversible. Even for the future, the anticipated images move only toward the actual perception. Movements (being the consciousness of the change of the images in Space) can have all directions with respect to the perceiving Self. However, as for Time, *a given Movement is not reversible* (except when a film is shown in reverse) since it consists in the comparison of a given succession of perceived images, a succession that can not be changed. Only successive Movements can an opposite direction.

For example, if I go from Viareggio to Lucca and I return the following day, Movement again brings me to the point of departure (return to the original images, inversion of the direction of Movement), but neither the day already spent nor the movement of the trip to Lucca will ever return; nor the movement can change direction. If the movement perceived in a certain way and stored in the memory could change direction, we would become thoroughly confused. To have meaning and usefulness, memory must be an accurate record of successive mental events.

As far as Movement is concerned, the images that succeeded each other in a certain order while I went to Lucca present themselves in reverse order when I return to Viareggio. The particular order with which the images succeed each other (e.g., the name of the stations) make me conscious of the direction of Movement and therefore whether I am going or returning. But it is the direction of **two** Movements (two way trip) that is opposite, no the direction of the same Movement. Similarly, whether going or returning, Time is created by the consciousness that the images perceived are replaced by other (unidirectional passage from the present to the past), although not necessarily at the same speed during the two trips.

If the train stops in an intermediary station for half an hour for technical reasons, I am aware that there is no movement because the image of the train does not change in Space. But I am aware that Time passes all the same, because I am aware that the image that I perceive is the same as those perceived before (and I would expect that they should change if the train moved). Furthermore, while the image of the train remains unchanged, other images change (people that stir, or trains that transit in other tracks).

If I fall asleep in the train and I wake up in Lucca, I deduce that there must have been Movement, since the image that I perceive (station of Lucca) is different from the image that I had before falling asleep (station of Viareggio). I am also aware that some Time must have passed since the transfer from Viareggio to Lucca could not have been instantaneous: this is a deduction that I confirm and quantify by looking at the clocks of the station of Lucca.

Naturally, I do not know anything of the Movement and Time that I have not perceived while I sleep. For example, I do not know that the train stopped for half an hour or at which intermediate stations it stopped or when.

The order in Time: chronology

Whatever the direction of Movement (that is, the particular order with which the images are perceived by the mind), that *movement is inserted in a well defined point in the orderly and irreversible sequence of the images that I remember (and that I call past Time). This point of insertion is at the immediate passage from the present (perception) to the past (remembrance) and that point of insertion moves ever more in the past as new perceptions are added to the memory.* It is in this manner that the past acquires "depth of field" and the chronology of remembrances is established in the mind. It is in this manner that "time passes" as the perceptions stored in the memory recede further, relentlessly pushed by new ones, until the oldest ones are bumped off into the nothingness of oblivion. In this manner, we grow old in the mind under the increasing weight of an ever lengthening chronology.

The temporal process is irreversible, because a remembrance can not be transferred from the Past to the Present or the Future: we can recall an event (memory), but we can not again perceive it (sensation). We can not even alter its insertion in a particular point of the past (e.g., of the memory) without denaturing Time and becoming disoriented by modifying its order. If we return to a place that we visited in the past, we perceive it anew, but we do not transfer the Past (the first visit) into the Present: simply we add to the Past the new visit and then we remember that we visited that place twice.

Perceived Movement and remembered Movement

Here, we need to distinguish among perceived Movement and remembered Movement. The **perceived** Movement requires the consciousness of the changing of the images coming from outside: it belongs to the present, because one is aware of the transfer of the images from perception to memory. *When a perceived image is compared to the preceding images that we remember, Movement is perceived because the comparison between images is made in the present.*

Instead, *the* **remembered** *Movement is not the comparison of successive perceived spatial images, but a notion (e.g., trip to Lucca) inserted at a particular point in the sequence of the remembrances that constitutes the past (Time).* What we remember can be perceived only as a remembrance (where most details have disappeared), and not as vivid actual perception.

Naturally, *it is necessary that the events be remembered in the* **same** *order in which they occurred. Chronology is the correct recollection of the sequence of the events stored in the memory.* It is for this reason that returning from Lucca to Viareggio, I am conscious that I return to the original images, but a day after. The trip to Lucca is inserted in the sequence of Time in the mind at a certain point of the personal chronology and the return trip is inserted in the remembrances of the following day.

Even if the following day we return to the original images (e.g., the station of Viareggio), in reality there are a series of changes that make the images different from the original ones. E.g., the following day can be colder, or it rains, or I am tired or I arrive later than when I departed, or I had different experiences, etc.

In other words, we physically return to the same place, but not to the same point of our mental life. *The Self that returns to the same place is not (and can not) be the same: that is like saying that we do not even return to the same place since the perceiver (and therefore his perceptions) has changed.* To be the same Self, the mind (and therefore Time) should have stopped at the previous day: in such a case, the trip would not exist for us. But if the trip did not exist, there would be nothing with which to compare the place and therefore even in that case we could not conclude that it is the same: the same as what? It might be added that a place is what each mind perceives it to be. For this reason, the same place not only is different for different minds, but it is different also for the same mind as the latter matures and has new experiences.

The mind does not stop working unless it loses consciousness (but in that case, it is not conscious that it has stopped). If the mind remembers what has happened in a given day, it is different from the mind of the previous day, since the previous day the mind had not experienced yet what it now remembers. *The existence of the Self is made possible by what we remember in an orderly fashion. One needs only to consider the consequences of the total loss of memory: one becomes a stranger to himself and he has to start again from zero.* The mind not only exists, but grows (becoming therefore even more different) as a function of age, when it learns from what it experiences and remembers, and when it creates the new. And it decays when it shrinks in its ability to experience, reason, remember, feel and create. In one day, the Self may be little changed (although not necessarily so), but *each day we add our experiences (physical, mental and affective) to our mind: in that process largely consists our life.*

We perceive Movement also if we have a weak memory, but, if the memory is weak, later both Movement and Time becomes uncertain ("Did I go to Lucca two or three weeks ago? Or did I not go there at all?"). Therefore, the remembered Movement depends entirely on memory (and not longer from perception), and it becomes a notion that is integrated in that orderly sequence of the remembrances that we call Time.

Similar considerations can be made for Space. In my mind, I can evoke from memory the image of Saint Peter square in Rome (remembered Space), but I am aware how different my recollection is from an actual perception (perceived Space)

Relation to the Self

Naturally, Space, Movement and Time are relative to the Self: to go or return, to go fast or slow, to go to the right or left, up or down, sooner or later etc. have a meaning only in relation to the Self. Also, the perceptions at successive times are never the same for the mind even if what is perceived is absolutely the same, since the perceptions incessantly and progressively become remembrances (and remembrances are different from perceptions).

In reality, this is the basis for "panta rei", in the sense that what continually changes is the mind and its content. A river does not change as a river from one hour to the next (no map would be possible), and also the water that runs in the river remains water. It is true that the molecules of the running water are never the same, but all are made of H_2O and are indistinguishable: this is why even if the single molecules change the water does not.

But certainly the content of the mind of the observer changes, in the sense that, in observing the river, the mind goes from the perception of the river to the remembrance of the previous perceptions. What the mind has perceived before exists only as a remembrance and it is different from what it perceives at the moment, in the same manner in which all remembrances are different from the actual perceptions.

Therefore, strictly speaking, it is not that I can not step twice in the same river, but that *the Self that steps in the river twice is not the same Self:* the first time the Self perceived the river, and the second time the Self remembers the previous experience and perceives the river again. And the difference in the Self can be considerable if, for example, the first time the Self risked drowning

Conclusions

When a new human mind perceives the physical world for the first time, it creates Space. Immediately, the creation of Time follows, in the sense that the images of the space go from perception to remembrance. The creation of Movement follows when successive images of the same object become different. Naturally, these processes are not instantaneous, as they are related to the degree of development of consciousness. *But it is in this way that a new (and different) human reality is born that will develop with the maturing of that mind, and eventually it will disappear with it.*

For each mind, Movement is therefore the changing of images perceived from Space, changing that may exist only in Time (passage of images from perception to remembrance). One could also say that *Space is a cone of perception that may have different dimensions (from a room to the firmament); Time is the perception **in the present** of images (present), of remembrances (past) and of anticipations (future); Movement is the consciousness that the image of the object that we perceive becomes gradually different from those perceived before.*

If we shut our eyes, Space disappear and we see nothingness. Nevertheless, one can still hear, for example, the birds singing and the rustling of the leaves. These sounds develop sequentially and therefore involve successive perceptions that are typical of Time.

If we also close also the ears, we hear nothingness. In that case, space is assumed to exist, but it only has the details perceived through touch. If we do not touch anything, only the perceptions from our own body are left. In such a case, successive perceptions become rather similar: the uniformity of nothingness. Space, Time and Movement become empty of content and remain only as concepts.

20 Maggio 2000

L'ARTE

Il problema

Durante una visita ad un museo d'arte moderna, sono rimasto colpito dalla varietà delle opere presentate e più ancora dalla varietà delle opinioni dei visitatori. La cosa mi ha reso perplesso dal momento che la stessa opera non può essere allo stesso tempo bella e brutta. Per chiarirmi le idee, ho cominciato a domandare alla gente *che cosa sia l'arte.*

Solo conoscendo la risposta a questa domanda, si può sperare di essere in una posizione migliore per formarsi un'opinione motivata su opere artistiche. Purtroppo, la mia indagine non ha progredito molto, dal momento che spesso la risposta non era sufficientemente specifica da essere soddisfacente, o consisteva in un'espressione perplessa, una lunga pausa e poi un "Non lo so". Questa risposta non era del tutto sorprendente, dal momento che facevo quella domanda perché io stesso non sapevo la risposta. Così, spinto dal desiderio di saperne di più sull'arte, mi sono messo a rifletterci sopra. Non so quanto abbia progredito in questa mia analisi, ma desidero condividere le mie riflessioni con chi desidera leggerle.

Definizione dell'arte

L'arte consiste nella creazione della bellezza, qualunque sia il soggetto rappresentato o lo stile adottato. Per esempio, non la bruttezza, ma la rappresentazione della bruttezza deve essere bella. Reciprocamente, la rappresentazione della bellezza fisica può anche essere formale e leziosa, cioè brutta. *Ci sono quadri belli di persone brutte e quadri brutti di persone belle.* Naturalmente, la rappresentazione di un soggetto bello può essere brutta o perché l'artista non è bravo, o perché vuol esserlo adottando la stranezza del metodo come strumento di originalità.

Emozioni e bellezza

Indipendentemente dal soggetto scelto e dallo stile, *l'arte può provocare differenti emozioni* (pietà, esaltazione, tristezza, melanconia, abbandono, ecc.), *ma nel provare queste emozioni si deve necessariamente sentire allo stesso tempo un piacere estetico, cioè il piacere che la bellezza dà.* Per farlo, è necessario che la creazione sia bella. Se un opera non dà piacere estetico, o non è arte (l'opera non è bella) o l'osservatore non ha buon gusto.

*Come nella vita, l'arte può rappresentare il bene ed il male, il bello e il brutto, il morale e l'immorale, ecc., ma in maniera che noi troviamo bella, **indipendentemente dalla natura delle emozioni che il soggetto***

rappresentato suscita in noi quando considerato fuori del campo dell'arte.
Di quello che vede, l'artista sceglie quello che emozionalmente lo colpisce. Non ha importanza se tende a cogliere aspetti tristi della vita, come la povertà, il declino, la disperazione del fallimento, una rassegnazione cronica, l'abitudine al grigiore di una vita vinta, una vita che non ha mai cominciato a vivere, l'affondare progressivo nell'alcol, la depressione della disperazione, il digiuno degli affetti, la solitudine, una generale bruttezza ambientale, una morte insignificante dopo una vita insignificante, la mancanza di sogni, ecc.

Una rappresentazione magistrale della tristezza, tragedia, tradimento, povertà o crudeltà ci può rattristare, ma allo stesso tempo proviamo piacere nella bellezza che ci ha commosso. In un'opera che ci commuove fino alle lacrime, il piacere è tanto più grande quanto più siamo commossi, il piacere che dà la perfezione di un capolavoro. Si versano lacrime non di tristezza, ma di commozione per la bellezza della sua drammatica tristezza. In ultima analisi, *la bellezza di un'opera è proporzionale all'intensità delle emozioni che ci fa provare.* Di fatto, il contrasto tra tristezza e piacere estetico che si prova allo stesso tempo contribuisce al pathos di quello che proviamo. *Se l'artista coglie le emozioni con la sua arte, è la loro acutezza che dà un'anima alla creazione. È l'anima che dà la bellezza alla creazione.*

Se il trattamento dello stesso soggetto è assai mediocre (cioè non artistico), invece di essere commossi, siamo delusi e irritati dal fatto che non vi è bellezza nella musica, canto, recitazione, intreccio, o psicologia del comportamento, ecc. *Nell'arte, il fallimento è la mancanza di bellezza.*

Emozioni senza bellezza
Se non vi è bellezza senza emozione, vi possono essere emozioni senza bellezza. Se nella vita quotidiana si è esposti ad un evento triste (essendo quello solo triste e non bello), si prova solo tristezza. Se si assiste ad un serio incidente stradale o si vedono in televisione le devastazioni di un terremoto proviamo orrore, tristezza e compassione, ma certamente non piacere. In quello che si vede ci può essere una tragedia, ma non vi è bellezza. Anzi, viene spontaneo dire: "Che brutto incidente!". Si prova tristezza per la presenza di compassione; non proviamo piacere nell'essere tristi per mancanza di bellezza.

Se poi anche in un atto della vita quotidiana vi è bellezza (per es., uno sfortunato atto eroico), si prova tristezza per la sfortuna, ma anche il piacere che deriva da un bella azione. È possibile che Giulio Cesare abbia voluto una bella morte, una morte nobile e coraggiosa, degno coronamento di una vita straordinaria. Una morte che ponesse un tocco finale alla scenografia di una vita che aspirava ad una gloria eterna. Non bisogna dimenticare che Cesare era anche un grande scrittore, cioè un artista.

La creazione

Per definizione, *la creazione risulta in qualcosa che non esisteva prima: la creazione è sempre originale e unica.* Anche se un quadro od un libro si ispirano a oggetti e persone che esistono in natura, questi non rappresentano la realtà esterna, ma la realtà sviluppata dal modo di sentire, sensibilità, creatività, immaginazione e bravura dell'autore. Si può anche affermare che *ogni creazione è unica perché il suo creatore è unico.*

Questo spiega perché i quadri falsi hanno ben poco valore anche se copiati in maniera così perfetta che è difficile stabilire se si tratta di una falsificazione o di un originale. Persino una riproduzione dello stesso quadro da parte del suo autore avrebbe poco valore. Una copia (anche eccellente) è senza valore, perché non è una creazione, soltanto una copia di una creazione, un semplice duplicato.

Lo stesso concetto si applica al dipinto originale. Se un artista copia fedelmente la natura, la mancanza di originalità squalifica la sua opera: *le copie originali non esistono, neanche della natura.* Se l'artista copiasse la natura, ne farebbe una fotografia, invece di ricreare la natura secondo quello che la sua immaginazione, sensibilità, fantasia, e stile gli suggeriscono. <u>Se l'arte copiasse la natura, i lati negativi della vita non potrebbero mai sperare di essere rappresentati in maniera bella</u>: quello che mancherebbe sarebbe l'emozione umana che suscitano e che è riflessa nella bellezza della creazione. Similmente, la bellezza della natura verrebbe semplicemente duplicata senza poesia personale. *La natura spesso provvede lo stimolo per l'ispirazione, e l'artista traduce la sua ispirazione nell'espressione dei suoi sentimenti.* Similmente, se uno scrittore copiasse la natura, invece di un romanzo scriverebbe una cronaca.

Per lo stesso motivo, un ritratto può essere fedele, ma non può essere una fotografia. Il ritratto è una interpretazione soggettiva dell'artista, non una descrizione oggettiva di una persona. Cosa l'artista può creare, se non quello che è nella **sua** mente? *Un ritratto non è la riproduzione di come uno si crede di essere, ma la creazione di quello che l'artista vede e sente di quella persona.*

A questo riguardo, bisogna notare che questa non è una peculiarità dell'artista, ma una legge generale: *ciascuno di noi è una persona differente a seconda di chi lo percepisce.* Siamo differenti per gli altri, perché differenti persone hanno una percezione di noi diversa. La percezione è diversa qualitativamente e quantitativamente a seconda di quanto sanno di noi (per es., a causa di una continua vicinanza); e a seconda della loro finezza e capacità nel percepirci. Le persone più percettive si formano un ritratto degli altri assai più somigliante all'originale. In un certo senso, ciascuno di noi si forma nella sua mente un ritratto diverso di una data persona, per quanto generalmente non vi sia nulla di artistico. In alcuni casi, se abbiamo troppa fantasia, ci si forma nella mente il ritratto di una persona che non esiste, talmente il ritratto è differente dall'originale.

Nel fare un ritratto, l'artista è fortemente influenzato dalle esigenze estetiche del quadro, oltre che dalla fisionomia del soggetto da ritrarre. Quello che è considerato bello varia a seconda dell'artista e pertanto varia anche quello che l'artista sceglie di rappresentare e lo stile che usa.

Creazione e "soggetto originale"

Nel ritratto, l'artista vuol creare un quadro esteticamente coerente secondo la sua interpretazione, finezza psicologica, sensibilità, abilità e stile. *Il quadro vive di una vita propria (indipendentemente dal soggetto originale), precisamente perché non è una copia.* Col tempo, l'originale (che sia bello o brutto) cessa di essere, ed il quadro (se è bello) sopravvive. Per un artista, la cosa più importante è che il ritratto sia bello, indipendentemente da chi vi è ritratto. Lo sfondo può essere così importante come la carnagione del viso.

Per avere una vita propria, il ritratto deve avere un'anima, un'anima rivelata da come il corpo è ritratto (per esempio, l'acutezza della mente nella luce degli occhi, o la nobiltà dei tratti). *Il ritratto ci fa vedere la creatura dell'artista.*

Dal momento che lo scopo principale del ritratto è quello di essere artistico, nel quadro vi può essere una poesia, una nobiltà d'animo, una forza morale o una mente acuta che quella persona non ha mai avuto. È possibile attribuire alla persona ritratta queste e altre qualità perché certe caratteristiche della mente sono generalmente rivelate dall'espressione del viso e dal portamento di una persona. Pertanto, è possibile riconoscere in differenti persone la superbia, la bontà, la nobiltà dell'anima, l'umiltà, l'intelligenza, l'astuzia, la forza di carattere, la sicurezza che deriva dal potere, l'insignificanza, ecc. O per lo meno, certe espressioni fisiche corrispondono a certe qualità mentali: di qui, la possibilità che l'espressione nel dipinto suggerisca qualità che un individuo non possiede.

Certi ritratti vogliono essere l'apoteosi di un'istituzione piuttosto che di un individuo: il ritratto di un Re o di un Imperatore non può che essere magnifico, indipendentemente dalla mediocrità di chi ha ereditato il trono. In questo caso, è il soggetto stesso che non vuole essere ritratto come vede se stesso, ma come vuole che lo vedano gli altri. Nessun Re si farà mai ritrarre in vestaglia, col berretto da notte, e le ciabatte. Quello che è ritratto è "l'Io Ufficiale" (per una definizione di "Io Ufficiale", vedi l'aforisma 1035).

Se uno vuole un ritratto "fedele", deve rivolgersi ad un fotografo e non ad un pittore. E anche il fotografo professionale cercherà di fare una bella fotografia, dove, per esempio, il cranio calvo sparisce in una penombra discreta e la posa è eretta e piena di dignità.

La persona ritratta e chi la ritrae

Per quanto indirettamente, *il ritratto di una persona ritrae allo stesso tempo la personalità dell'artista*: non si tratta solo di un ritratto, ma di un ritratto fatto da quell'artista. Al punto che spesso ci si riferisce al ritratto col nome dell'artista (per esempio, un ritratto di Leonardo, intendendo un ritratto fatto da Leonardo, non un ritratto rappresentante Leonardo) piuttosto che col nome della persona che vi è ritratta.

Il fatto è che *quella persona l'ha fatta Dio e il suo ritratto l'ha fatto l'artista*. In questo senso, una persona provvede solo il soggetto per la creazione dell'artista. Il ritratto coglie e fissa per sempre uno stadio particolare (e transitorio) della vita fisica e mentale del soggetto quale la vede l'artista. Della Monna Lisa si vede solo quello che Leonardo ha dipinto: persino le sue ceneri sono sparite da gran tempo, per quanto Leonardo viva nelle nostre menti mediante le sue opere.

Per convincersi del fatto che il soggetto provvede solo la materia prima per la creazione artistica, basterebbe ordinare il ritratto della stessa persona a dieci artisti diversi. Ne risulterebbero non tanto dieci differenti ritratti della stessa persona, quanto il ritratto di dieci persone differenti. A questo riguardo, basta pensare alle differenze che vi sarebbero tra un ritratto fatto da Raffaello e quello fatto da Picasso. Ogni artista coglierebbe di quella persona le caratteristiche che lo interessano e le rappresenterebbe secondo le esigenze (o le pretese) del suo stile.

L'arte e la "verità"

Similmente, nella letteratura vicende e personaggi storici variano a seconda di chi le rievoca: ogni artista ha una sua "versione" che è reale in termini d'arte. È reale in quanto una creazione ha una sua propria vita, non storica ma artistica. Non si confronta un'opera con la vicenda storica originale, perché l'originale è solo lo spunto per l'artista. *Un artista crea, non descrive*. Romeo e Giulietta vivono il loro sogno d'amore nell'arte di Shakespeare: Romeo e Giulietta originali non si sarebbero riconosciuti in quel "ritratto". Si potrebbe anche dire che la vicenda storica e l'opera letteraria sono due creazioni parallele con scopi completamente differenti.

Una descrizione fedele di una vicenda storica è compito non di un artista, ma di uno storico. Uno storico deve descrivere gli eventi che si svolgono sulla scena del mondo con assoluta obiettività e esattezza. Tuttavia, se uno storico è molto bravo può farlo anche con arte usando il suo stile personale (conciso, pittoresco, ricco di sfumature psicologiche e di intuizioni, ecc.). Nell'interpretare motivi, interessi, aspirazioni, cospirazioni, eroismi, tradimenti, convinzioni, audacie, paure, ecc., un bravo storico può fare un ritratto pieno di stile, finezza e penetrante psicologia, non inferiore a quello di un bravo pittore.

L'acutezza della sua comprensione illumina gli oscuri recessi dell'anima umana e individua i motivi che hanno determinato le azioni. Allora, nel leggere quel brano di storia si apprezza la bellezza, la finezza e l'eleganza con cui è scritto (anche se l'interpretazione può essere ipotetica). Anzi, vi sono storie scritte così bene (Tucidide, Plutarco, Tacito, Livio, Giulio Cesare, ecc.) che appartengono alla letteratura, oltre che alla storia.

Anche lo storico può creare un personaggio, ma il personaggio che crea deve essere storicamente corretto. Senza l'analisi dello storico, esisterebbe quello che quel personaggio ha fatto, ma il personaggio non esisterebbe nella complessità che lo storico rivela sulla base dei fatti raccolti. Per esempio, i grandi della storia possono perdonare i nemici per motivi che hanno tutto a che fare con il calcolo politico e nulla a che fare con la generosità. In questo comportamento, sono certo superiori a chi è stupidamente crudele. La differenza tra uno storico ed un artista è che *in uno storico la verità è obbligatoria e l'arte facoltativa; e in un artista l'arte è obbligatoria e la "verità" è facoltativa.* La verità nell'arte consiste nella bellezza (di un'opera bella si dice che è *vera* arte).

Si possono estendere questi concetti in ogni campo. Mi ricordo di aver letto quando ero studente di medicina nel libro di anatomia del Chiarugi una descrizione delle modificazioni dell'utero durante il ciclo mensile, una descrizione che al suo acme raggiungeva l'acuta bellezza del dramma di una vita mancata.

Lo stile

Lo stile è la maniera personale di rappresentare quello che l'artista sente. In ogni epoca, nelle tendenze dell'arte, gli artisti cercano di esprimere nuove forme di bellezza cercando di sviluppare uno stile personale ispirato anche dai valori prevalenti al momento (per es., religiosità, romanticismo, materialismo, teorie sociali, ecc.). *Ma non ci può essere né bellezza né stile personale se non c'è talento artistico.*

Per avere uno stile personale, non basta volerlo avere, servendosi delle sottigliezza della logica o di distorsioni emotive. *Non si sceglie uno stile più di quanto uno possa scegliere la propria personalità: lo stile è una maniera di essere artisticamente. Lo stile risulta dal fatto che* <u>*l'individualità di ciascuna mente può esprimersi solo in una propria*</u> <u>*maniera personale.*</u> La maniera di esprimersi è la conseguenza diretta dell'individualità di ciascuno. Per esempio, è improbabile che una mente confusa si esprima chiaramente; o una prosaica si esprima poeticamente. Nel caso dell'artista, lo stile personale risulta dalla struttura della sua mente (caratteristiche congenite e influenze acquisite come addestramento, ambiente, educazione, mode, tendenze e persino il caso) e si associa ad un'abilità eccezionale nel "sentire" e creare la bellezza.

Questo è lo stesso che dire che *non si diventa artisti a meno che uno non nasca con talento artistico: il talento artistico deve essere parte della struttura della sua mente come altre caratteristiche che uno possa avere (come una comprensione acuta, tenacia, passione, energia, generosità, ecc.).*

È perfettamente inutile chiedere all propria natura quello che non ha. Se lo si fa, la nostra natura può rispondere solo offrendoci la nostra mediocrità. Ma quest'ultima è rivelata dalla mancanza di talento, per lo meno a quelli che hanno buon gusto e un talento critico sicuro. Similmente, è inutile chiedere alla nostra natura comprensione, tenacia, passione, energia o generosità, se non abbiamo questi attributi.

Stile ed arte

Dal punto di vista della bellezza, lo stile personale dell'artista ha poca importanza nel senso che (quale che sia lo stile) il risultato deve essere la bellezza. *Non è lo stile per sé a creare la bellezza: lo stile è solo una maniera personale di rappresentarla.* Anzi, se la creazione non è bella, può anche darsi che vi abbia contribuito il fatto che lo stile "scelto" è brutto. *La distinzione tra stile ed arte consiste nel fatto che lo stile è un mezzo e l'arte il fine.*

Ma, qualsiasi cosa si crei, la si crea con uno stile personale (o per lo meno in maniera personale). *Lo stile è il marchio con cui la bellezza è creata: un autore si riconosce dallo stile.* Non è necessario cercare la firma: *lo stile è la firma.*

Lo stile è importante per altre ragioni. Lo stile risulta in <u>una necessaria varietà nella creazione</u>. Lo stile è uno strumento potente con cui l'artista rappresenta il **suo** mondo, un mondo unico e irrepetibile. Dal momento che lo stile risulta dalla struttura mentale, è improbabile che un'artista debole abbia uno stile "forte" (tutt'al più, lo stile potrebbe essere enfatico). È altrettanto improbabile che chi è sensibile alle cose delicate abbia uno stile epico. Per averlo, bisogna avere una personalità che abbia il gusto del grandioso e pertanto uno stile adatto a quello.

Ma lo stile dovrebbe risultare dalla maniera di sentire dettato dalla personalità dell'artista, e non essere una scelta intellettuale fatta calcolando e riflettendo sulle mode e teorie correnti. Prima di tutto, bisognerebbe aver dentro "qualcosa" che uno non solo vuole ma piuttosto sente di *dover* esprimere; e poi esprimerlo secondo come uno è. Quando non è naturale, lo stile riflette l'artificiosità di scelte intellettuali. Questo lo si vede dall'artificiosità di quello che è creato. Uno stile artificiale ancora riflette l'individualità di una persona, ma allo stesso tempo rivela la mancanza di un ingrediente essenziale: il talento artistico.

Alcuni scelgono a freddo un metodo (per lo più strano purché sia differente) per dire quello che non sentono; o per lo meno, quello che non sentono appassionatamente. *C'è il desiderio di creare qualcosa di unico, ma non la naturale capacità di creare qualcosa di bello.* Il che è l'equivalente a parlare senza aver nulla da dire. In altri casi, si può anche avere qualcosa da dire, ma o non lo si sa dire oppure non vale la pena dirlo. *In questi casi, c'è solo una mancanza di talento artistico espressa con uno stile confuso.*

In altri casi, lo stile può essere strano come quello che rappresenta. Se l'artista è strano, la sua concezione della bellezza può essere talmente eccentrica da non essere comprensibile.

Evoluzione dello stile ma non della bellezza

Come il ricercatore scientifico, *l'artista sperimenta*: prova questa o quella maniera di creare, finché ne trova una di cui è istintivamente soddisfatto. Questo spiega come vi possa essere un'evoluzione nello stile dello stesso artista. Più spesso, il modificarsi della sua mentalità col passare del tempo e sotto l'influenza di passate esperienze può trovare più soddisfacente una nuova maniera di creare. Naturalmente, l'evoluzione è solo nello stile, dal momento che *non vi è evoluzione nella bellezza*. Se c'è bellezza, è nel risultato, non nello stile. Anzi, adottando un nuovo stile si può essere più originali, ma nella bruttezza. In tal caso, invece di evoluzione, si ha involuzione. *Per esservi un'evoluzione della bellezza, bisognerebbe che la genetica cambiasse e con quella il nostro senso estetico.* La bellezza creata da Prassitele sorpassa quella di molte opere contemporanee. *Non è possibile migliorare la perfezione nella bellezza.*

La bellezza o la bruttezza di un opera non cambia col tempo, per quanto possa variare temporaneamente quello che la gente pensa dell'opera. Ma l'evoluzione dalla bellezza alla bruttezza (e reciprocamente) di una particolare opera si verifica solo nel gusto della gente ed è il risultato del "sedimentare" dei fattori estranei (per es., mode o teorie o novità dello stile). In ogni caso, la natura dell'opera non cambia: o è bella o è brutta, e si sbagliava o quando la si considerava bella o quando la si considerava brutta.

Arte e moda

In genere, questa "evoluzione" nella valutazione di un'opera si verifica solo per le opere nuove e recenti. È un'evoluzione dovuta a molti fattori: la moda che influenza il gusto generale, novità della concezione, stile non convenzionale, mancanza di un gusto sicuro, paura di sbagliare nel non apprezzare quello che non ci piace, desiderio di acutezza che porta a vedervi quello che non c'è, influenza dei critici sull'incertezza dei più, protezione che vi è nel conformarsi all'opinione prevalente, paura di essere considerati retrivi o senza gusto, desiderio del nuovo, ecc.

Un motivo di incertezza è che *si diffida di quello a cui non siamo abituati*, perché non siamo capaci di esprimere un giudizio critico sicuro. Abbiamo paura di sbagliare, perché abbiamo esperienza del cambiare, anche radicale, delle opinioni su opere d'arte che nel passato erano d'avanguardia. *Abbiamo visto sia l'apprezzamento della bellezza di opere che prima sembravano strane, sia il rendersi conto della stranezza di opere che prima erano considerate belle.* Il giudizio dei critici professionali aiuta ma non molto, dal momento che i giudizi dei critici sono spesso così discordanti come quelli della gente comune. Inoltre, un'opera mediocre può sembrare bella ad una persona mediocre.

Ma il giudizio che si forma dopo un periodo di "sedimentazione" più o meno lungo in genere rimane inalterato nei secoli. I fallimenti spariscono dalla scena (e dai musei) e i successi diventano opere classiche. A seconda dei critici, in un'opera classica vi si può vedere di più o di meno, ma il giudizio rimane sostanzialmente invariato. *La bellezza di un'opera classica persiste perché le leggi della genetica umana non cambiano: in questo caso, non cambia quello che consideriamo bello.*

Naturalmente, non ci si può aspettare che tutti gli esperimenti abbiano successo. Anzi, relativamente pochi hanno successo come artisti, perché *molti creano non nuove forme di bellezza, ma solo nuove forme.* Il problema è che hanno una maniera personale di esprimersi, ma non uno stile reale. O se si preferisce, hanno uno stile personale, ma solo quello. Ma, come si è detto, lo stile non è sinonimo con l'arte. *Lo stile è una maniera di creare, ma l'arte è la creazione di bellezza. Essere sedotti dalla bellezza (come lo sono tutti gli artisti) non è sinonimo con la capacità di creare la bellezza.*

Rapporti tra variabilità dello stile e del gusto

Lo stile ha un'altra importante funzione. *Come vi è diversità di sentire tra gli artisti, così vi è diversità di sentire e di apprezzare tra il pubblico.* Ci si sente più attratti dalle opere d'arte che più si confanno al gusto della nostra personalità. Quando troviamo bello quello che un particolare artista ha creato, quell'artista diventa allora il nostro artista preferito.

A queste preferenze contribuisce prima di tutto il nostro modo di sentire, che (come per l'artista) è legato alla nostra personalità, educazione, esperienze, sviluppo mentale e sensibilità. Un buon gusto istintivo poi fa sì che le nostre preferenze scelgano tra le cose belle, e non siano irretite dalle cose brutte, anche se quest'ultime sono di moda. Ma, in generale, una persona ordinata e "ragionevole" considera strane certe novità e una persona estrosa considera nuove (e attraenti) le stranezze.

Queste diversità nelle preferenze conferma che il senso estetico è determinato dalla genetica. *Tutti noi si obbedisce alle regole della genetica umana, nel senso che tutti abbiamo un senso estetico. Ma ciascuno individuo ha le sue variazioni genetiche (determinate dalle mescolanze dei geni).* Pertanto, non sorprende per nulla che il senso estetico vari non solo nella "quantità", ma anche nella "qualità" in individui diversi.

Per la "quantità", vi sono individui completamente indifferenti alle cose belle ed altri che non vivono che per la bellezza ("esteti"). Per la "qualità", tra quelli che apprezzano la bellezza, di alcuni si dice che non hanno gusto (*trovano bello quello che noi troviamo brutto*) e di altri si dice hanno un gusto raffinato ("arbiter elegantiae").

Pertanto, istintivamente ciascuno preferisce quegli artisti che il suo gusto apprezza. *Se però uno ha una considerevole sensibilità, allora è capace di apprezzare la bellezza nelle sue diverse forme*: trova piacere nelle delicate sfumature di certe immagini poetiche (per esempio, il timido pudore dell'innocenza) come nelle ondate di passione di una musica eroica. Reciprocamente, se l'artista ha una straordinaria genialità viene apprezzato da un numero larghissimo di persone.

Nuove forme d'arte

Così come Cristoforo Colombo conobbe l'incertezza dell'inesplorato, similmente ci si muove con incertezza tra le novità delle nuove "scuole". Vi sono sempre nuovi "movimenti" nell'arte, che nell'esplorare l'ignoto conoscono i successi della moda per periodi più o meno lunghi. Vengono attribuiti ai continui cambiamenti delle condizioni di vita e alle varie teorie sociali e filosofiche prevalenti al momento.

A questo proposito, viene da domandarsi se sia possibile che l'arte abbia bisogno di teorie. La risposta sembrerebbe essere che non l'arte, solo gli artisti ne possono avere bisogno. *Ciascun artista vive nel mondo della sua epoca ed è soggetto alle influenze a cui è esposto.* Se l'artista è fortemente attratto da certe teorie sociali del momento, può darsi che trovi interessante solo il rappresentare le miserie e sofferenze degli strati più poveri della società. In altre epoche, la moda riflette il predominio della nobiltà ed allora si rappresentano i nobili nella "gloria" di fastosi abbigliamenti. La miseria semplicemente non esiste, per lo meno come soggetto di rappresentazione. *Queste oscillazioni di interesse creano la precondizione per la successiva ondata della moda, se non altro perché ci si abitua a tutto. E pochi resistono al fascino di voler essere innovatori o perfino rivoluzionari.*

Se la miseria o la ricchezza (o qualsiasi altra cosa) possono essere motivi di ispirazione per un dato artista, per sé non sono sufficienti a creare dell'arte. Se l'artista non è bravo non fa dell'arte, ma solo della propaganda alle sue convinzioni. E se è bravo, dal punto di vista dell'arte ha poca importanza quello che rappresenta. Per esempio, vi sono bellissimi romanzi che trattano dei più svariati temi (inclusa la povertà e la ricchezza).

Non a caso, quando si parla di una moda si parla di "ultima moda": *ultima* perché le precedenti sono passate di moda. L'importanza delle mode nasce dall'universale desiderio di novità, o meglio dalla necessità di creare il nuovo. Ma soprattutto *tutte le mode nascono dal fatto che una società non rimane mai la stessa: più che un desiderio, lo sviluppo del nuovo è una spinta insopprimibile.*

Siccome nascono sempre individui nuovi, l'espressione di se stessi non può essere che diversa e pertanto originale. Ma nell'esprimersi, si è potentemente influenzati da quello che ha influenzato lo sviluppo della nostra mente. *Si vive non tanto **nella** nostra epoca quanto **della** nostra epoca.* Si assorbe l'ambiente in cui si vive. Di qui ne segue che il nuovo è la necessaria conseguenza di nuovi individui con una differente formazione.

La ricerca del nuovo è un'assoluta necessità per evitare la stagnazione, creare varietà e qualche volta nuove forme di bellezza. Ma anche le creazioni brutte hanno una loro funzione. Stimolano a pensare e ci spingono a cercare le ragioni per le quali riteniamo che una creazione non sia bella. *Si cerca di giustificare il giudizio del nostro gusto, che è una maniera per voler dimostrare che abbiamo buon gusto.*

Inoltre, la bellezza deve molto alla bruttezza: il confronto con la bruttezza la fa apprezzare molto di più Anzi, *se non ci fosse la bruttezza, ipso facto non ci sarebbe la bellezza.* Nuove forme di bellezza possono essere trovate solo seguendo il sentiero affollato dai fallimenti della bruttezza.

La libertà nell'arte

Per le sue caratteristiche, *l'arte esige libertà*: è impossibile imporre all'artista un particolare soggetto o una particolare maniera di presentarlo (per es., realismo o cubismo). Sarebbe come chiedere all'artista di non essere se stesso. Lo si può anche fare, come fanno certe dittature in nome delle loro esigenze politiche. Ma allora si ottiene della (brutta) propaganda e non dell'arte. L'unica maniera in cui la politica può sfruttare l'arte per i suoi fini è di influenzare lo sviluppo dell'artista durante la sua formazione prima che raggiunga l'età adulta, o le sue convinzioni da adulto.

Non vi è nulla di più libero della creazione, perché l'artista ha a sua completa disposizione tutti gli elementi per creare. Prima di tutto, le caratteristiche della sua personalità e una mente creativa che ha completo controllo della creazione come la va concependo; e poi i mezzi per realizzare le proprie concezioni (come parole, colori, scalpello, scrittura musicale, volumi di spazio, ecc.).

L'arte è libera perché origina all'interno del mondo della mente: l'artista esprime se stesso, indipendentemente da, e qualche volta contro, le tendenze del momento. Assolutamente sua è la scelta del colore, delle sfumature, degli sfondi, delle espressioni, della prospettiva, delle malinconie, dei merletti, ecc. Nell'arte, non esistono libri di istruzione come per la cucina o per l'ingegneria. Inoltre, un critico può approvare o disapprovare un'opera con ragione, ma non certo dirigerne la realizzazione. *L'unica cosa che l'artista* **non può fare** *è di scegliere di non esprimersi o di esprimersi come gli altri vorrebbero che facesse.*

La licenza nell'arte

Dall'altra parte, c'è chi confonde la libertà dell'arte con la licenza. Qualcuno si crede che la libertà consista solo nel fare quello che piace a lui, senza rendersi conto che si diventa artisti solo quando quello che si fa è bello. Non ha importanza se quello che piace all'artista è bello o brutto, ma è essenziale che quello che ha fatto sia bello. Se la rappresentazione di qualcosa (bello o brutto) è brutta, in che cosa l'arte potrebbe mai consistere? *Naturalmente, tutti coloro che lavorano nel campo dell'arte fanno quello che piace a loro, ma solo chi crea la bellezza è un artista.* Gli altri contribuiscono solo delle "novità", le novità del momento che possono sorprendere l'intelletto e lasciare indifferente il gusto.

L'arte non può essere arbitraria, perché *deve creare la bellezza*. Sotto questo punto di vista, l'arte deve creare una sua *coerente realtà*. *L'incoerenza per se stessa non crea bellezza: può semplicemente non aver significato per essere incomprensibile.* Per esempio, il fare un viso con un orecchio molto più grande dell'altro o tre narici acquisterebbe significato solo se fosse esteticamente giustificato. Neanche la coerenza per se stessa crea la bellezza, ma per lo meno può essere valutata dal buon gusto, senza il bisogno di giustificare scelte arbitrarie.

In un romanzo, un personaggio può essere buono o cattivo, superbo o umile, onesto o disonesto, ecc.; oppure essere buono e cattivo a seconda delle situazioni. Ma in ogni caso, vi deve essere una coerenza interna senza la quale non vi è un personaggio, ma una marionetta. Se si vuol creare un eroe, non ne deve venir fuori un personaggio così goffo da sembrare un buffone. Uno può voler creare un personaggio incoerente, ma anche in questo caso la caratterizzazione dell'incoerenza deve essere fatta coerentemente.

Non si può scrivere un romanzo ignorando la realtà della psicologia umana, perché altrimenti il lettore non potrà formarsi nella sua immaginazione un ritratto mentale dei personaggi e apprezzare il significato delle loro vicende. Non leggiamo semplicemente un bel romanzo, ma piuttosto lo viviamo nella nostra immaginazione e nelle emozioni che suscita in noi. *Quello che l'artista esprime può essere apprezzato dalla nostra mente solo se è compreso nei confini di caratteristiche mentali che abbiamo in comune con l'artista.* L'opera di un artista pazzo non comunica con la maggior parte delle persone; e l'arte è sprecata per un osservatore pazzo.

È necessario aggiungere che la coerenza nell'arte è una coerenza artistica, non letterale. Se un certo colore è esteticamente necessario per un certo oggetto, non ha la *minima* importanza se in natura quell'oggetto non ha mai quel colore. Similmente, la forma di un oggetto può esistere solo in un certo quadro, ed essere esteticamente coerente. In altre parole, **nell'arte la bellezza ha la precedenza su tutto**, inclusa la coerenza e l'incoerenza.

L'arte e la bellezza

Se l'arte deve creare la bellezza, bisognerà domandarci cosa sia la bellezza. *La bellezza è un modo di sentire che risulta dalla nostra struttura genetica*, come ne risultano altri modi di sentire della nostra mente, per esempio, la moralità, la fede o gli affetti di famiglia. *Questa particolare facoltà della mente ci fa provare piacere per quello che ci fa giudicare bello.* A seconda dello sviluppo di questa facoltà in differenti individui, si apprezza di più o di meno la bellezza.

Quello che si considera bello, lo si "sente" bello. Non sappiamo spiegare perché una cosa è bella, perché la bellezza non ha una base logica e dipende da un tratto genetico. *Possiamo analizzare le ragioni per cui una cosa è bella, ma non "spiegare" l'essenza della bellezza.* Non a caso, si dice "È bello quello che piace".

In questo, il buon gusto non è differente da altri sentimenti: se siamo geneticamente normali, si ama il bello, si prova affetto per la famiglia, si distingue il giusto dall'ingiusto, il vero dal falso, il delicato dal grossolano, ecc. Nei casi patologici, ci possono essere distorsioni o degli affetti, o della morale o del buon gusto. Ma anche nei casi normali, la rozzezza di taluni ignora le seduzioni, gli abbandoni e le emozioni della sensibilità estetica.

L'ispirazione

Se il buon gusto è necessario per *apprezzare* la bellezza di un'opera d'arte, si richiede assai di più per *creare* un'opera d'arte.

Qualcuno per creare ha bisogno dell'ispirazione. Uno scrive o dipinge quando un'emozione viene suscitata nella sua mente da quello che vede, prova o pensa. Un'emozione che si desidera intensamente esprimere con parole, poesia, musica, o un quadro in maniera tale da soddisfare il proprio desiderio di bellezza. Si vuole dar vita a quello che si prova.

Ne risulta una creazione unica con una sua propria bellezza che è differente da quello che l'ha ispirata. *Come la natura, l'arte crea. Ma l'arte non imita la natura, perché non riproduce quello che l'artista vede (come invece fa la comune fotografia), ma la maniera con cui l'artista vede, sente, concepisce ed esprime il soggetto scelto.*

L'arte umana crea, ma non dal nulla. E quando lo facesse sarebbe incomprensibile. *Si può concepire solo nei termini in cui siamo stati concepiti.* È vero che l'arte umana non copia la bellezza della natura creata da Dio, ma spesso ne è ispirata. O ascolta gli insegnamenti della natura, come quelli di un maestro dell'arte.

A sua volta, la bellezza di una creazione ispira un piacere estetico in chi vi è esposto. Come già detto, *l'arte rende bello quello che crea, sia il soggetto bello, tragico, delicato, triste, o persino brutto.* È la bellezza della creazione che suscita emozione in chi la rimira.

Quello che viene creato deve catturare l'emozione di quello che ha ispirato l'artista. *L'ispirazione è un'emozione causata da quello che ci colpisce per essere bello in una maniera o nell'altra. L'ispirazione stimola l'immaginazione, che a sua volta vuole realizzare quello che concepisce attraverso un'espressione personale di bellezza.* Una volta che sia stimolata, l'immaginazione non più dipende da quello che si è visto, ma consiste in un fermento emotivo che sviluppa nella mente un tema (per esempio, una nuvola spinta dal vento) usando parole, immagini e concetti che soddisfino le proprie esigenze estetiche. *L'immaginazione è la capacità della mente di creare immagini, pensieri e sentimenti che non dipendono direttamente dalla ricezione sensoriale dal mondo fisico. Così facendo, l'immaginazione crea una nuova realtà secondo le caratteristiche della mente di ciascuno.* Senza immaginazione, uno è arido; e con troppa immaginazione indisciplinata, uno può essere un sognatore alla deriva. Se non ci può essere arte senza immaginazione, l'immaginazione sola non basta: ha bisogno di essere tradotta in bellezza.

Senza l'ispirazione, non vi sono impulsi a creare perché l'immaginazione resta muta. Tutti i giorni, l'artista vede e sente, ma non tutti i giorni sente con un'emozione così acuta da imporgli l'impulso ad esprimerla. *L'ispirazione è necessaria (e possibile) per chi ha la necessaria sensibilità: se vi è talento, vi è allora anche la capacità di realizzare l'ispirazione nella creazione.*

Nell'esprimere un'emozione, si è creativi quando l'immaginazione trova nel suo mondo interiore i mezzi adatti per esprimere in maniera bella quella che la commuove. Essendo il mondo interiore personale, lo stesso stimolo emotivo può spingere artisti differenti a creare una canzone, una poesia, della musica, un romanzo, ecc. Quello che è espresso ha una realtà che gli deriva dalla bellezza creata, una realtà differente da quello che ha originato l'emozione e che riflette la personalità artistica dell'autore.

La bellezza nasce dall'espressione del mondo interiore dell'artista ed è apprezzata dal mondo interiore di chi ama l'arte. È solo nel mondo interiore (la mente, l'anima, gli affetti, o l'Io) di ciascuno che la bellezza può suscitare un'emozione estetica. Il ruolo del mondo interiore nei riguardi della bellezza spiega come ogni artista persegua differenti espressioni estetiche e come ciascuno abbia differenti preferenze estetiche.

La personalità artistica

Non tutti gli artisti sembrano dipendere dai capricci dell'imprevedibile ispirazione. Sono questi gli artisti professionali. Per esempio, vi sono degli scrittori che scrivono per un certo numero di ore ogni giorno. Come è possibile che tutti i giorni siano ispirati dalle nove di mattina a mezzogiorno e mezzo? Ispirazione a rate? Altri scrivono musica o poesie, perché hanno ricevuto una commessa. Ispirazione a pagamento?

La spiegazione è un'altra. Sono questi degli individui in genere eccezionali (quanto eccezionali lo stabilisce la qualità della loro opera) che sono stati "strutturati" dalla natura alla creazione in differenti campi dell'arte. *Per loro, il creare è una maniera di essere: a qualunque situazione siano esposti, vi rispondono con una mente capace di creare con fertile immaginazione un mondo proprio.*

Quando cominciano a lavorare sul soggetto che li occupa al momento, la loro sensibilità e il loro talento svolgono il tema secondo la regia della loro immaginazione e fantasia. Vivono nella loro immaginazione la vicenda che svolgono e si immedesimano volta a volta nei differenti protagonisti: non per nulla, gli scrittori sono acuti osservatori della natura umana.

Così, la passione dell'amore o la tragedia della morte dei personaggi trovano una maniera di essere espressi secondo la maniera di sentire, essere e concepire dell'artista (in un'opera, dramma, romanzo, quadro o poema, ecc.). Poiché l'artista si immedesima nei suoi personaggi, questi si esprimono a quelle altezze a cui li porta la bravura dell'artista. Quello che avrebbe potuto essere solo pettegolezzo o una delle tante (anche banali) evenienze della vita quotidiana (per es., gelosia o adulterio) diviene un dramma pieno di intense emozioni nella visione dell'artista. La sua abilità, fantasia, sensibilità poetica, drammaticità, immaginazione, acutezza psicologica, conoscenza degli impulsi umani, capacità di analizzare se stesso a fondo, ecc. creano quelle realtà che faranno vibrare le corde dell'arpa del cuore umano.

Così come si rende poetica una gita in campagna rappresentando la limpida trasparenza dell'acqua del fiume, le vele della barche nella brezza, i fiori generosi di colori, la pausa di riposo delle figure umane all'ombra di un albero, il cestino delle vivande e la bottiglia di vino rosso sulla tovaglia a scacchi rossi e bianchi stesa sull'erba. *Non è la gita che si dipinge, ma un quadro della varietà della vita umana così come lo sente l'artista.* O se si preferisce, uno dei quadri (questa volta idillico) del complesso dramma della vita così come è sentito dalla sensibilità della bellezza.

Arte e conoscenza

L'arte non vuole capire la vita nei suoi reconditi significati e nell'intreccio dei suoi misteri. L'arte crea invece espressioni di vita che diventano parte della vita di tanti, aggiungendovi significati nuovi, coltivandone la sensibilità, rendendola più ricca di emozioni e più sensibile alla bellezza. Si arricchisce e si sviluppa una parte del nostro Io che ci dà un piacere puro e incontaminato anche quando risulta dalla rappresentazione della torbidezza delle passioni e dei vizi umani da parte dell'artista.

Se l'arte fa delle domande, non è per trovare delle risposte, ma per esprimere quello che vi è di drammatico nel mistero della nostra esistenza. Quel mistero che le cure dell'attività quotidiana esilia dalla coscienza della nostra mente e relega alle indagini della filosofia. Non solo non si indaga il significato della nostra esistenza, ma spesso nemmeno ci si domanda se ve ne sia uno.

Se qualcuno pone la domanda, quella persona sembra se non strana per lo meno indiscreta nel porre delle domande imbarazzanti e "teoriche" [imbarazzanti sono le domande di cui non si sa la risposta]. Al contrario della filosofia, le domande dell'arte suscitano emozioni, non ragionamenti.

Nell'arte, le domande sono le risposte: si chiede solo che le domande siano piene di intensità bella e emotiva.

La bellezza e le menti individuali

Dal momento che la bellezza è legata alla genetica, necessariamente *la bellezza esiste solo nella mente e per la mente*. Si ricevono immagini dal mondo esterno ed alcune le troviamo belle, altre brutte e altre ancora esteticamente indifferenti secondo il gusto della nostra struttura mentale. Siccome la struttura genetica dei vari individui ha una considerevole somiglianza di base, spesso si giudicano belle le stesse immagini provenienti dal mondo esterno.

Ma la struttura genetica dei vari individui ha sempre delle variazioni individuali, rese ancora più marcate da fattori acquisiti (per es., l'educazione, l'età o l'ambiente). Pertanto, quello che ciascuno considera bello può variare nell'intensità ("È bellissimo", "È bello", "Non c'è male") o persino nella qualità ("Non so cosa ci trovi di bello: per me, è brutto"). Perfino l'interesse nella bellezza ha ampie variazioni a seconda delle persone. C'è chi è così rozzo da non apprezzare nessuna forma di bellezza. E chi è così raffinato che per lui non esiste nulla di importante al di fuori della bellezza.

Questi atteggiamenti sono meno differenti per quanto riguarda i fenomeni naturali, con i quali si cresce e che diventano parte della nostra vita quotidiana. Le divergenze si moltiplicano quando si tratta di giudicare della bellezza delle creazioni umane. Vi contribuisce il fatto che le creazioni umane si verificano in campi diversi (musica, poesia, architettura, scultura, pittura, ecc.), ciascuno dei quali è "specializzato" e interessa alcune persone ma non altre. Inoltre, tra le persone che apprezzano una forma d'arte, per esempio la poesia, alcuni apprezzano una particolare forma di poesia e altri ne apprezzano un'altra. Ma anche chi apprezza la stessa forma di poesia, la conoscenza del campo, il buon gusto e la competenza nel giudicare variano notevolmente da un individuo all'altro.

Nell'apprezzare la bellezza della natura naturalmente si apprezza l'arte di Dio, anche se normalmente ci si limita ad ammirare la bellezza di un fiore o della luce serica della luna nel silenzio pensoso della notte senza domandarci chi sia il loro autore. Il che è un po' curioso, perché di un quadro si domanda subito chi ne sia l'autore. Anzi, pochi comprerebbero un quadro di cui non si sapesse chi è l'autore. Inoltre, in genere è da considerare che anche i più grandi artisti sono creature della natura come lo sono le foglie che giocano nel vento, la cresta delle onde spumosa o il silenzio di cristallo dei picchi nevosi.

Come la natura, anche l'artista ci offre il *suo* mondo individuale, che consiste o nella maniera in cui ricrea quello che vede e sente, o crea quello che la sua immaginazione gli fa vivere nella mente. In tutti e due i casi, l'artista persegue la creazione della bellezza. Ma, *al contrario della natura, la bellezza umana non è "universale" come quella naturale, ma una bellezza "individuale" che porta lo stile e l'impronta non di Dio (come nella natura), ma di un individuo (creato da Dio).* Come ricordato più sopra, è assai più difficile giudicare di questa bellezza individuale, perché spesso si presenta in forme nuove a cui non siamo abituati, e altre volte si tratta di creazioni "nuove" ma non belle.

Natura e bellezza artistica

La natura è così ricca di bellezza che è il paradigma della bellezza. La sua bellezza è il risultato dell'arte di Dio. Ed è apprezzata istintivamente dalla maggior parte della gente. Si cresce con la bellezza naturale e la si dà per scontata. A tal punto che alcuni non la considerano nemmeno una forma d'arte. Eppure, *è la bellezza della natura che il più delle volte ispira l'artista.*

Vi è dell'arte anche negli impeti più selvaggi della natura. Per esempio, un uragano che suscita onde violente la cui schiuma copre di spruzzi la spiaggia abbandonata, mentre le palme scuotono impazzite le loro chiome al vento che si abbandona senza moderazione alla propria ira, quell'uragano ha una sua bellezza primordiale che è impossibile non apprezzare. Per lo meno, finché non risulta nella tragedia della perdita di vite.

L'artista cerca di catturare l'anima della bellezza della natura: la grazia, i colori, la delicatezza, la malinconia, la solitudine, la selvatichezza, la maestà, l'impetuosità, la forza spaventosa, la ferocia, ecc. L'anima di un quadro è un'emozione umana che l'artista ha provato e che l'osservatore condivide.

Se in un quadro viene rappresentato un terremoto in maniera tale da coglierne l'intensità della tragedia, la crudeltà delle devastazioni, le sofferenze umane, la desolazione delle distruzioni, ecc., vi si può reagire con la commozione intensa ed il piacere con cui si apprezza un dramma tragico. Non ci si può trattenere dal sentire quanto il quadro sia drammaticamente bello. La differenza con un terremoto reale è che nel quadro non si riproduce il terremoto, ma lo si "interpreta". Il quadro non fotografa il terremoto, ma crea quella realtà che l'emozione dell'artista vi ha visto, quei sentimenti che la tragedia ha suscitato in lui.

Fotografia e arte

Anche un fotografo può fare dell'arte, ma in tal caso fotografa con effetti speciali solo quello che lo ispira: *come tutti gli artisti, non riproduce quello che vede, ma crea quello che sente.* Interpreta la sua sensibilità. Lo spettatore ammira la bellezza che vi è nella fotografia (per esempio, l'ombra di un muro di pietre su un viottolo di campagna e sulla erba vicina), non nell'oggetto (il muro) che di per sé può non dir nulla. Dal che si vede che l'arte imita la natura solo in quanto, come la natura, crea la bellezza.

In un terremoto, il fotografo cercherà non di documentare il danno, ma di presentare le proprie emozioni. Riprenderà quello che lo colpisce per essere particolarmente triste, o tragico o epico o acutamente umano. Si servirà della macchina fotografica come il pittore del pennello per creare la sua visione di quello che sente. O meglio di quello che la sua sensibilità estetica sente, perché nel fotografare sceglierà solo quello che in una maniera o nell'altra gli sembrerà bello. Bello non oggettivamente (anzi potrebbe essere orribile), ma bello emotivamente. Cioè, bello in quanto suscita un'emozione estetica e contribuisce a creare quel dramma e quello sgomento che il terremoto suscita nell'anima umana. *È la bellezza della fotografia che piace, non la distruzione.*

Naturalmente, vi è una differenza notevole tra fotografo e artista. La creazione del fotografo richiede un sensibilità acuta, un buona macchina fotografica ed alcuni minuti. La creazione dell'artista richiede sensibilità, l'immaginazione che rielabora lo stesso oggetto, l'abilità di tradurre l'immaginazione nella creazione e uno stile personale nel creare. Il fotografo coglie la bellezza che vede nell'opera di Dio. L'artista fa altrettanto, ma la ricrea in maniera originale. Un buon fotografo ha sensibilità, e un buon artista ha sensibilità e talento creativo.

La valutazione dell'arte

Non è difficile valutare la realtà dal punto di vista fisico. Per esempio, è facile misurare la distanza tra due città, o quanto acciaio occorrerà per la costruzione di un ponte. Similmente, si possono calcolare le fondamenta di un palazzo, lo spessore dei muri, la lunghezza delle volte, ecc. Queste misure sono basate sulla prestazione meccanica dei materiali usati e su dati ben precisi.

Invece, la valutazione estetica del palazzo è soggetta a criteri, molti dei quali sono assai soggettivi. I criteri dipendono dal gusto individuale e pertanto sono variabili da individuo a individuo. La bellezza non ha un'unità di misura oggettiva, un'unità che abbia una dimensione definita e valida per tutti, come, per esempio, la scala Richter per i terremoti. *Il fatto è che la bellezza non può avere per nulla un unità di misura oggettiva, perché la bellezza è nella mente, e la mente è differente nelle differenti persone.* Le dimensioni della bellezza sono stabilite dal gusto della mente dell'osservatore.

Bellezza "soggettiva" e bellezza "oggettiva"

La bellezza è un'esperienza emotiva individuale e, in questo senso, è sempre soggettiva. Ma le emozioni suscitate dalla bellezza sono di diversa natura. Anzi, si dà il caso che o la bellezza suscita le emozioni o le emozioni suscitano la bellezza.

Un esempio del primo caso (*la bellezza suscita le emozioni*) è fornito da alcuni attori e attrici famosi, di cui ciascuno apprezza la bellezza fisica e la bravura artistica. La loro bellezza è "oggettiva" perché è apprezzata da quasi tutti.

Il secondo caso (*le emozioni suscitano la bellezza*) è assai più comune ed è in genere il risultato dell'amore: la persona amata è raramente brutta per l'innamorato. Questa bellezza "soggettiva" e "individualizzata" è naturalmente alla base di un ordinato sviluppo della società, dal momento che permette a tutti di sposare la persona scelta. Se tutti si innamorassero delle stesse persone "oggettivamente" belle, sarebbe il caos. A questo riguardo, si deve aggiungere che *la bellezza fisica è importante ma non è la sola forma di bellezza che può rendere una persona attraente.* Qualche volta, altre belle qualità (gentilezza, comprensione, generosità, affettuosità, ecc.) possono essere di gran lunga più importanti della bellezza fisica.

Inoltre, i nostri figli sono sempre belli e così sono i nostri nipotini. Anche se si vedono dei bambini più belli dei nostri nipotini, la mancanza di una relazione personale apprezza la loro bellezza in maniera "teorica", vale a dire senza l'affetto che proviamo per i nostri nipotini. Per gli estranei possiamo provare un piacere estetico, ma per la nostra famiglia si prova prima di tutto affetto che dà anche piacere estetico. *Reciprocamente, una madre è sempre bella per i suoi figli.*

Bellezza e varietà

La varietà è già una forma di bellezza, ovverosia la bellezza deve essere varia. Supponiamo che tutti andassero a giro con lo stesso vestito (anche bellissimo): ben pochi ne sarebbero contenti. Basta considerare l'imbarazzo e l'irritazione di una signora che ad un ricevimento ne incontra un'altra con lo stesso vestito. L'implicazione è che non si ha un gusto abbastanza personale.

Quello che rende personale il gusto di ciascuno è la mescolanza dei geni. Come ciascuno ha un suo viso unico, similmente ciascuno ha un suo gusto unico. Le scelte personali che ne derivano contribuiscono a quella varietà che dà piacere estetico. *La varietà nella bellezza dunque risulta non solo nel fatto che ogni creazione è personale e unica, ma anche nel fatto che il gusto individuale di ciascuno è personale e unico.* Più in generale, si può dire che *la nostra personalità è il frutto delle mescolanze della genetica: la nostra mente è la sorgente di ogni forma di varietà, sia nel creare che nell'apprezzare.* Nei gemelli identici non c'è una copia solo perché non c'è un originale. L'importanza delle mescolanze della genetica si vede dal fatto che se la partenogenesi fosse la sola maniera di riprodursi, saremmo tutti gemelli, cioè, un esercito di copie.

Arte e moralità

Nel creare la bellezza, l'arte può impunemente rappresentare la violenza, la volgarità, la nudità, ecc. Significa questo che l'arte è immorale o amorale? Immorale certamente no, perché *l'arte non offende le nostre concezioni morali: nell'arte, solo la bruttezza offende le nostre concezioni estetiche.* Non è neanche amorale, se per amorale s'intende l'essere indifferenti alla virtù e al vizio (come può esserlo, per esempio, un gatto). L'arte non ignora la morale, nel senso che in un'opera o in un romanzo i valori che regolano la condotta dei personaggi vengono valutati al metro della morale: virtù e vizi sono visti per quello che sono.

Anzi, *spesso è il contrasto tra virtù e vizi che crea una situazione drammatica che è alla base del pathos di un'opera.* Il vizio può anche prevalere, ma non per questo è giustificato, più di quanto lo sia quando prevale nella vita. La crudeltà può esser rappresentata in maniera magistrale, ma non per questo diviene bontà. Anzi, suscita un senso di revulsione. Similmente, l'arte può rappresentare in maniera vigorosa la volgarità, ma l'opera non deve essere volgare: la volgarità per sé non è mai bella. Queste considerazioni dimostrano che l'arte è certamente libera, ma altrettanto certamente non è amorale.

L'arte rappresenta il bene e il male nella stessa maniera in cui questi sono presenti nella vita. Tuttavia, nessuno si domanda per questa ragione se la vita sia morale, immorale o amorale. Questi aggettivi possono essere applicati soltanto a chi vive, non alla vita; e, nell'arte, solo ai suoi personaggi. *L'arte è innocente perché non commette i peccati che rappresenta. I peccati dell'arte sono solo contro la bellezza.*

Per la stessa ragione, l'arte non può essere moraleggiante. L'arte sacra può rappresentare un'intensa spiritualità, una completa dedizione a Dio, l'eroismo di un totale sacrificio di sé nel nome di una fede appassionata, e l'ardente desiderio dell'anima umana per l'amore perfetto dello spirito. Nel fare questo, l'arte può ispirare coloro che sono sensibili alla necessità di comunicare con il nostro Creatore, ma l'arte non predica.

Anche nel campo della moralità, la bellezza ha la precedenza sulle convenzioni sociali. Un bel quadro di una persona nella sua nudità può essere esposto in un museo ad visitatori di tutte l'età, perché *la bellezza è intrinsicamente innocente.* Se quella stessa persona apparisse ugualmente nuda davanti al suo quadro sarebbe uno scandalo (atti osceni in luogo pubblico). Anzi, basterebbe che uno distribuisse fotografie non del quadro, ma di quella stessa persona nuda, per suscitare reazioni risentite (accuse di indecenza, se non di pornografia). Eppure sarebbe la stessa persona e la stessa nudità nel quadro, nel museo e nella fotografia.

La differenza è nella mente di chi la rimira. Alla nudità rappresentata nel quadro (anche se vi è una connotazione sensuale) reagisce il nostro senso estetico: se il quadro è bello o brutto non dipende certo dalla nudità per sé. Alla nudità fisica o a una sua fotografia, si rimprovera la sfida alla comune decenza. Quel senso di decenza che è stato preposto come custode "esterno" (la moralità è il custode "interno") ad una sfera dell'attività umana dove gli istinti non hanno certo bisogno di stimoli extra. Di fatto, la decenza deve sopprimere le scintille di certi stimoli, dal momento che certi istinti appartengono alla categoria delle "sostanze infiammabili".

La reazione estetica alla bellezza permette all'arte quella libertà che deve avere se vuol essere arte. L'arte non potrebbe rappresentare la bellezza del corpo umano se le fossero imposti i limiti della comune decenza. *L'arte non è indecente, perché è innocente.*

Saffo ha cantato i suoi amori con appassionata delicatezza e intima tenerezza. Uno può non approvare le sue scelte, ma questo non ha nulla a che fare con la bellezza dei suoi poemi. *Saffo è apprezzata non per i suoi amori, ma per la poesia con cui ha espresso le sue emozioni d'amore.* Cioè, per le sue creazioni artistiche. *Vi può anche essere colpa in quello che l'arte sceglie di rappresentare, ma vi è solo merito nella bellezza che l'arte crea.* Gli stessi amori di Saffo senza la sua poesia avrebbero avuto ben poco significato e interesse, eccetto per il pettegolezzo locale di Mitilene nell'isola di Lesbo. Gli amori di Saffo sono morti con lei, ma la sua poesia vive nel piacere estetico che dà ad ogni nuova generazione. La sua poesia esprime con grande bellezza sentimenti d'amore (e spesso i tormenti d'amore) che ciascuno vive: la sua poesia dà quel piacere che deriva dal suo esprimere quei sentimenti con passione ardente e allo stesso tempo con tenerezza intensa e delicata.

Conclusioni

L'apprezzamento dell'arte è il risultato della componente estetica della mente umana. L'abilità di percepire ed apprezzare la bellezza è un dono della genetica di incalcolabile valore, non certo inferiore a quello della logica. A questo riguardo, non bisognerebbe dimenticare che *la genetica è uno strumento essenziale della bioingegneria di Dio.*

Il piacere che si prova nella bellezza è così importante che determina gran parte delle nostre azioni. La bellezza è il criterio con cui si sceglie una cravatta, i vestiti, la casa in cui si vuol vivere, il coniuge, le vacanze, i libri che vogliamo leggere, i quadri, le suppellettili, ecc. Dove la bellezza non ha importanza, la bruttezza regna incontrastata. Ma dove tutto è brutto, la nostra sensibilità ci fa sentire estranei perfino fisicamente.

*Oltre all'abilità di **apprezzare** la bellezza, un altro grande dono di Dio alla razza umana è quello di poter **creare** la bellezza.* Questi doni non ci obbligano, perché sono doni d'amore: non esigono il pedaggio della gratitudine. Per apprezzare le contribuzioni umane alla bellezza del nostro habitat, è sufficiente riflettere su quanto si perderebbe se città belle (per esempio, Firenze, Roma, Parigi o New York) e i loro tesori artistici sparissero per essere sostituite da boschi e prati, sia pure belli. Inoltre, solo attraverso le creazioni dell'arte le sofferenze umane possono essere sublimate nel piacere della bellezza.

Il dono di creare la bellezza viene usato a tutti livelli. Per quanto riguarda la vita di tutti i giorni, individualmente il nostro gusto personale cerca la bellezza che l'attività artigianale crea nelle nuove mode nell'abbigliamento (dalle scarpe ai cappelli) e negli oggetti che usiamo (per es., automobili, mobilia, drappeggi, telefoni, computers, ecc.). La gente cerca la bellezza personale nell'acconciatura o colore dei capelli, nel portamento e persino nella dizione e nell'accento. *Naturalmente, la maggior parte delle cose che si usano nella quotidiana attività appartengono alla categoria della decorazione piuttosto che a quella dell'arte*: la decorazione ci dà della piacevolezza, mentre l'arte ci dà piacere estetico. La decorazione svanisce con la moda successiva e non è più piacevole, mentre l'arte rimane per sempre, la differenza tra le opere di un artigiano e quelle di un artista. Ma c'è una continuità nello sviluppo della bellezza e in cima alla scala c'è l'arte creata da grandi talenti. L'arte che, come la natura, crea la bellezza e la varietà nella bellezza.

L'arte e l'apprezzamento della bellezza contribuiscono alla completezza della mente e a rendere più piacevole la vita umana. Vi aggiungono una sorgente di piacere immediato, permettendole di apprezzare quello che di bello vi è nell'ambiente che ci circonda. Non è un piacere intellettuale o fisico, ma delicatamente emotivo, un piacere puro che non lascia delusioni o postumi amari.

Una persona rozza è sfortunata perché non apprezza la bellezza, per quanto questo è moderato dal fatto che una persona rozza non sa quello che perde. Rimane il fatto che la sua mente è in un certo senso mutilata perché incompleta. E il suo mondo più triste per essere assai meno bello.

20 May 2000

ART

The problem

In a visit to a museum of modern art, I was struck by the variety of the works presented and even more by the variety of the opinions of the viewers. This seemed puzzling, because the same work of art can not be at the same time beautiful and ugly. To clarify my ideas, I began to ask people *what art is.*

Only by knowing the answer to that question, one may hope to be in a better position for developing an informed opinion about artistic works. However, my inquiries did not get me very far, for the answers were not sufficiently specific to be satisfactory, or consisted in a bewildered look, a long pause and then "I do not know". I understood that, for I was asking that very question because I myself did not know the answer. So, driven by the desire to learn more about art in order to have a better understanding, I started to think this matter over. I do not know how far I progressed in my analysis, but I wish to share my reflections with those who wish to read them.

Definition of art

Art consists in the creation of beauty, whatever the subject represented or the style adopted. For example, not ugliness, but the representation of ugliness must be beautiful. Reciprocally, the representation of physical beauty can also be formal and affected, that is, ugly. *There are beautiful paintings of ugly persons and ugly paintings of beautiful persons.* Naturally, the depiction of a beautiful subject may be ugly either because the artist is not good, or because he wants to be so by adopting the strangeness of the method as tool for originality.

Emotions and beauty

Independently from the selected subject and from the style, *art can arouse different emotions* (pity, exhilaration, sadness, melancholy, transport, etc.), *but in feeling these emotions one must necessarily feel at the same time an aesthetic pleasure, that is, the pleasure that beauty gives.* To do this, it is necessary that the creation be beautiful. If a work does not give an aesthetic pleasure, either it is not art (the work is not beautiful) or the observer does not have good taste.

*As in life, art can represent the good and the evil, the beautiful and the ugly, the ethical and the immoral, etc., but in a manner that we find beautiful, **independently of the nature of the emotions that the portrayed*** *subject arouses in us when considered outside the field of art.*

Of what he sees, the artist chooses what emotionally strikes him. It does not matter if he strives to capture the sad aspects of life, such as poverty and decay, hopelessness of failure, chronic resignation, habit to the grayness of a drab life, a life that never began to live, progressive sinking in alcohol, gloom of despair, starvation of affections, loneliness, pervasive surrounding ugliness, an insignificant death after an insignificant life, lack of dreams, etc.

A masterly picture of sadness, tragedy, betrayal, poverty or cruelty can make us sad, but at the same time we feel pleasure in the beauty that has moved us. In an opera that moves us to tears, the pleasure is greater the more we are moved, the pleasure of the perfection of a masterpiece. We shed tears not of sadness, but of emotion for the beauty of its dramatic sadness. In the end, *the beauty of an opera is proportional to the intensity of the emotions that makes us feel*. In fact, the contrast between sadness and the aesthetic pleasure that we feel at the same time contributes to the poignancy of what we feel. *If the artist captures emotions with his art, it is their poignancy that gives the creation a soul. It is the soul that gives beauty to the creation.*

If the treatment of the same subject is rather mediocre (that is not artistic), instead of being moved, we are disappointed and irritated by the fact that there is no beauty in the music, song, recitation, plot, psychology in the behavior, etc. *In art, failure is the lack of beauty.*

Emotions without beauty

If there is no beauty without emotions, there can be emotions without beauty. In our daily life, if we witness a sad event (being the event only sad and not beautiful), we feel only sadness. If we see a serious car accident or we see on television the devastation of an earthquake, we feel horror, sadness and compassion, but certainly not pleasure. In what we see, there can be a tragedy, but there is no beauty. In fact, it comes spontaneously to say: "What an ugly accident!". We feel sadness that derives from our compassion; we do not feel pleasure in being sad for the lack of beauty.

If there is beauty even in an act of daily life (i.e., an unlucky heroic action), we feel sadness about the bad luck, but also the pleasure that derives from a beautiful action. It is possible that Julius Caesar had wanted a beautiful death, a noble and courageous death, a worthy crowning to an extraordinary life. A death that would set a final touch to the script of a life that yearned for an everlasting glory. We should not forget that Caesar also was a great writer, that is, an artist.

The creation

By definition, *creation results in something that did not exist before: creation is always original and unique.* Even if a painting or a book are inspired by objects and persons that exist in nature, they do not depict the external reality, but the reality developed by the way of feeling, sensitivity, creativeness, imagination and ability of the author. One might also say that *each creation is unique because his creator is unique.*

This explains why forged paintings have very little value even if copied in such a perfect manner that it is difficult to establish whether it is a falsification or an original. Even a reproduction of the same painting by his author would have little value. A copy (no matter how good) is valueless, because it is not a creation, only the copy of a creation, a mere clone.

The same concept applies to an original painting. If an artist exactly copies nature, the lack of originality disqualifies the work: *original copies do not exist, not even of nature.* If the artist were to copy nature, he would make a photo of it, instead of re-creating nature according to what his imagination, sensitivity, and style suggest to him. If art were to copy nature, the negative aspects of life could never hope to be beautifully depicted: the missing ingredient would be the human emotion that they elicit and that is reflected in the beauty of creation. Similarly, the beauty of nature would be merely duplicated without any personal poetry. *Nature often provides the stimulus for inspiration, and the artist translates his inspiration in the expression of his feelings.* Similarly, if a writer were to copy nature, instead of a novel, he would write a chronicle.

For the same reason, a portrait may be like the subject, but it can not be a photograph. The portrait is a subjective interpretation of the artist, not an objective description of a person. What could an artist create if not what is in **his** mind? *A portrait is not the reproduction of what the subject thinks he is, but the creation of what the artist sees and feels of that person.*

In this respect, it should be noted that this is not a peculiarity of the artist, but a general law: *each one of us is a different person according to who perceives us.* We are different for others, because different persons have a different perception of us. The perception is different qualitatively and quantitatively according to how much they know of us (for example, because of a continuous proximity); and according to their finesse and ability in perceiving us. The more perceptive persons form a portrait of others, which is much more like the original. In a certain sense, each of us forms in the mind a different portrait of a given person, although generally there is nothing artistic about it. In some cases, if we imagine things, we form in our mind the portrait of a person who does not exist, so different is our portrait from the original.

In painting a portrait, the artist also is strongly influenced by the aesthetic constraints of the painting, in addition to the physiognomy of the subject to be painted. What is thought to be beautiful varies according to the artist and therefore what the artist chooses to depict also varies as well as the style that he uses.

Creation and the "original subject"

In the portrait, the artist wants to create an *aesthetically* coherent painting according to his interpretation, psychological finesse, sensitivity, skill, and style. *The painting lives its own life (independently from the original subject), precisely because it is not a copy.* With the passing of time, the original (whether beautiful or ugly) ceases to be, and the painting (if beautiful) survives. For the artist, the most important thing is that the painting be beautiful, independently from the subject portrayed. For an artist, the background may be as important as the complexion of the face.

To have its own life, the portrait must have a soul, a soul revealed by the way the body is portrayed (for example, the acuteness of the mind in the light of the eyes, or the nobility of the countenance). *The portrait shows us the creature of the artist.*

Because the principal purpose of the portrait is to be artistic, in the painting there may be a poetry, a nobility of soul, a moral strength or an acute mind that the person portrayed never had. It is possible to attribute these and other qualities to the portrayed person because certain characteristics of the mind are usually revealed by the expression of the face and by the mien. Therefore, it is possible to recognize in different people haughtiness, good nature, nobility of soul, humility, intelligence, shrewdness, strength of character, the assurance of power, insignificance, etc. Or, at least, certain physical expressions correspond to certain mental qualities: hence, the possibility that the expression in the painting might suggest qualities that a person does not have.

Certain portraits want to be the apotheosis of an institution rather than of an individual: the portrait of a King or an Emperor can not be but magnificent, independently from the mediocrity of the person who has inherited the throne. In this case, it is the subject who does not want to be portrayed as he sees himself, but as he wants others to see him. No King will ever have himself portrayed in a dressing gown, night cap and slippers. *What is portrayed is the "Official Self"* (for a definition of the "Official Self", see aphorism 1035).

If one wants an "objective" portrait, he must turn to a photographer and not to a painter. And even the professional photographer will try and make a beautiful photo, where, for example, the baldness of the head disappears in a demure faint light or the posture is erect and full of dignity.

The portrayed and the portrayer

Although indirectly, *a portrait of a person portrays at the same time the individuality of the artist*: it is not only a matter of a portrait, but that of a portrait made by a given artist. So much so that people often refer to the portrait with the name of the artist (for example, a portrait of Leonardo, meaning a portrait made by Leonardo, not a portrait featuring Leonardo) rather than with the name of the person portrayed.

The fact is that *the person portrayed was made by God and his portrait was made by the artist*. In this sense, a person provides only the subject for the creation of the artist. The portrait picks and fixes for all times a distinctive (and transient) stage of the physical and mental life of the subject as the artist sees it. Of Mona Lisa, one only sees what Leonardo painted: even her ashes are long gone, although Leonardo lives in our minds through his work.

To become convinced that the subject provides only the raw material for the artistic creation, it would suffice to commission the portrait of the same person to ten different artists. The result would be not so much ten different portraits of the same person, as the portrait of ten different persons. In this respect, it suffices to consider the differences that there would be between a portrait made by Raffaello and that made by Picasso. Each artist would pick of that person the characteristics that interest him and would depict them according to the demands (or the pretense) of his style.

Art and "truth"

Similarly, in literature historic events and characters are different depending on who re-evokes them: each artist has his version that is real in terms of art. It is real in that a creation has its own artistic, not historical, life. A literary work should not be compared with the original historic event, because the original provides only the inspiration for the artist. *An artist creates, he does not describe.* Romeo and Juliet live their dream of love in the art of Shakespeare: the original Romeo and Juliet would not have recognized themselves in that "portrait". One could say that the literary work and historical events are parallel creations with completely different aims.

An accurate description of a historic event is the task not of an artist, but of an historian. An historian must describe the events that unfold on the human stage with absolute objectivity and exactness. Nevertheless, if an historian is very good he can also do it artistically, using his personal style (concise, picturesque, rich of psychological hues and insights, etc.). In interpreting motives, interests, aspirations, conspiracies, ambitions, heroism, betrayals, convictions, audacity, fears, etc., a good historian can do a portrait full of style, finesse and penetrating psychology not inferior to that of a good painter.

The acuteness of his comprehension illuminates the dark recesses of the human soul and uncovers the motives that have determined the actions. Then, in reading that passage of history one appreciates the beauty, finesse and elegance with which it is written (even if the interpretation may be hypothetical). In fact, there are books of history written so well (Thucydides, Plutarch, Tacitus, Livius, Julius Caesar, etc.) that belong to literature, in addition to history.

Also the historian can create a character, but the character that he creates must be historically correct. Without the analysis of the historian, what that character has done would exist, but the character would not exist in the complexity that the historian reveals on the basis of the collected information. For example, the great of history may forgive their enemies for motives that have all to do with political calculations and nothing to do with generosity. In this behavior, they are certainly superior to those who are stupidly cruel. *The difference between an historian and an artist is that for an historian the truth is obligatory and art optional; and for an artist art is obligatory and the "truth" is optional.* The truth in the arts consists in beauty (of a beautiful work one says that is *real* art [in Italian, *true* art]).

These concepts can be extended to every field. I remember that when I was a medical student I read in the book of anatomy of Chiarugi a description of the modifications of the uterus during the monthly cycle, a description that at its peak attained the acute beauty of the drama of a missed life.

Style

Style is the personal way of depicting what the artist feels. In every epoch, in the trends of art, artists try to express new forms of beauty seeking to develop a personal style inspired also by the values prevailing at the moment (i.e., religious feelings, romanticism, materialism, social theories, etc.). *But there can be neither beauty nor personal style if artistic talent is not there.*

In order to have a personal style, it is not enough to be wanting to have one, using the subtlety of logic or emotional distortions. *Style can not be chosen any more than one can choose his own individuality: style is a way of being artistically. Style results from the fact that the individuality of each mind can express itself only in its own personal way.* The way of expressing oneself is the direct consequence of the individuality of that person. For example, it is unlikely that a confused mind should express itself clearly; or a prosaic mind should express itself poetically. In the case of the artist, the personal style results from the fabric of his mind (congenital characteristics and acquired influences, such as training, environment, education, fashions, tendencies and even chance) and is associated with an exceptional ability in "sensing" and creating beauty.

This is the same as saying that one does not become an artist unless one is born with artistic talent: *artistic talent needs to be a part of the structure of his mind, like other characteristics that one might have (such as keen understanding, tenacity, passion, drive, generosity, etc.).*

It is perfectly useless to ask our nature for what it does not have. If we do, our nature can respond only by offering us our mediocrity. But the latter is revealed by the lack of talent, at least to those who have good taste and an unfailing critical talent. Similarly, it is useless to ask our nature for keen understanding, tenacity, passion, drive or generosity, if we do not have these attributes.

Style and art

From the point of view of beauty, the personal style of the artist has little importance, in the sense that (whatever the style) the result must be beauty. *It is not the style in itself that creates beauty: style is only an individual manner of depicting it.* Nay, if the creation is not beautiful, it is also possible that the ugliness of the "chosen" style might have contributed to it. *The distinction between style and art consists of the fact that the style is a means and art is the goal.*

However, whatever is created, it is created with a personal style (or at least in a personal way). *Style is the imprint with which beauty is created: an author is recognized by his style.* One does not need to look for the signature: *the style is the signature.*

Style is important for other reasons. Style results in a necessary variety in the creation. Style is a powerful tool with which the artist represents **his own** world, a unique and unrepeatable world. Since style results from the mental make up, it is improbable that a weak artist should have a "strong" style (at most, the style may be emphatic). Likewise, it is as improbable that a person sensitive to delicate things should have an epic style. To have it, one has to have a personality that has a taste of the grandiose and therefore a style appropriate for that.

However, the style should result from the manner of feeling dictated by the personality of the artist and not be an intellectual choice made on the basis of calculations and reflections on the current fashions and theories. First of all, one should have within "something" that not only he wants to express but rather that *he feels compelled* to express; and then express it according to the way he is. When the style is not natural, it reflects the artificiality of intellectual choices. This becomes apparent from the artificiality of what is created. An artificial style still reflects the individuality of a person, but at the same time reveals the lack of an essential ingredient: artistic talent.

Some coolly choose a method (most often a strange one, as long as it is different) to say what they do not feel; or at least do not feel passionately. *There is a desire to create something unique, but not the natural ability of creating something beautiful.* That is equivalent to speaking without having anything to say. In other instances, one could even have something to say, but either he does not know how to say it or it is not worth saying it. *In those cases, there is only a lack of artistic talent expressed with a confused style.*

In other cases, the style can be as strange as that which it depicts. If an artist is strange, his conception of beauty is so eccentric as to be incomprehensible.

Evolution of style but not of beauty

Like the scientific researcher, *the artist experiments*: he tries this or that manner of creating, until he finds one with which he is instinctively satisfied. This explains how there might be an evolution in the style of the same artist. More often, the change in his mentality with the passing of the time and under the influence of past experiences may find more satisfactory a new manner of creating. Naturally, the evolution is only in the style, since *there is no evolution in beauty*. If there is beauty, it is in the result, not in the style. Nay, in adopting a new style one could become more original, but in ugliness. In that case, instead of evolution, there is involution. *For beauty to evolve, genetics should change and with it our esthetic sense.* The beauty created by Praxiteles by far surpasses that of many contemporary works. *There is no way to improve perfection in beauty.*

The beauty or the ugliness of a work does not change with time, although what people think of a work may temporarily change. But the evolution from beauty to ugliness (and vice versa) of a given work only occurs in the taste of people and it is the result of the "sedimentation" of extraneous factors (i.e., fashions or theories or novelty of the style). In any case, the nature of the work does not change: it is either beautiful or ugly, and people were mistaken when it was considered beautiful or when it was considered ugly.

Art and fashion

In general, this "evolution" in the evaluation of a work only occurs for new and recent works. It is an evolution due to many factors: fashion that influences the general taste, novelty of conception, non-conventional style, lack of a sure taste, fear of being mistaken in not appreciating what we do not like, desire of being sharp-witted that leads one to see what is not there, the influence of critics on the uncertainty of most people, protection that there is in conforming to the prevailing opinion, fear of being considered reactionary or without taste, desire of the new, etc.

A reason for uncertainty is that *we distrust that to which we are not accustomed*, because we are incapable of forming a sound critical opinion. We are afraid of making a mistake, because we have experience of the changing (even drastic) of the opinions on works of art that in the past were considered vanguard. *We have seen both the appreciation of the beauty of works that before seemed strange and the becoming aware of the strangeness of works that before were deemed beautiful.* The opinion of professional critics helps but not much, since the opinions of critics often are as discordant as those of common people. Furthermore, a mediocre work may seem beautiful to a mediocre person.

However, the opinion that people form after a variable period of "sedimentation" in general remains unaffected in the following centuries. The failures disappear from the scene (and from museums) and the successes become classical work. Depending on the critics, more or less is seen in a classical work, but the opinion is substantially unchanged. *The beauty of a classical work persists because the laws of human genetics do not change: in this case, it does not change what we consider beautiful.*

Naturally, not all experiments can be expected to be successful. On the contrary, relatively few are successful as artists, because *many create not new forms of beauty, but only new forms.* The problem is that they have a personal way of expression, but no real style. Or if you prefer, they have a personal style, but only that. But, as I said, style is not synonymous with art. *Style is a way of creating, but art is the creation of beauty. Being seduced by beauty (as all artists are) is not synonymous with the ability to create beauty.*

Relationship between the variability of style and of taste

Style has another important function. *As there is diversity of feeling among the artists, likewise there is a diversity of feeling and of appreciation among the public.* We feel more attracted by the works of art that appeal to the taste of our individuality. If we deem beautiful what a given artist has created, that artist becomes our favored artist.

To this preference contributes first of all our way of feeling, that (as for the artist) is linked to our individuality, education, experience, mental development and sensitivity. An instinctive good taste guides our preferences to choose among things that are beautiful, and not to be enmeshed by things that are ugly, even if the latter are fashionable. In general, an orderly and "reasonable" person considers certain novelties strange and a whimsical person considers strangeness new (and attractive).

This difference in one's preferences confirms that the aesthetic sense is determined by genetics. *All of us obey the general rules of human genetics, in that all of us have an aesthetic sense. But each individual has his own genetic variations (determined by the mixtures of genes).* Therefore, it not in the least surprising that aesthetic sense should vary not only in the "quantity", but also in the "quality" in different individuals.

For the "quantity", there are individuals who are completely indifferent to beautiful things and others who live only for beauty ("aesthetes"). As for "quality", among those who appreciate beauty, of some we say that they do not have good taste (*they find beautiful what we find ugly*) and of others we say that have a sophisticated good taste ("arbiter elegantiae").

Therefore, each one instinctively prefers those artists whose taste agrees with his own. However, *if someone has a considerable sensitivity, then he is capable of appreciating beauty in its different forms*: he finds pleasure in the delicate nuances of certain images (e.g., demure modesty of innocence) as in the sweeping waves of passion of a heroic music. Conversely, if the artist has an extraordinary genius he is appreciated by a very large number of persons.

New forms of art

As Cristoforo Colombo experienced the uncertainty of the unexplored, likewise we move with uncertainty among the novelties of the new schools. There always are new movements in the arts, which, in exploring the unknown, meet with the success of fashion for variable periods of time. These movements are attributed to the continuous changes in living conditions and to the various social and philosophical theories prevailing at the moment.

In this regard, one can not but ask himself whether it is possible that art should need theories. The answer would seem to be that not art, but only artists may need them. *Each artist lives in the world of his epoch and he is subject to the influences to which he is exposed.* If the artist is strongly attracted by certain social theories of the moment, it is possible that he may only find interesting dealing with the misery and sufferings of the poorest layers of society. In other epochs, fashion reflects the predominance of nobility and then the noble are portrayed in the "glory" of their flamboyant attires. Poverty does not exist, at least as a subject for portrayal. *These swings in interest create the precondition for next wave of fashion, if nothing else because we get used to everything. And few resist the fascination of being innovative or even revolutionary.*

If poverty or affluence (or any other thing) can be stimuli for inspiration for a given artist, in themselves they are not sufficient to create art. If the artist is not good, he does not create art, but only propaganda according to his convictions. And if he is good, from the point of view of art, the subjects that he chooses have little importance. For example, they there are beautiful novels that treat of most varied themes (including poverty and wealth).

Not by chance, when we speak of a current fashion, we say the "last fashion": *last* because the precedent ones are no longer fashionable. The importance of fashions is related to the universal desire of novelty, or rather by the necessity to create the new. But, *above all, all fashions are determined by the fact that a society never remains the same: more than a desire, the development of the new is an insuppressible drive.*

Since new individuals are born all the time, self-expression can not be but different and therefore original. In expressing ourselves, we are mightily influenced by what has influenced the development of our mind. *We live not so much in our epoch as of our epoch.* We absorb the influence of the environment where we live. Hence, the new is the necessary consequence of new individuals with a different formation.

The search for the new is an absolute necessity to avoid stagnation, create variety and sometimes new forms of beauty. But even ugly creations have a function of their own. They stimulate thinking and they drive us to look for the reasons which make us believe that a creation is not beautiful. *We try to justify the judgment of our taste, which is a manner by which we want to demonstrate that we have good taste.*

Furthermore, beauty owes much to ugliness: the comparison with ugliness makes us appreciate beauty much more. Nay, *if there were no ugliness, ipso facto there would be no beauty.* New forms of beauty can only be found only by following the path strewn with the failures of ugliness.

Freedom in art

Because of its characteristics, *art demands freedom*: it is impossible to force upon on an artist a given subject or a given way to depict it (e.g., realism or cubism). It would be the same as asking the artist not to be himself. One can even try to do it, as some dictatorships do in the name of their political necessities. But then the result is (an ugly) propaganda, and not art. The only way in which politics could exploit art for its ends is to influence the development of the artist during his formation before he reaches adulthood, or his convictions when he is an adult.

There is nothing more free of creation, because the artist has at his complete disposal all the ingredients to create. First of all, the characteristics of his individuality and a creative mind that have a complete control of the creation as the artist is conceiving it; and then the means to realize his own conceptions (such as words, colors, scalpel, musical script, volumes of space, etc.).

Art is free because it originates within the world of the mind: the artist expresses himself, independently from, and sometimes against, the trends of the moment. Absolutely his is the choice of colors, nuances, backgrounds, expressions, perspective, melancholy, laces, etc. In art, there are no instruction books as for cooking or for engineering. Furthermore, a critic may approve or disapprove of a given work and rightly so, but he certainly can not direct its realization. *The only thing that the artist **can not do** is choosing not to express himself or express himself as others would want him to do.*

License in art

On the other hand, there are those who confuse freedom of art with license. Some believe that liberty consists only in doing whatever pleases them, without realizing that one becomes an artist when what he does is beautiful. It is of no consequence if what the artist likes is beautiful or ugly, but it is essential that what he does should be beautiful. If the depiction of something (beautiful or ugly) is ugly, in what might art possibly consist? *Naturally, all those who work in the field of art do what pleases them, but only those who create beauty are artists.* The others contribute only "novelties", novelties of the moment that may surprise the intellect and leave indifferent the taste.

Art can not be arbitrary, because *it **must** create beauty.* In this sense, art must create *a coherent reality of its own. Incoherence in itself does not create beauty: it may simply have no meaning in that it is incomprehensible.* For example, making one ear much larger than the other or three nostrils would acquire coherence only if aesthetically justified. Coherence in itself does not create beauty either, but at least it can be assessed by taste without the need to justify arbitrary choices.

In a novel, a character may be good or bad, haughty or humble, honest or deceitful, etc.; or be good and bad according to the situation. But in any case, there must be an internal coherence without which there is not a character, but a puppet. If one wants to create a hero, the result should not be a character so awkward as to seem a buffoon. One may want to create an incoherent character, but even in that case the depiction of incoherence needs to be done coherently.

One can not write a novel while ignoring the reality of human psychology, because otherwise the reader will not form in his imagination a mental portrait of the characters and appreciate the meaning of the events. We do not merely read a beautiful novel, rather we live it in our imagination and in the emotions that it elicits in us. *What the artist expresses can be appreciated by our mind only it falls within the boundaries of mental characteristics that we have in common with the artist.* The work of a mad artist does not communicate with most people; and art is wasted on a mad viewer.

It must be added that coherence in art is an aesthetic, not literal, coherence. If a given color is aesthetically necessary for a given object, it is not *in the least* important whether in nature that object has never that color. Similarly, the form of an object may exist only in a given painting and be aesthetically coherent. In other words, **in art beauty must prevail over everything**, including coherence and incoherence.

Art and beauty

If art must create beauty, we need to ask ourselves what beauty is. *Beauty is a way of feeling that results from our genetic structure,* as do other ways of feeling of our mind, for example, morality, faith or family affections. *This particular faculty of the mind makes us find pleasure in what it make us find beautiful.* Depending on the development of this faculty in different individuals, one appreciates beauty to a greater or smaller extent.

What we consider beautiful, we "feel" it to be beautiful. We are unable to explain why, because beauty does not have a logic foundation and depends on a genetic trait. *We can analyze why a thing is beautiful, but not "explain" the essence of beauty.* Not by chance, we say: "It is beautiful what one likes". In this, good taste is not different from other feelings: if we are genetically normal, we love the beautiful, we feel affection for our family, we distinguish just from unjust, true from false, delicate from coarse, etc. In pathological cases, there can be distortions either of affections, or of ethics or of good taste. But even in the normal cases, the roughness of some ignores the seductions, transport and emotions of aesthetic sensitivity.

Inspiration

If good taste is necessary to *appreciate* the beauty of a work of art, a great deal more is required to *create* a work of art.

In order to create, some people need inspiration. One writes or paints when an emotion is aroused in his mind by what he sees, feels or thinks. This is an emotion that one intensely desires to express in words, poetry, music, or a painting in such manner as to satisfy one's desire of beauty. One wants to give life to what he feels. The outcome is a unique creation with a beauty of its own which is different from what inspired it. *Like nature, art creates. But art does not imitate nature because it does not reproduce what the artist sees (like a common photograph does), but the manner in which the artist sees, feels, conceives and expresses the chosen subject.*

Human art creates, but not from nothing. And if it did that, it would be incomprehensible. *We can conceive only within the terms in which we have been conceived.* It is true that human art does not copy the beauty of the nature created by God, but is often inspired by it. Or it listens to the teachings of nature, like those of a master of art.

In turn, the beauty of a creation inspires an aesthetic pleasure in those who are exposed to it. As already mentioned, *art makes beautiful what it creates, be the subject beautiful, tragic, delicate, sad , or even ugly.* It is the beauty of the creation that elicits an emotion in those who are exposed to it.

What is created must capture the emotion of what has inspired the artist. *Inspiration is an emotion caused by what strikes us as being beautiful in one way or another. Inspiration stimulates the imagination, which in turn wants to realize what it conceives through a personal expression of beauty.* Once aroused, imagination no longer depends on what we have seen, but consists in emotive ferment that develops in the mind a theme (for example, a cloud pushed by the wind) using words, images and concepts that satisfy one's own aesthetic demands. *Imagination is the ability of the mind to create images, thoughts and feelings that do not depend directly on the sensory input from the physical world. In doing so, imagination creates a new reality according to the characteristics of one's mind.* Without imagination, one is arid; and with too much undisciplined imagination, one may be a drifting dreamer. But if there can not be art without imagination, imagination alone is not enough: it needs to be translated into beauty.

Without inspiration, there are no impulses to create, because imagination remains mute. Every day the artist sees and feels, but not every day he feels an emotion so keen as to impose an impulse to express it. *Inspiration is necessary (and possible) for those who have the necessary sensitivity: if there is talent, then there is also the capability of realizing the inspiration in a creation.*

In expressing an emotion, one is creative when imagination finds in its inner world the appropriate means for expressing in a beautiful manner what moves it. The inner world being personal, the same emotional stimulus can drive different artists to create a song, a poem, music, a novel, etc. What is expressed has a reality that arises from the beauty created, a reality different from what has originated the emotion and that reflects the artistic individuality of the author.

Beauty is born by the expression of the inner world of the artist and it is appreciated by the inner world of those who love art. It is only in the inner world (the mind, the soul, the affections, or the Self) of everyone that beauty can arouse an aesthetic emotion. The role of the inner world (the world of each mind) in regard to beauty explains why each artist pursues different aesthetic expressions and why each one has different aesthetic preferences.

The artistic individuality

Not all artists seem to depend from the whims of the unpredictable inspiration. These are the professional artists. For example, there are writers who write each day for a certain number of hours. How could it be possible that every day they should be inspired from 9 AM to 12:30 PM? Inspiration on installments? Others write music or poems, because they have received a commission. Inspiration on payment?

The explanation is another one. These are generally exceptional individuals (how exceptional is established by the quality of their work) who have been "structured" by nature for creating in different fields of art. *For them, to create is a way of being: no matter to which situation they are exposed, they respond to it with a mind capable of creating with a fertile imagination a world of their own.*

When they start to work on the subject that occupies them at the moment, their sensitivity and their talent develop the theme under the direction of their imagination and fantasy. They live in their imagination the events that they develop and identify themselves with the different characters: not by chance, writers are acute and alert observers of human nature.

Thus, the passion of love or the tragedy of death of the characters find a way of being expressed according to the way of feeling, being and conceiving of the artist (in an opera, a drama, a novel, a painting, a poem, etc.). Since the artist identifies himself with his characters, these express themselves at those heights to which the ability of the artist brings them.

What could have been only gossip or one of the many (even banal) eventualities of daily life (e.g., jealousy or adultery) becomes a drama full of intense emotions in the vision of the artist. His ability, fantasy, poetic sensitivity, sense of the dramatic, imagination, psychological acuteness, knowledge of the human drives, capability of analyzing himself in depth, etc. create those realities that set into vibration the strings of the harp of the human heart.

Just like a picnic in the country is made poetic by depicting the clear transparency of the water of the river, the sails of the boats in the breeze, the flowers generous of colors, the pause of rest of the human figures in the shade of a tree, the basket with food and the bottle of red wine on the tablecloth with red and white squares spread on the green grass. *It is not the picnic that is being painted, but a picture of the variety of the human life as the artist feels it.* Or if one prefers, one of the pictures (this time idyllic) of the complex drama of life as it is perceived by the sensitivity of beauty.

Art and knowledge

Art does not want to understand life in its recondite meanings and in the intertwining of its mysteries. Instead, art creates expressions of life that become part of the life of many, adding to it new meanings, cultivating its sensitivity, rendering it richer of emotions and more sensitive to beauty. It enriches and develops a part of our Self that gives us a pure and uncontaminated pleasure even when results from the depiction by the artist of the turbidity of human passions and vices.

If art asks questions, it is not to find answers, but to express what there is of dramatic in the mystery of our existence. That mystery that the cares of our daily activity banish from the consciousness of our mind and relegate to the investigations of philosophy. Not only we do not inquire into the meaning of our existence, but often we do not even ask if there is one.

If someone asks the question, that person seems, if not strange, at least indiscreet in asking embarrassing and "theoretical" questions [a question is embarrassing when we do not know the answer]. In contrast to philosophy, the questions of art arouse emotions, not reasoning. *In art, the questions are the answers: we demand only that the questions have a beautiful and emotional intensity.*

Beauty and the individual minds

Since beauty is linked to human genetics, necessarily beauty exists only in the human mind and for the human mind. We receive images from the external world and we find some beautiful, others ugly and other still aesthetically indifferent according to the taste of our mental structure. Since the genetic structure of different individuals has a considerable basic similarity, people often judge beautiful the same images originating from the external world.

But the genetic structure of different individuals always has individual variations, made even more marked by acquired factors (i.e., education, age, or environment). Therefore, what each person considers beautiful can vary in the quality ("it is very beautiful", "it is beautiful", "it is not bad") or even in the quality ("I do not see what you find beautiful in it: to me, it is ugly"). Even interest in beauty has great variations depending on the persons. There are people who are so coarse as not to appreciate any form of beauty. And those who are so refined that for them nothing important exists outside beauty.

These attitudes are less different as far as natural phenomena are concerned, since we grow with these phenomena and they become part of our daily lives. Divergences increase when people judge of the beauty of human creations. To it contributes the fact that human creations take place in different fields (music, poetry, architecture, sculpture, painting, etc.), each of which is "specialized" and interests some persons but not others. In addition, among persons who appreciate a form of art, for example poetry, some appreciate a given form of poetry and others appreciate another. But even among those who appreciate the same form of poetry, the knowledge of the field, good taste and competence in judging beauty varies considerably from one individual to the next.

In appreciating the beauty of nature, naturally we appreciate the art of God, even if commonly we confine ourselves to admiring the beauty of a flower or of the silken light of the moon in the pensive silence of the night without asking ourselves who their author is. That is somewhat curious, because of a painting or of a novel we immediately ask who the author is. Nay, few would buy a painting of which the author is not known. Furthermore, it has to be considered that even the greatest artists are creatures of nature as are the leaves playing in the wind, the foamy crest of the waves or the crystalline silence of the snowy peaks.

Like nature, also the artist offers us *his* world, a personal world that consists in the manner in which either he re-creates what he sees in nature, or creates what his imagination makes him live in his mind. In both cases, the artist pursues the creation of beauty. However, *in contrast to the beauty of nature, human beauty is not "universal". It is an "individual" beauty that bears the style and the imprint not of God (like in nature), but of an individual (created by God).* As mentioned above, it is a great deal more difficult to judge this individual beauty, because often it presents itself in new forms to which we are not accustomed, and at other times we deal with creations that are "new" but not beautiful.

Nature and artistic beauty

Nature is so rich in beauty that it is the paradigm of beauty. Its beauty is the result of the art of God and it is instinctively appreciated by most people. We grow with it and we take it for granted. So much so that some may not even consider it a form of art. Yet, *it is the beauty of nature that most often inspires the artist.*

There is beauty also in the wildest outbursts of nature. For example, a hurricane that arouses fierce waves whose foam sprays the deserted beach, while the palms, gone mad, savagely shake their leaves in the wind that unleashes its fury without restraint, that hurricane has a primordial beauty that is impossible not to appreciate. At least, as long as it does not result in the tragedy of the loss of lives.

The artist endeavors to capture the soul of the beauty of nature: the grace, colors, delicacy, melancholy, peace, loneliness, wilderness, majesty, impetuosity, frightening power, savagery, etc. The soul of the painting is a human emotion that the artist felt and that the viewer shares.

If in a painting an earthquake is depicted in such a way as to capture the intensity of the tragedy, the cruelty of the devastation, the human suffering, the desolation of destruction, etc., one can react to it with the intense emotion and with the pleasure with which a tragic play is appreciated. We can not avoid feeling how dramatically beautiful the painting is. The difference with a real earthquake is that in the painting the earthquake is not described, but it is "interpreted". The painting does not photograph the earthquake, but it creates that reality that the emotion of the artist has seen in it, those feelings that the tragedy has aroused in him.

Photography and art

Also a photographer can do something artistic, but in such a case he takes a picture with special effects of only what inspire him: *like all artists, he does not reproduce what he sees, but creates what he feels*. He interprets his own sensitivity. The viewer admires the beauty that there is in the photo (for example, the shadow of a stonewall on a country lane and on the adjacent grass), not in the object (the wall) that in itself may not mean much. From that, it is clear that art imitates nature only in so far as, like the nature, it creates beauty.

In an earthquake, the photographer will try not to document the damage, but to present his own emotions. He will photograph what strikes him as being particularly sad, tragic, epic or keenly human. He will use the camera like the painter uses the brush to create his vision of what he feels. He will depict what his aesthetic sensitivity feels, because in taking pictures he will choose only what in one way or another will seem to him beautiful. Beautiful not objectively (in fact what is photographed could be horrible), but beautiful emotionally. That is, beautiful in so far as it arouses an aesthetic emotion and contributes to create that drama and that dismay that the earthquake arouses in the human soul. *It is the beauty of the photo that we like, not the destruction.*

Naturally, there is a considerable difference between photographer and artist. The creation of the photographer requires a keen sensitivity, a good camera and a few minutes. The creation of the artist requires sensitivity, imagination that elaborates the same object, ability in translating imagination into creation and a personal style in creating. The photographer captures the beauty that he sees in the creation of God. The artist does likewise, but he re-creates it in an original manner. A good photographer has sensitivity, and a good artist has sensitivity and creative talent.

The evaluation of art

It is not difficult to evaluate reality from a physical point of view. For example, it is easy to measure the distance between two cities, or how much steel will be needed for the construction of a bridge. Similarly, one can calculate the foundations of a palace, the thickness of the walls, the length of the vaults, etc. These measurements are based on the mechanical performance of the materials used and on well established data. Instead, the aesthetic evaluation of the palace is subject to criteria many of which are rather subjective. The criteria depend on the individual taste and therefore are variable from individual to individual.

Beauty does not have an objective unit of measure, a unit that has a definite dimension and it is valid for everyone, like, for example, the Richter scale for earthquakes. *The fact is that beauty can not have a unit of measure at all, because beauty is in the mind, and the mind is different in different persons.* The dimensions of beauty are established by the taste of the mind of the observer.

Subjective beauty and objective beauty

Beauty is an emotional individual experience and, in that sense, is always subjective. But the emotions aroused by beauty are of different nature. Furthermore, it happens that either beauty arouses emotions or emotions arouse beauty.

An example of the first case (*beauty arouses emotions*) is provided by some famous actors and actresses, of whom everyone appreciates the physical beauty and artistic brilliance. Their beauty is "objective" because it is appreciated by nearly all.

The second case (*emotions arouse beauty*) is a great deal more common and is in general the result of love: the person with whom one falls in love is rarely ugly for the lover. This "subjective" and "individualized" beauty is naturally the basis for an orderly development of society, since it permits everyone to marry the chosen mate. If everyone were to fall in love with the same "objectively" beautiful persons, chaos would ensue. In this connection, it should be added that *physical beauty is important, but it is not the only form of beauty that can make a person attractive.* Sometimes, other beautiful qualities (gentleness, understanding, consideration, generosity, affectionateness, etc.) may be far more important than physical beauty.

Furthermore, our children are always beautiful and so are our grandchildren. Even if we see children who are more beautiful than our own children or grandchildren, the lack of a personal relationship appreciates their beauty in a "theoretical" manner, i.e., without the affection that we feel for our children. For strangers we may feel an aesthetic pleasure, but for our own family we feel first of all an affection that then gives an aesthetic pleasure as well. *Reciprocally, a mother is always beautiful to her children.*

Beauty and variety

Variety is already a form of beauty, i.e., beauty must be varied. Let us assume that everyone were to go around with the same suit (even if very beautiful): very few would be thrilled. It suffices to consider the embarrassment and irritation of a lady who were to meet another with the same dress at a party. The implication would be that one's taste is not sufficiently personal.

What makes personal the taste of everyone is the mixing of genes. As everyone has his own unique face, similarly each one has his own unique taste. The consequent personal choices contribute to that variety that gives an aesthetic pleasure. *Therefore, variety in beauty results not only from the fact that each creation is personal and unique, but also from the fact that each individual taste is personal and unique.* More over, in general, it can be stated that *our individuality is the result of the mixtures of genetics: our mind is the source of every form of variety, both in creating and in appreciating beauty.* In identical twins, there is no copy because there is no original. The importance of the mixing by genetics is seen from the fact that if parthenogenesis were the only manner of reproduction, we all would be twins, i.e., an army of clones.

Art and morality

In creating beauty, art can with impunity depict violence, vulgarity, nudity, etc. Does this mean that art is immoral or amoral?

Immoral certainly not, because *art does not offend our moral convictions: in art, only ugliness offends our aesthetic conceptions.* It is not amoral either, if for amoral one means being indifferent to virtues and vices (as, for example, a cat would be). Art does not ignore morality, in the sense that in an opera or in a novel the values that regulate the behavior of the characters are evaluated in the light of ethics: virtues and vices are seen for what they are.

Nay, *often it is the contrast between virtues and vices that creates a dramatic situation which is the basis of the pathos of an opera.* Vice may even prevail, but it is not justified for that reason, no more than it is justified when it prevails in life. Cruelty can be depicted in masterly manner, but it does not become goodness because of this. On the contrary, it arouses a sense of revulsion. Similarly, art can vigorously depict vulgarity, but the work must not be vulgar: vulgarity in itself is never beautiful. These considerations show that art is certainly free, but with equal certainty art is not amoral.

Art depicts the good and the evil in the same way these are found in life. However, nobody asks whether for this reason life is moral, immoral or amoral. These adjectives can be applied only to the living, not to life; and in art, only to its characters. *Art is innocent, because it does not commit the sins that it depicts. The sins of art are only against beauty.*

For the same reason, art can not be moralizing. Sacred art may depict an intense spirituality, a complete devotion to God, the heroism of total self-sacrifice inspired by a passionate faith, and the yearning of the human soul for perfect love of the spirit. In doing so, the sacred art may inspire those who are sensitive to the need to communicate with our Creator, but art does not preach.

Also in the field of morality, beauty has the precedence over social conventions. A beautiful painting of a person in its nudity can be exposed in a museum to visitors of all ages, because *beauty is intrinsically innocent.* If that same person were to appear equally nude next to its painting it would be a scandal (obscenity in a public place). Nay, it would suffice to give away photos not of the painting, but of that same nude person to arouse resentful reactions (accusations of indecency, if not of pornography).Yet, it would be the same person and the same nudity in the painting, in the museum and in the photo.

The difference is in the mind of observer. To the nudity depicted in the painting (even if there is a sensual connotation to it) reacts our aesthetic sense: if the painting is beautiful or ugly, it certainly does not depend on the nudity in itself. To the physical nudity or to its photo, we reproach the challenge to common decency. That sense of decency that has been assigned as "external" custodian (morality is the "internal" custodian) to a sphere of human activity where the instincts do not need extra stimuli. In fact, decency must suppress the sparks of certain stimuli, since certain instincts belong to the category of "inflammables".

The aesthetic reaction to beauty permits art that freedom that it must have to be art. Art could not depict the beauty of the human body if the limits of common decency were to be imposed to it. *Art is not indecent, because it is innocent.*

Sappho sung her loves with impassioned delicacy and intimate tenderness. One may not approve her choices, but this has nothing to do with the beauty of her poems. *Sappho is appreciated not for her loves, but for the poetry with which she expresses her emotions of love.* That is, for her artistic creations. *There can be even guilt in what art chooses to depict, but there is only merit in the beauty that art creates.*

The same loves without her poetry would have had rather little meaning and interest, except for the local gossip of Mitylene in the island of Lesbos. The loves of Sappho have died with her, but not her poetry which lives in the aesthetic pleasure that it gives to each new generation. Her poetry beautifully expresses feelings of love (and often the torments of love) that each one lives: her poetry gives the pleasure that derives from her expressing those feelings with ardent passion and at the same time with intense and delicate tenderness.

Conclusions

The appreciation of art is the result of the aesthetic component of the human mind. The capability of perceiving and appreciating beauty is a gift of genetics of incalculable value, not certainly inferior to that of logic. In this connection, we should not forget that *genetics is an essential instrument of the bioengineering of God.*

The pleasure that we feel in beauty is so important that it determines most of our actions. Beauty is the criterion with which we select a tie, our clothes, the house where we want to live, our consort, vacations, the books that we want to read, paintings, furnishings, etc. Where beauty is not important, ugliness reigns uncontested. But where everything is ugly, our sensitivity makes us feel extraneous even physically.

*In addition to the ability of **appreciating** beauty, another great gift of God to human kind is that of being capable of **creating** beauty.* These gifts do not even oblige us, because they are gifts of love: they do not demand the toll of gratitude. To appreciate the human contributions to the beauty of our world, it suffices to reflect how much would be lost if beautiful cities (for example, Florence, Rome, Paris or New York) and their artistic treasures were to disappear to be substituted by woods and meadows, no matter how beautiful. Furthermore, only through the creations of art can human suffering be sublimated into the pleasure of beauty.

The gift of creating beauty is made use of at all levels. As far as daily life is concerned, individually our personal taste seeks the beauty that artisan activity creates in new fashions in clothing (from shoes to hats) and in the objects that we use (e.g., cars, furniture, draperies, telephones, computers, etc.). People seek personal beauty in hairstyle or color, in gait and even in diction and accent. *Of course, most of the items used in our daily activity belong to the category of decoration rather than to that of art*: decoration gives us pleasantness, whereas art gives aesthetic pleasure. Decoration fades with the next fashion and it is no longer pleasant, whereas art is there for good, the difference between the works of an artisan and those of an artist. But there is a continuum in the development of beauty and at the top of the ladder there is the art created by great talents. Art that, like nature, creates beauty and variety in beauty.

Art and the appreciation of beauty contribute to the completeness of the mind and to make human life more pleasant. They add a source of immediate pleasure by allowing the mind to appreciate the beauty in the environment that surrounds us. It is not an intellectual or physical pleasure, but a delicately emotional one, a pure pleasure that does not leave behind disappointments or bitter after-effects.

A coarse person is unlucky because he does not appreciate beauty, although this is mitigated by the fact that a coarse person does not know what he misses. Yet, the fact remains that his mind is in a certain sense mutilated because it is incomplete. And his world is sadder because it is much less beautiful.

18 Marzo 1993

DIO

Intelligenza e onnipotenza

Di Dio si sa ben poco, ma non necessariamente nulla.
Ragioniamoci un po' sopra. Un architetto che fa un palazzo splendido con
un parco di grande eleganza certamente dimostra una grande intelligenza
(talvolta ai limiti della genialità) e un grande sensibilità estetica.

Come sarebbe stato possibile aver creato le meraviglie infinite
dell'universo senza un'intelligenza altrettanto infinita? Senza un'intelligenza
associata all'onnipotenza? Per esempio, durante una conferenza è stata
presentata la foto di un neurone che aveva circa 30000 connessioni con altre
cellule nervose. Ora, nelle due cellule iniziali dell'embrione evidentemente
ci sono le istruzioni che eventualmente portano allo sviluppo di tale neurone
e delle sue connessioni con altri neuroni. E queste istruzioni vanno
incorporate nelle cellule che portano al successivo embrione. Chi ha fatto
questo non può che avere un'intelligenza e potere infiniti.

Se uno avesse bisogno di una conferma dell'intelligenza di Dio, può
solo considerare la capacità di pensare: il passaggio dalla cellule nervose
alla formulazione del pensiero è un processo incredibilmente straordinario.
*Il dubitare dell'intelligenza di Dio dovrebbe solo farci dubitare della
nostra.* Se poi si dubita dell'onnipotenza, basta considerare l'universo o il
ruolo del sole nell'economia della biologia: chi avrebbe potuto crearli se
non un Essere onnipotente? Ma, a questo riguardo, bisogna considerare che
creare una "semplice" lucertola dal nulla non è un'impresa molto più facile.
Per rendersene conto, basta provarcisi.

La mente e la libertà

Si può ancora negare Dio, ma è chiaro che *solamente uno che sia
stato creato da Dio può avere la prerogativa di negare Dio: basta avere
solo una mente miope che non si rende conto della necessità di essere stata
creata.* Ma senza la mente (miope o no), non si afferma né si nega niente.

Se poi la mente non fosse stata creata da Dio e si fosse sviluppata
"da sé" sarebbe un miracolo. Ma per spiegare il miracolo, avremmo pur
bisogno di un autore del miracolo, cioè di Dio. Bisogna anche considerare
che la mente è talmente straordinaria da essere di per se stessa di fatto un
miracolo, un miracolo di Dio.

Dio ha dato alla mente il pensiero e la libertà di usarlo come vuole.
Non stupidamente, ma arditamente. Proprio perché siamo liberi ma spesso
non abbastanza intelligenti, si fanno degli errori. *Se non fossimo liberi, nel
fare degli errori si eseguirebbero solo istruzioni sbagliate.* Che la libertà sia
un privilegio assai difficile lo dimostra il fatto che è difficile non solo

servirsene in maniera appropriata, ma perfino definirla in maniera soddisfacente.

Il caso

Dunque, *sarebbe difficile negare che Dio possiede un'intelligenza infinita e la capacità di tradurla in opere eccezionali (onnipotenza). Se poi si volesse negare l'esistenza di Dio, si sarebbe forzati a divinizzare il caso.* Il caso che non solo creerebbe un ordine straordinario (che è già difficilmente concepibile e intrinsecamente contraddittorio), ma anche la materia dal nulla. Ma lì sorge un altro problema: dal nulla non si crea nulla, *neanche a caso.*

Senso estetico

Ma, per ritornare all'esempio dell'architetto, per fare qualcosa di pregevole sono necessari non solo un'intelligenza notevole e i mezzi materiali, ma anche senso estetico. Se apprezziamo la bellezza di un palazzo, quanto più dovremmo apprezzare la bellezza della natura, una bellezza che è diretta solo a rallegrare l'anima umana e che contribuisce così tanto a fare della terra il paradiso terrestre.

Per esempio, consideriamo la bellezza dei fiori e la loro grande varietà. Che cosa giustifica la bellezza e varietà dei fiori? O la loro "necessità"? La risposta non può essere che la creazione di bellezza in forme diverse per il godimento di coloro che possono apprezzarla, e cioè degli esseri umani.

Se si toglie la bellezza e la sua varietà, che cosa rimane dei fiori? *Quale altra funzione hanno i fiori, se non di essere belli? E perché tanti fiori diversi se non per creare forme diverse di bellezza?* Quando i fiori sono appassiti e non sono più belli, forse che non vengono tirati via? Ora, chi può creare una cosa bella senza avere senso estetico? *Se Dio ha creato tante cose meravigliose, come è possibile che non abbia uno straordinario senso estetico e l'abilità di creare con grande varietà secondo tali criteri estetici?*

Certamente non si vorrà sostenere che i fiori sono belli e vari "per caso" o come risultato dell'evoluzione. *L'evoluzione non potrebbe esistere se non ci fosse già qualcosa che esiste. Almeno che non si ammetta un'evoluzione dal nulla. Ma allora sarebbe qualcosa di più dell'evoluzione: sarebbe creazione.* Ed inoltre, sulla base del caso, dovremmo assistere ad esempi di evoluzione ed involuzione. Il risultato netto sarebbe una sequenza di variazioni senza un piano strategico né una direzione particolare. Cioè, non ci sarebbe evoluzione (netta).

Si potrebbe dire che oggettivamente i fiori non sono belli, ma ci appaiono tali a noi. Come ho già detto altrove, obiettivamente i fiori non solo non sono belli, ma non sono nemmeno fiori: diventano fiori e sono considerati belli solo quando percepiti dalla nostra mente. Ma, quando sono percepiti dalla mente, alcuni fiori ci piacciono molto ed altri ci piacciono assai meno. Anzi, a qualcuno alcuni fiori non piacciono. Questo significa che *la bellezza comincia ad esistere quando quello che si percepisce soddisfa i criteri estetici della mente o, più semplicemente, ci piace.* E la bruttezza quando questi criteri sono "offesi" o, più semplicemente, qualcosa ci dispiace. Ma questi criteri estetici non li abbiamo scelti noi. Tutt'al più, vi sono variazioni individuali determinate da svariati fattori (genetica, educazione, sensibilità, gusto, ecc.).

Il percepire la bellezza ci dà piacere (per esempio, vedere un bel fiore) e la varietà aumenta questo piacere (per esempio, vedere un campo di fiori diversi). È questo un dono riservato solo alla specie umana: un gatto risponde agli ormoni od altri stimoli, ma non alla bellezza. Se poi si apprezza la bellezza solo perché siamo stati condizionati geneticamente a farlo, di questo "obbligo" non potremmo che essere profondamente grati dal momento che la bellezza ci dà molti delicati piaceri.

Le cose create si apprezzano a seconda della loro bellezza, sia pure così come la intendiamo noi. E noi la intendiamo in una certa maniera perché siamo stati fatti così. Ma comunque la intendiamo, per noi vi sono cose che sono belle o brutte e ci rendiamo conto che la bellezza è l'unica funzione di certe cose belle. Se noi abbiamo un senso estetico, come negarlo a Chi ha dotato la nostra mente di senso estetico per cui certe cose ci colpiscono per la loro bellezza e non hanno altra funzione all'infuori di questa?

Etica

Dal che si deduce che *Dio possiede intelligenza, onnipotenza, sensibilità e creatività.* Ma né le qualità di Dio né le nostre si esauriscono in queste categorie. I nostri principi morali dividono quello che si fa in bene o male. In genere, non facciamo le cose che ci ripugnano vivamente. È difficile vedere una madre che picchia a morte il figlio o un figlio che lascia morire di fame il proprio padre. Succede anche quello, ma sono rare eccezioni che tutti condannano. Una precondizione essenziale della libertà è la possibilità di scelta tra bene e male.

Pertanto, tutti sappiamo che ci sono cose morali ed immorali, anche se nella nostra debolezza non facciamo sempre quello che dovrebbe essere fatto. Ma *se noi abbiamo un'etica, lo dobbiamo alla nostra genetica. Come è possibile che Chi ci ha dato l'etica, non ne abbia alcuna?* Evidentemente, se abbiamo un sistema etico, è perché Dio ne ha uno Lui stesso. Se un infanticidio spietato ci fa orrore, come è possibile che sia un evento indifferente per Dio? Anche se Dio lo perdonasse, questo pur implica una condanna, anche se non seguita da punizione.

L'etica di Dio può essere differente e superiore alla nostra, ma deve pur comprendere il concetto di bene e, automaticamente, quello di male. Non si insegnerebbe ai nostri figli che cosa è il bene, se non ne avessimo noi stessi la minima idea di che cosa sia il bene. O se non si credesse al bene. Se Dio ci ha dato un'etica, evidentemente ha un'etica lui stesso ed ha ritenuto che fosse necessario che l'avessimo anche noi.

Amore

Il che introduce un altro aspetto di Dio. Come è possibile che Dio abbia fatto le infinite meraviglie dell'universo e gli spettatori di queste meraviglie e li senta estranei a sé? Non è legge umana che si ama quello che si crea? A cominciare dai figli? E Dio dovrebbe essere meno di noi? Noi amiamo i nostri figli, eppure siamo solo gli strumenti della loro procreazione. Diamo loro i nostri cromosomi che noi stessi non abbiamo scelto. Quanto più sarebbero nostri se noi avessimo creato li stessi cromosomi, invece di averli ereditati per un processo in cui il caso può fare tutta la differenza.

Ma se noi amiamo i nostri figli, come pensare che Dio ha creato quello in cui non aveva il minimo interesse o verso cui provava la più completa indifferenza? *Il fatto stesso che esistiamo è già una prova dell'interesse di Dio in noi.* Una prova confermata dalle cose che sono state fatte per allietare la nostra breve esistenza, come per l'appunto la bellezza.

L'ambiente fisico è stato creato per la nostra sopravvivenza fisica (vedi il sole, l'atmosfera, le piante, ecc.) e un sistema di valori etici per la nostra sopravvivenza spirituale. La mente ci è stata data perché, imparando, fossimo in grado di capire, creare e svilupparci. Emozioni ci agitano che danno significato alla nostra vita. Una gran varietà di cose sono state create solo per abbellire il nostro ambiente.

Se questi non sono atti di un Padre verso i figli e se questo non implica amore verso le creature, che cosa significano? Come potrebbe essere possibile che Dio avesse creato l'uomo e la donna, suoi capolavori, con indifferenza? O per caso? Né l'una né l'altro si accordano col concetto di un Creatore. Perché creare una realtà tanto complessa, se non la si fosse considerata altrettanto importante. Che cosa può essere più importante di quello che si ama? E come si può non amare quello che noi stessi abbiamo voluto creare? *La creazione è già un atto di amore.*

Ma chi tra noi vorrebbe che i suoi figli non sapessero che lui è il padre? Chi procrea dei figli e poi li abbandona a se stessi o nasconde loro la propria identità? Chi non vuole rapporti di affetto tra lui e le sue creature? Chi non dice con orgoglio presentando i suoi figli: "Questo è mio figlio o mia figlia"? *Se noi creature mortali, la cui traccia sulla terra è alla fine solo un pugno di polvere, abbiamo bisogno di affetti profondi tra noi e i nostri figli, come potremmo negare al nostro Creatore la necessità di un rapporto tra Lui e le sue creature?*

La fede

Di qui nasce la fede, cioè la necessità di un rapporto intimo della nostra anima con Dio. La fede è basata su emozioni piuttosto che sulla logica, così come i rapporti tra genitori e figli sono basati sull'affetto e non sui ragionamenti. *La fede nasce dalla necessità di non lasciare l'uomo solo con la sua solitudine.* La fede nasce con ogni nuova creatura, perché lo spirito di ciascuno di noi ha il diritto di non essere orfano del suo Creatore. Chi dubiterebbe degli affetti tra genitori e figli solo perché sono basati su emozioni e non ragionamenti? E allora perché la fede dovrebbe essere meno reale perché basata su emozioni piuttosto che su ragionamenti?

Conclusioni

Da queste considerazioni si vede che Dio dimostra intelligenza, sensibilità, senso di giustizia, amore e un legame verso l'uomo. Necessariamente, ha dato all'uomo alcune delle sue caratteristiche: naturalmente, la differenza tra Dio e uomo è quantitativa e qualitativa. Differenza tanto grande da richiedere la protezione dell'uomo dalla grandezza della Divinità attraverso il mistero. Eppure quanto sopra indica che Dio ci ha fatto a sua immagine e somiglianza.

Dopo tutto, se non fosse per Dio e le sue creature, l'immensità dell'Universo sarebbe più piccola della sua solitudine.

18 March 1993
GOD
Intelligence and omnipotence
Of God little is known, but not necessarily nothing. Let us reason a little about it. An architect who builds a splendid palace with a park of extraordinary elegance certainly demonstrates a great intelligence (sometimes bordering on genius) and a great aesthetic sensitivity. How could it have been possible for God to have created the infinite marvels of the universe without an infinite intelligence? Without an intelligence associated to omnipotence?

For example, during a seminar the photo of a neuron was presented that had about 30000 connections with other neurons. Now then, in the two initial cells of the embryo evidently there are the instructions that eventually lead to the development of such neuron and of its connections with other neurons. And these instructions are incorporated in the cells that will bring about the next embryo. The One who has done this can not have but an infinite intelligence and power.

If one were to need a confirmation of the intelligence of God, he should only consider our ability to think: the transition from nerve cells to the formulation of thoughts is an incredibly extraordinary process. *To doubt the intelligence of God should only makes us doubt ours.* If then we doubt his almightiness, it would suffice to consider the universe or the role of the sun in the economy of biology: who could have created them if not an almighty Being? But, in this respect, we need to consider that creating a "simple" lizard from the nothing is not a much easier enterprise. For anyone to become convinced of that, it suffices for one to try and do it.

Mind and freedom
One can still deny God, but it is clear that *only someone to whom God has given a mind can have the prerogative of denying God: it only suffices that his mind is myopic and is not aware of the necessity of having been created.* But without the mind (myopic or not), we can not assert or deny anything.

If the mind had not been created by God and had developed "by itself", it would be a miracle. But to explain the miracle, we would still need the author of the miracle, that is God. We need also to consider that the mind is so extraordinary that in fact it is in itself a miracle, a miracle of God.

God has given the mind the ability to think and the liberty to use it as it wants. Not stupidly, but daringly. Just because we are free but not enough intelligent, we make mistakes. *If we were not free, in making mistakes we would only carry out mistaken instructions.* That the liberty is a rather difficult privilege is demonstrated by the fact that it is difficult not only to use it in an appropriate manner, but even to define it in an satisfactory manner.

Chance

Then, *it would be difficult to deny that God possesses an infinite intelligence and the ability of translating it into exceptional works (omnipotence).* If then we would want to deny the existence of God, we would be forced to deify chance. A chance that not only would create an extraordinary order (and this already is hardly conceivable and intrinsically contradictory), but also matter from nothing. But there another problem arises: nothing is created from nothing, *not even by chance.*

Aesthetic sense

But, to return to the example of the architect, to do something worthwhile not only a considerable intelligence and material means, but also aesthetic sensibility are necessary. If we do appreciate the beauty of a palace, how much more should we appreciate the beauty of nature, a beauty which is meant to gladden the human soul and contributes so much to make the earth the garden of Eden.

For example, consider the beauty of flowers and their great variety. What justifies the beauty and variety of flowers? Or their "necessity"? The answer can not be but the creation of beauty in different forms for the enjoyment of those who can appreciate it, namely, the human beings.

If one takes away the beauty and variety, what remains of the flowers? *Which other function do flowers have, if not that of being beautiful? And why so many different flowers if not to create different forms of beauty?* When the flowers are wilted and no longer are beautiful, are they not thrown away?

Now, who can create beauty without having aesthetic sensitivity? *If God has created so many marvelous things, how is it possible that He does not have an extraordinary aesthetic sensitivity and the ability of creating with great variety according to such aesthetic criteria?*

Certainly, we would not want to maintain that the flowers are beautiful and varied "by chance" or as the result of evolution. *Evolution could not exist if something did not already exist. Unless we admit an evolution from nothing. But, in that case, it would be something more than evolution: it would be creation.* And besides, on the basis of chance, we should see examples of evolution and involution. The net result would be a sequence of changes without either a strategic plan or a particular direction. That is, there would not be a (net) evolution.

One could say that flowers objectively are not beautiful, but they only appear so to us. As I have already wrote elsewhere, "objectively" flowers not only are not beautiful, but they are not even flowers: they become flowers and are considered beautiful only when they are perceived by our mind. But, when they are perceived by the mind, some flowers are liked very much and others a great deal less. Nay, some people dislike some flowers. This means that *beauty starts to exist when what we perceive satisfies the aesthetic criteria of our mind or, more simply, we like it.* And ugliness when these criteria are "offended" or, more simply, we dislike something. But these aesthetic criteria have not been chosen by us. At most, there are individual variations determined by various factors (genetics, education, sensitivity, taste, etc.).

Perceiving beauty gives us pleasure (for example, seeing a beautiful flower) and the variety increases that pleasure (for example, seeing a field of different flowers). This is a gift reserved only to the human kind: a cat responds to hormones or other stimuli, but not to beauty. If then we appreciate beauty only because we have been genetically conditioned to do so, we can not be but deeply thankful for this "obligation" since beauty gives us many delicate pleasures.

The things created are appreciated according to their beauty, even if only according to the way we understand it. And we understand it in a certain manner because we have been made in that manner. But no matter how we understand it, for us there are things that are beautiful or ugly, and we become aware that beauty is the unique function of certain beautiful things. If we have an aesthetic sense, how can we deny it to One who has endowed our mind with aesthetic sense so that certain things strike us for their beauty and do not have any other function but that?

Ethics

From this, we deduce that God possesses intelligence, omnipotence, sensitivity and creativeness. But neither the attributes of God nor ours become are limited to these categories. Our moral principles divide what we do into good or evil. In general, we do not do things that are vividly repugnant to us. It is unlikely that a mother would beat her child to death or that a son would let his own father die of starvation. That also happens, but these are rare exceptions that everyone condemns. An essential precondition for liberty is the capability of choosing between good and evil.

Therefore, we all know that there are moral and immoral things, even if in our weakness we do not always do what should be done. But *if we have an ethics, we owe it to our genetics. How could it be possible that the*

One who has given us ethics, should not have any? Evidently, if we have an ethical system is because God has one himself. If a merciless infanticide horrifies us, how is it possible that God should remain indifferent to it? Even if God were to forgive it, still this implies a condemnation, even if not followed by punishment.

The ethics of God can be different and superior to ours, but it must include the concept of good and, automatically, that of evil. We would not teach to our children what is good, if we did not have ourselves the least idea of what good is. Or we did not believe in good. If God has given us an ethics, evidently He has an ethics himself and He felt it necessary that we too should have it.

Love

This introduces an other aspect of God. How is it possible for God to create the infinite marvels of the universe and the spectators of these marvels and feel them extraneous? Is not a human law that we love what we create? Beginning with our children? Should God be less than us? We love our children, yet we are only the tools for their procreation. We give them our chromosomes that we ourselves have not chosen. How much more they would be ours if we have created the chromosomes instead of having inherited them through a process in which chance can make all the difference.

But if we love our children, how can we think that God created that in which He did not have the least interest or toward which he feels the complete indifference? *The very fact that we exist is already proof of the interest of God in us.* A proof confirmed by the things that have been made to cheer our brief existence, as indeed beauty.

The physical environment has been created for our physical survival (see the sun, the atmosphere, the plants, etc.) and a system of ethical values for our spiritual survival. The mind has been given to us so that, by learning, we could understand, create and develop ourselves. Emotions stir us that give meaning to our existence. A great variety of things has been creates only to adorn our environment.

If these are not the acts of a Father toward his children and if this does not mean love toward the creatures, what does it mean? How could it be possible that God created man and woman, his masterpieces, with indifference? Or by chance? Neither indifference nor chance fit the concept of a Creator. Why create such a complex reality, if it were not considered likewise important. What could be more important than what one loves? And how we could not love what we ourselves had wanted to create? *Creation is already a act of love.*

But who among us would want that his children should not know that he is the father? Who procreates children and then abandon them to themselves or hides from them his own identity? Who does not want a relation based on affection between himself and his creatures? Who does not say with pride on introducing his children: "This is my son or my daughter?" *If we mortals, whose trace on earth is in the end only a handful of dust, need deep affections between us and our children, how could we deny our Creator the necessity of a relation between Him and his creatures?*

Faith

From this the faith is born, that is, the necessity of an intimate relation of our soul with God. Faith is based on emotions rather than on logic, as the relation between parents and children is based on affection and not on reasoning. *The faith is born out of the necessity of not leaving man alone with his solitude.* Faith is born with each new creature, because the spirit of each one of us has a right not be orphan of his Creator. Who would doubt the affections between parents and children only because they are based on emotions and not logic? But then why should faith be less real because is based on emotions and not on reasoning?

Conclusions

From these considerations is follows that God has intelligence, omnipotence, sensitivity, sense of justice, love and a bond toward human beings. Necessarily, He has given to man some of his characteristics: naturally, the difference between God and man is quantitative and qualitative. The difference is so great as to require the protection of man from the greatness of Divinity by means of mystery. Yet, the above considerations indicate that God made us in his image and resemblance.

After all, if it were not for God and his creatures, the immensity of the Universe would be smaller than its solitude.

INDICE ANALITICO

INDEX

INDICE ANALITICO
degli aforismi

I numeri identificano i rispettivi aforismi.

674, 1762, 1788, 1804, 1845, 1876, 1956, 1958, 1980, 1992

Bene 1031, 1098, 1184, 1522, 1547, 1582, 1790, 1815, 1850, 1887

Biologia 1791

Bontà 1202, 1239, 1278, 1299, 1815

Bravura 1623

Brillante 1007, 1764

Bruttezza 1376, 1389, 1620

Bugia 1183, 1426, 1694, 1849, 1873, 1970

Calunnia 1173

Cambiamento 1271, 1358

Capacità 1393, 1457, 1759, 1932, 1935, 1997

Capire 1013, 1025, 1100, 1102, 1217, 1224, 1262, 1455, 1587, 1623, 1905, 1941, 1985

Caso 1073, 1084, 1346, 1469, 1479, 1485, 1815

Cattivo 1033, 1057, 1143, 1523, 1547, 1867

Certezza 1071

Cervello 1051, 1256, 1404, 1429, 1489, 1581, 1830

Chiarezza 1406, 1766, 1989

Cinismo 1482,1572

Civiltà 1253

Classico 1842

Coerenza 1333, 1807

Colpa 1013,1039, 1549, 1636, 1664

Commedia 1713

Comodo 1390,1546

Compassione 1537, 1548, 1753

Complessità 1451

Comportamento 1060, 1159, 1244, 1258, 1456, 1887

Comprensione 1023, 1038, 1097, 1116,1167, 1239, 1265, 1274, 1323, 1509, 1530, 1568, 1629, 1657, 1658, 1662, 1672, 1738, 1785, 1795, 1846, 1892, 1899, 1905, 1955

Compromessi 1471, 1577, 1872

Confusione 1047, 1118, 1317, 1850, 1892

Conoscenza 1566, 1672, 1734, 1869

Consapevolezza 1432

Consiglio 1026, 1147, 1333, 1393,1401

Contraddizione 1706, 1807, 1971

Contrasto 1191, 1422, 1954

Controllo 1191, 1750, 1821

Convenienza 1249, 1301, 1794

Conversazione 1221

Convinzioni 1100, 1126, 1249, 1275, 1396, 1443, 1455, 1460, 1492, 1568, 1662, 1665, 1709, 1830, 1910, 1997

Coraggio 1070, 1131, 1137, 1536, 1598, 1625, 1715, 1900

Corpo 1005, 1110, 1263, 1277, 1377, 1478, 1498, 1588, 1675, 1830, 1874, 1986, 1992

Correttezza 1406

Coscienza 1178, 1331, 1206, 1506, 1576, 1578, 1583, 1644, 1771, 1813

Creare 1055, 1097, 1271, 1552, 1560

Creatività 1041, 1048, 1195,

Dubbio 1025, 1069, 1181, 1395,
    1566, 1662, 1788, 1798
Durezza 1174, 1559, 1571, 1652,
    1792, 1990

Eccellere 1187, 1249, 1346,
    1632, 1675, 1703
Efficienza 1559
Egoismo 1038, 1063, 1068, 1110,
    1115, 1124, 1201, 1274,
    1439, 1509, 1572, 1574,
    1717, 1794
Eleganza 1023, 1078, 1569,
    1753, 1808, 1915
Emozioni 1019, 1062, 1071,
    1074, 1094, 1127, 1173,
    1184, 1209, 1225, 1293,
    1416, 1460, 1462, 1472,
    1482, 1517, 1525, 1548,
    1596, 1599, 1605,1606,
    1737, 1750, 1786, 1799,
    1800, 1816, 1844, 1878,
    1923, 1941, 1947, 1984,
    1991
Energia 1232, 1726, 1865, 1982,
    1997
Equilibrio 1469, 1479, 1701,
    1788
Eroismo 1038, 1335
Errore 1023, 1038, 1318, 1399,
    1654, 1723, 1763, 1805,
    1809, 1826
Esperienza 1005, 1008, 1026,
    1405, 1460, 1587, 1621,
    1659, 1849, 1850, 1885,
    1935
Espressione 1048, 1337, 1342,
    1397, 1551, 1571, 1603,
    1604, 1618, 1643, 1745,
    1750, 1771, 1825, 1971
Estetica 1023, 1607, 1826, 1983

Età   1005, 1190, 1222, 1230,
    1351, 1422, 1464, 1633,
    1772, 1809, 1894, 1921,
    1935, 1960, 1992
Euforia 1615

Faccia 1142, 1377
Fallimento 1128, 1374, 1559,
    1572
Falso   1110, 1148, 1442, 1548,
    1752, 1926
Fantasie 1208, 1230, 1457, 1639,
    1694, 1735, 1904
Fede   1025, 1069, 1141, 1181,
    1212, 1379, 1458, 1507,
    1526, 1617, 1657, 1830
Felicità 1141, 1214, 1228, 1245,
    1320, 1367, 1425, 1430,
    1449,1509, 1518, 1732,
    1784, 1821, 1963, 1993
Fiducia 1461, 1554
Figli   1052, 1120, 1222, 1250,
    1496, 1650, 1690, 1761,
    1942, 1977
Filosofia 1060, 1192, 1262, 1319,
    1360, 1460, 1503, 1507,
    1161, 1837, 1890, 1946,
    1999
Fine   1181, 1221, 1325, 1495,
    1516, 1831, 1907
Finezza 1340, 1348, 1362, 1410,
    1517, 1776, 1778, 1818
Fiori   1024, 1104, 1328, 1361,
    1571, 1605
Follie 1321
Fortuna 1084, 1469
Forza   1085, 1110, 1254, 1404,
    1415, 1742, 1755, 1912,
    1931, 1954, 1990, 1992,
    1994
Futilità 1112

Futuro 1341, 1350, 1356, 1554, 1586, 1626, 1834, 1886, 1986

Garbo 1722, 1852
Gelosia 1937
Generazione 1342, 1527, 1573, 1825, 1994
Generosità 1038, 1080, 1141, 1201, 1325, 1739, 1964
Genetica 1196,1242, 1258, 1262, 1305, 1346, 1357, 1403, 1485, 1522, 1568, 1641, 1791, 1812, 1824, 1826, 1830
Genio 1085, 1656
Genitori 1250, 1824, 1977
Gente 1134, 1153, 1316, 1450, 1676, 1829, 1864, 1982
Gentilezza 1080, 1104, 1141, 1239, 1747, 1775
Gioia 1740, 1842
Giovane 1114, 1135, 1193, 1209, 1240, 1351, 1470, 1478, 1616, 1659, 1865, 1894, 1935
Gioventù 1019, 1222, 1361, 1399, 1443, 1587, 1620, 1885, 1921
Giustizia 1091, 1283, 1314, 1585, 1910, 1912, 1957
Governo 1860
Grandezza 1040, 1528, 1624, 1922

Ideale 1455, 1561, 1779, 1792, 1904
Ignoranza 1188, 1529, 1610, 1686, 1885, 1941, 1987
Illusione 1002, 1210, 1511, 1535,

1552, 1592, 1792
Imbecillità 1234, 1981
Imitazione 1003
Immortalità 1536, 1725
Imparare 1271, 1289, 1327, 1504, 1651, 1882
Inclinazione 1380, 1640, 1814
Incompetenza 1115, 1630
Indifferenza 1023, 1031, 1093, 1098, 1156, 1173, 1355, 1408, 1431, 1589, 1794, 1850, 1891
Infanzia 1825
Infelicità 1038, 1367, 1396, 1446, 1661
Infinito 1495, 1540, 1560, 1748 1788
Ingratitudine 1754, 1823
Inibizioni 1402, 1415, 1500, 1522, 1567, 1664
Insipidezza 1465, 1807
Intelligenza 1036, 1065, 1108, 1503, 1663, 1905, 1961, 1997
Interessante 1063, 1072, 1247, 1280, 1359, 1364, 1371, 1418, 1460, 1477, 1623, 1661, 1666, 1734, 1776, 1787, 1881, 1978, 1997
Interesse 1006, 1061, 1072, 1090, 1106, 1143, 1177, 1274, 1344, 1352, 1359, 1400 1433, 1455, 1474, 1544, 1556, 1585, 1611, 1640, 1665, 1668, 1679, 1779, 1781, 1783, 1821, 1912, 1938, 1941, 1957, 1978, 1984, 1998
Intimità 1025, 1035, 1040, 1169, 1179, 1250, 1276, 1328, 1587, 1599, 1613, 1697,

1705, 1747, 1794, 1801, 1928

Intuizioni 1406, 1505, 1617, 1883, 1905

Invidia 1045, 1089, 1265, 1313, 1428, 1497, 1924

Inutile 1564, 1606, 1616, 1633, 1731, 1760, 1949

Io 1027, 1035, 1066, 1075, 1135, 1206, 1365, 1590, 1606, 1682, 1697, 1794, 1836, 1960

Ipocrisia 1028, 1294, 1381, 1474, 1881

Ironia 1713, 1758

Irrequietezza 1259, 1371, 1433, 1553, 1693, 1708

Istinti 1036, 1166, 1260, 1455, 1567, 1585, 1771, 1941, 1943

Leggi 1100, 1155, 1217, 1299, 1388, 1395, 1558, 1585, 1646, 1791, 1797, 1803, 1813, 1818, 1876, 1913

Liberazione 1693

Libertà 1112, 1184, 1343, 1349, 1531, 1603, 1810, 1819, 1926

Licenza 1622, 1810

Limiti 1063, 1074, 1132, 1181, 1182, 1348, 1496, 1509, 1516, 1570, 1587, 1625, 1629, 1710, 1748, 1836, 1905, 1932, 1934

Lingua 1287, 1322, 1746, 1788, 1876

Logica 1005, 1023, 1025, 1069, 1094, 1145, 1152, 1160, 1175, 1186, 1212, 1262, 1270, 1323, 1458, 1460,

1496, 1505, 1568, 1570, 1575, 1607, 1608, 1614, 1657, 1663, 1710, 1869, 1890

Lotta 1081, 1243, 1531, 1781, 1917

Luce 1206, 1261, 1320, 1647, 1699, 1892, 1909, 1934, 1952, 1976, 2000

Madre 1496, 1711

Magnanimità 1513, 1615, 1753

Male 1031, 1098, 1184, 1491, 1522, 1547, 1582, 1588, 1780,.1850, 1887

Malevolenza 1630

Malinconia 1077, 1239, 1788, 1804, 1811

Meccanismi 1277, 1417, 1581, 1701

Mediocrità 1249, 1345, 1615, 1632, 1684, 1872

Memoria 1088, 1266, 1480, 1699, 1802, 1836

Mente 1005, 1041, 1060, 1076, 1084, 1088, 1100, 1126, 1135, 1138, 1142, 1160, 1163,1181, 1190, 1208, 1209, 1220, 1228, 1240, 1256, 1258, 1261, 1270, 1271, 1277, 1284, 1297, 1311, 1312, 1317, 1323, 1327, 1346, 1375, 1377, 1378, 1392, 1409, 1410, 1416, 1429, 1432, 1440, 1470, 1478, 1489, 1494, 1498, 1501, 1517, 1519, 1521, 1527, 1540, 1544, 1547, 1552, 1567, 1575, 1576, 1580, 1583, 1586, 1588, 1590, 1591, 1595,

Oggettivo 1006, 1400, 1470, 1489, 1494, 1633, 1694, 1966

Oggetto 1170, 1463, 1470, 1633, 1822, 1898, 1937, 1950, 1983

Onestà 1083, 1137, 1232, 1451, 1873

Opere 1021, 1160, 1538, 1642, 1656, 1844, 1958

Opinione 1126, 1272, 1280, 1428, 1455, 1633, 1780, 1837, 1865, 1866, 1869, 1892, 1950

Ordine 1073, 1122, 1184, 1227, 1270, 1299, 1343, 1357, 1561, 1562, 1571, 1646, 1810, 1824, 1876

Orgoglio 1273, 1593

Originalità 1003, 1153, 1342, 1618, 1877

Ostacoli 1023, 1069, 1331

Ostilità 1011, 1403, 1843, 1908

Ostinatezza 1162

Padre 1649, 1690, 1711

Parole 1078, 1162, 1287, 1385, 1519, 1612, 1748, 1756, 1794, 1852, 1890, 1905

Passato 1017, 1022, 1133, 1341, 1350, 1356, 1422, 1480, 1481, 1504, 1586, 1586, 1626, 1734, 1886, 1986

Passioni 1019, 1106, 1123, 1192, 1226, 1463, 1487, 1584, 1589, 1604, 1611, 1614, 1660, 1698, 1712, 1730, 1784, 1858, 1923, 1941, 1957, 1991, 1997

Paura 1139, 1293, 1369, 1455, 1729, 1905

Pazzia 1032, 1591

Peccati 1012, 1448, 1549, 1565, 1851, 1913, 1928

Pensare 1036, 1126, 1236, 1286, 1302, 1579, 1581, 1583, 1627, 1689, 1822, 1828, 1866, 1869, 1930, 1935, 1969, 1986, 1994

Pensieri 1047, 1127, 1160, 1276, 1296, 1302, 1315, 1322, 1370, 1487, 1519, 1580, 1581, 1605, 1627, 1678, 1706, 1709, 1828, 1839, 1869, 1919

Pensione 1046

Percezioni 1146, 1365, 1366, 1489, 1596, 1766, 1819, 1846, 1869, 1886, 1904, 1950, 1983

Perdonare 1011, 1038, 1070, 1080, 1140, 1201, 1399, 1537, 1607, 1749, 1802, 1924, 1942

Perfezione 1021, 1141, 1251, 1516, 1972, 1992

Pericolo 1224, 1301, 1504, 1570, 1715, 1904

Pessimismo 1119, 1229

Piacere 1038, 1060, 1121, 1214, 1228, 1245, 1263, 1276, 1367, 1449, 1502, 1509, 1562, 1567, 1588, 1600, 1607, 1719, 1844, 1845, 1900

Piacevole 1138, 1263, 1307, 1309, 1391, 1405, 1449, 1521, 1627, 1679, 1689, 1719, 1808, 1847, 1875, 1916

Piccolezza 1642, 1748, 1788

Pietà 1234, 1299, 1537

1784, 1833, 1869, 1893,
    1979
Scandali 1854
Schiavitù 1181, 1584, 1910, 1833
Scienza 1063, 1110, 1423, 1458,
    1656, 1788, 1938
Sciocchezza 1204, 1607
Scopo 1257, 1977
Scrittore 1858
Selezione 1035, 1469, 1830
Semplicità 1099, 1162, 1239,
    1466, 1530, 1533 1637,
    1702, 1958, 1974, 1989
Sensibilità 1072, 1107, 1117,
    1164, 1172, 1385, 1596,
    1755, 1846, 1915, 1997
Sentimenti 1152, 1157, 1193,
    1328, 1559, 1571, 1658,
    1706, 1747, 1784, 1963,
    1988
Serietà 1483, 1727, 1793
Sesso 1282, 1638
Sfogo 1147, 1435
Sforzi 1036, 1455, 1516
Significato 1064, 1335, 1367,
    1376, 1416, 1432, 1484,
    1495, 1521, 1540, 1548,
    1623, 1626, 1900, 1919,
    1941, 1965
Silenzio 1130, 1236, 1580, 1643,
    1677, 1788, 1888, 1940,
    1976
Simpatia 1157, 1594
Società 1321, 1381, 1469, 1825,
    1860, 1964
Sofferenza 1141, 1367, 1449,
    1516, 1589, 1606, 1706,
    1816, 1900
Sogni 1054, 1062, 1172, 1230,
    1256, 1571, 1966, 1993
Sole 1058, 1138, 1281,1320,

1647, 1766, 1770, 1788,
    1804, 1853, 1892, 1914,
    1952, 2000
Solitudine 1082, 1169, 1198,
    1326, 1688, 1769, 1811,
    1840, 1888
Sonno 1297, 1716
Sopportare 1454, 1524, 1525,
    1757
Sopprimere 1174
Sopravvivenza 1366
Sorriso 1770, 1848
Sorte 1485
Sottigliezza 1778
Specchio 1027, 1057, 1135,
    1199, 1284, 1377, 1590,
    1794
Specializzazione 1282
Specie 1562
Speranza 1071, 1180, 1416,
    1443, 1458, 1513, 1535,
    1552, 1565, 1706, 1732,
    1898
Spinte 1060, 1090, 1166, 1622,
    1629
Spirito 1006, 1063, 1110, 1209,
    1225, 1252, 1253, 1263,
    1355, 1449, 1490, 1693,
    1992
Spiritoso 1111, 1134, 1445,
    1483, 1760, 1793
Spiritualità 1252, 1355, 1693
Squilibrio 1144
Stagioni 1364, 1804
Stagnazione 1654
Stile 1551, 1560, 1808
Stimoli 1060, 1138, 1191, 1258,
    1272, 1308, 1371, 1386,
    1440, 1489, 1494, 1557,
    1561, 1583, 1666, 1741,
    1765, 1776, 1846, 1904,

INDEX
of the aphorisms

Since the same number identifies the same aphorism in Italian and in the English translation, the Index does not repeat the same numbers for the same entries. Instead, the Index indicates for each entry the equivalent Italian word under which the numbers of the related aphorisms are to be found in the above Indice Analitico. For example, for the word "Ability", the related aphorisms are to be found listed under the corresponding Italian word "Abilità".

Ability = Abilità
Actions = Azioni
Activity = Attività
Actor = Attore
Acts = Atti
Advantage = Vantaggio
Advice = Consiglio
Aesthetics = Estetica
Affections = Affetti
Age = Età
Aim = Scopo
Ambition = Ambizione
Amuse = Divertire
Analysis = Analisi
Animal = Animale
Answers = Risposte
Anxiety = Ansietà
Aphorism = Aforisma
Appearance = Apparenza
Aridity = Aridità
Arrogance = Arroganza
Aspirations = Aspirazioni
Attention = Attenzione
Avarice = Avarizia

Bad = cattivo
Balance = Equilibrio
Beauty = Bellezza

Behavior = Comportamento
Biology = Biologia

Birth = Nascita
Body = Corpo
Boldness = Audacia
Boredom = Noia
Brain = Cervello
Brilliant = Brillante

Capacity = Capacità
Certainty = Certezza
Chance = Caso
Change = Cambiamento
Children = Bambini, Figli
Civilization = Civiltà
Clarity = Chiarezza
Classic = Classico
Cleverness = Abilità, Bravura
Coarseness = Rozzezza
Coherence = Coerenza
Comedy = Commedia
Compassion = Compassione
Complexity = Complessità
Comprehension = Comprensione
Compromise = Compromesso
Confusion = Confusione
Conscience = Coscienza
Consciousness = Consapevolezza

Contradiction = Contraddizione
Contrast = Contrasto
Control = Controllo
Convenience = Convenienza
Convenient = Comodo
Conversation = Conversazione
Convince = Convincere
Convictions = Convinzioni
Correctness = Correttezza
Corruption = Corruzione
Courage = Coraggio
Create = Creare
Creativity = Creatività
Criticism = Critica
Criticize = Criticare
Crowd = Folla
Cruelty = Crudeltà
Crying = Pianto
Culture = Cultura
Curiosity = Curiosità
Cynicism = Cinismo

Danger = Pericolo
Death = Morte
Decadence = Decadenza
Decisions = Decisioni
Deep = Profondo
Defects = Difetti
Defense = Difesa
Delicacy = Delicatezza
Demagoguery = Demagogia
Demerit = Demerito
Democracy = Democrazia
Depression = Depressione
Derelicts = Derelitti
Desires = Desideri
Detachment = Distacco
Diet = Dieta
Dignity = Dignità
Direction = Direzione
Discipline = Disciplina

Discretion = Discrezione
Disinhibitions = Disinibizioni
Dislike = Antipatia
Disorder = Disordine
Disputes = Dispute
Distinction = Distinzione
Doubt = Dubbio
Drama = Dramma
Dreams = Sogni
Drives = Spinte
Duty = Dovere

Ease = Agio
Efficiency = Efficienza
Efforts = Sforzi
Egoism = Egoismo
Elegance = Eleganza
Emotions = Emozioni
End = Fine
Endurance = Sopportazione
Enemy = Nemico
Energy = Energia
Envy = Invidia
Equality = Uguaglianza
Error = Errore, Sbaglio
Erudition = Erudizione
Esteem = Stima
Euphoria = Euforia
Evil = Male
Excel = Eccellere
Expedient = Espediente
Experience = Esperienza
Expression = Espressione

Face = faccia
Failure = Fallimento
Faith = Fede
False = Falso
Fantasies = Fantasie
Fashion = Moda

Father = Padre
Fault = Colpa
Fear = Paura
Feelings = Sentimenti
Finesse = Finezza
Flowers = Fiori
Follies = Follie
Force = Forza
Forget = Dimenticare
Fortune = Fortuna
Freedom = Libertà
Friendship = Amicizia
Frivolity = Frivolezza
Futility = Futilità
Future = Futuro

Generation = Generazione
Generosity = Generosità
Genetics = Genetica
Genius = Genio
Goal = Scopo
God = Dio
Good = Bene
Goodness = Bontà
Government = Governo
Graciousness = Garbo
Greatness = Grandezza
Grow = Crescere

Habit = Abitudine
Happiness = Felicità
Hardness = Durezza
Hardship = Difficoltà
Hate = Odio
Heart = Cuore
Heroism = Eroismo
History = Storia
Honesty = Onestà
Hope = Speranza
Hostility = Ostilità

Humanity = Umanità
Humility = Umiltà
Humor = Umorismo
Hypocrisy = Ipocrisia

Ideal = Ideale
Ignorance = Ignoranza
Illusion = Illusione
Imbecility = Imbecillità
Imitation = Imitazione
Immortality = Immortalità
Inclination = Inclinazione
Incompetence = Incompetenza
Indifference = Indifferenza
Infancy = Infanzia
Infinite = Infinito
Inhibitions = Inibizioni
Ingratitude = Ingratitudine
Insipidity = Insipidezza
Instincts = Istinti
Instruments = Strumenti
Intelligence = Intelligenza
Interest = Interesse
Interesting = Interessante
Intimacy = Intimità
Intuitions = Intuizioni
Irony = Ironia

Jealousy = Gelosia
Joy = Gioia
Justice = Giustizia

Kindness = Gentilezza
Knowledge = Conoscenza

Laughter = Riso

Laws = Leggi
Learn = Imparare

Liberation = Liberazione
Liberty = Libertà
License = Licenza
Lie = Bugia
Life = Vita
Light = Luce
Limits = Limiti
Live = Vivere
Logic = Logica
Love = Amore

Madness = Pazzia
Magnanimity = Magnanimità
Malevolence = Malevolenza
Man = Uomo
Meaning = Significato
Meanness = Meschinità
Means = Mezzi
Mechanisms = Meccanismi
Mediocrity = Mediocrità
Melancholy = Malinconia
Memory = Memoria
Merit = Merito
Mind = Mente
Miracles = Miracoli
Mirror = Specchio
Mistake = Errore, Sbaglio
Moderation = Moderazione
Modernity = Modernità
Modesty = Modestia
Money = Denaro
Morality = Moralità
Mother = Madre
Music = Musica
Myth = Mito

Nature = Natura
Necessity = Necessità
Nonsense = Sciocchezza
Normality = Normalità

Nothing = Nulla

Object = Oggetto
Objective = Oggettivo
Obligations = Obblighi
Obstacles = Ostacoli
Occasions = Occasioni
Offense = Offesa
Old age = Vecchiaia
Opinion = Opinione
Order = Ordine
Originality = Originalità
Others = Altri
Outlet = Sfogo

Pain = Dolore
Pardon = Perdonare
Parents = Genitori
Passions = Passioni
Past = Passato
Pension = Pensione
People = Gente
Perceptions = Percezioni
Perfection = Perfezione
Perspicacity = Accortezza
Pessimism = Pessimismo
Pettiness = Piccolezza
Philosophy = Filosofia
Pity = Pietà
Pleasant = Piacevole
Pleasure = Piacere
Poetry = Poesia
Politics = Politica
Potentialities = Potenzialità
Poverty = Povertà
Power = Potere
Practical = Pratico
Preaching = Prediche
Present = Presente
Pride = Orgoglio

Problems = Problemi
Profession = Professione
Progress = Progresso

Quality = Qualità
Questions = Domande

Reality = Realtà
Realizations = Realizzazioni
Reason = Ragionc
Reasonableness =
              Ragionevolezza
Reasoning = Ragionamento
Rebels = Ribelli
Refinement = Raffinatezza
Reflect = Riflettere
Reflections = Riflessioni
Reflexes = Riflessi
Religion = Religione
Reputation = Reputazione
Resoluteness = Risolutezza
Respect = Rispetto
Responsibility = Responsabilità
Restlessness = Irrequietezza
Rhythm = Ritmo
Rigor = Rigore
Risk = Rischio
Routine = Routine
Rudeness = Rudezza
Rules = Regole

Sacrifices = Sacrifici
Sadness = Tristezza
Scandals = Scandali
Science = Scienza
Seasons = Stagioni
Selection = Selezione
Self = Io
Sensibility = Sensibilità
Seriousness = Serietà

Sex = Sesso
Sharpness = Acutezza
Silence = Silenzio
Simplicity = Semplicità
Sins = Peccati
Slander = Calunnia
Slavery = Schiavitù
Sleep = Sonno
Smallness = Piccolezza
Smile = Sorriso
Snow = Neve
Society = Società
Solitude = Solitudine
Sorrow = Dolore
Soul = Anima
Specialization= Specializzazione
Species = Specie
Spirit = Spirito
Spirituality = Spiritualità
Stagnation = Ristagno
Stimuli = Stimoli
Strategy = Strategia
Struggle = Lotta
Stubbornness = Ostinatezza
Stupidity = Stupidità
Style = Stile
Subconscious = Subconscio
Subtlety = Sottigliezza
Success = Successo
Suffering = Sofferenza
Sun = sole
Superficiality = Superficialità
Suppress = Sopprimere
Survival = Sopravvivenza
Sympathy = Simpatia

Temptations = Tentazioni
Tensions = Tensioni
Tests = Prove
Theories = Teorie
Think = Pensare

Thoughts = Pensieri
Time = Tempo
Tolerance = Tolleranza
Tongue = Lingua
Trust = Fiducia
Truth = Verità

Ugliness = Bruttezza
Unbalance = Squilibrio
Understand = Capire
Unhappiness = Infelicità
Universe = Universo
Useful = Utile
Useless = Inutile

Vacuum = Vuoto
Vanity = Vanità
Variety = Varietà
Vengeance = Vendetta
Vices = Vizi

Virtue = Virtù
Vivacity = Vivacità
Vulgarity = Volgarità

Weakness = Debolezza
Wealth = Ricchezza
Will = Volontà
Win = Vincere
Wine = Vino
Wisdom = Saggezza
Woman = Donna
Words = Parole
Works = Opere
Writer = Scrittore

Years = Anni
Young = Giovane
Youth = Gioventù